Chiang Kai-shek's Secret Past

CHIANG KAI-SHEK'S SECRET PAST

The Memoir of His Second Wife,
Ch'en Chieh-ju

edited & with an introduction by
Lloyd E. Eastman

WESTVIEW PRESS
Boulder • San Francisco • Oxford

English edition copyright © 1993 by Westview Press, Inc.

English edition published in 1993 in the United States of America by Westview Press, Inc., 5500 Central Avenue, Boulder, Colorado 80301-2877, and in the United Kingdom by Westview Press, 36 Lonsdale Road, Summertown, Oxford OX2 7EW

Chinese edition published in 1992 in Taiwan by Biographical Literature Press as *Ch'en Chieh-ju Hui-yi-lu Ch'üan-Yi-pen* and by The Journalist Press as *Ch'en Chieh-ju Hui-yi-lu*

Library of Congress Cataloging-in-Publication Data
Ch'en, Chieh-ju, d. 1971.
  Chiang Kai-shek's secret past : the memoir of his second wife /
Ch'en Chieh-ju ; edited & with an introduction by Lloyd E. Eastman.
    p. cm.
  ISBN 0-8133-1824-6—ISBN 0-8133-1825-4 (pbk.)
  1. Chiang, Kai-shek, 1887–1975. 2. Presidents—China—wives.
3. Ch'en, Chieh-ju, d. 1971. I. Eastman, Lloyd E. II. Title.
DS777.488.C5C464 1993
951.05'092—dc20   93-21728
                                                                        CIP

Printed and bound in the United States of America

The paper used in this publication meets the requirements
of the American National Standard for Permanence of Paper
for Printed Library Materials Z39.48-1984.

10   9   8   7   6   5   4   3   2   1

For Meya
Through mostly good times
But also some tough times
Together

—L.E.E.

CONTENTS

A BRIEF
HISTORICAL FOREWORD

During the period encompassed by this memoir (1919–1927), China was in the grip of warlordism. The Revolution of 1911 had proved to be a disappointing failure: It had accomplished the overthrow of the Ch'ing Dynasty, but this had been followed by the breakup of China's political system. Regional militarists dominated the political landscape, their armies warring with each other for control of territories and for whatever tax revenues could be squeezed from those territories.

Joining this chaotic and devastating struggle for power and revenue was the battered band of revolutionaries led by Dr. Sun Yat-sen. Sun had briefly served as the first provisional president of the newly founded Republic of China in early 1912. In 1913, he and his Nationalist Party, the Kuomintang, launched the Second Revolution in a feeble effort to oust the dictatorial new president, Yuan Shih-k'ai. After the revolt collapsed, Sun and his adherents were outlawed, forced to seek refuge on the political and geographical periphery of China.

In 1917, Sun joined forces with a coalition of warlords to form a military government in Canton. Although Sun was nominally commander in chief of the new regime, he was helpless in the hands of the generals who commanded troops. This experience instilled in him the conviction that he could achieve his revolutionary goal of unifying the nation under his Nationalist Party only if he had an army dedicated to himself and to his revolutionary principles.

Sun's decision to form a party army presented Chiang Kai-shek with a fresh opportunity. Until this time, he had been a revolutionary of no particular distinction. But he was one of the few trained soldiers among Sun's followers, and Sun soon leaned on him for military advice. In 1924, Sun picked him to command the Whampoa Military Academy, then being formed with Russian advice and material aid. Many of the graduates of the academy became intensely loyal to Chiang, and they thereafter served as his most dedicated supporters during his rise to party and national leadership.

His rise to power was, however, by no means smooth. Dr. Sun died in March 1925, and several of his followers had stronger claims to his mantle of leadership than did Chiang. By 1928, however, Chiang had surpassed each of his rivals, both inside and outside the Kuomintang, and he became the supreme leader of the Nationalist government.

Ch'en Chieh-ju was married to Chiang Kai-shek throughout most of these tempestuous times. She writes of his battles with the various warlords as he consolidated a revolutionary base in Canton. And she describes his struggles with rival claimants for leadership of the Kuomintang. On the threshold of seizing national power, however, Chiang disavowed Ch'en Chieh-ju as his wife so that he could marry the politically more useful Soong Mei-ling, who soon gained international recognition as Mme Chiang Kai-shek.

Lloyd E. Eastman

EDITOR'S NOTE

I have edited the manuscript with a relatively light hand. Jennie's version was 425 pages long; this one is 417 pages in typescript. Only material of no conceivable historical value, such as the first ten pages of Jennie's work, has been deleted. Most of the editing has involved correcting the English or making the text comprehensible. No attempt has been made to bring to the original English a high polish. James Lee, the ghostwriter of the manuscript, possessed an extensive vocabulary, sometimes using quite elegant phrases. I cannot take credit for those. But English for him was a second language, and sometimes the syntax and phraseology did require some adjusting if the meaning was to become clear. That I tried to do. When possible, the romanization of Chinese proper names has been changed to the Wade-Giles system; otherwise, the spelling has been left in the form of the original manuscript, which usually reflected the Cantonese pronunciation.

Acknowledgments

In bringing this manuscript from obscurity to publication, I have received help from numerous people. First was the scholar who told me that the manuscript was located in the Hoover Archives. She or he must still remain anonymous. Ginny Connor, who also still prefers anonymity, has throughout this long process been of invaluable assistance and inspiration. I am deeply grateful to her, first, for preserving her notes of Jennie Ch'en's manuscript and the Lee brothers' correspondence—in the face of what she felt was grave peril to herself and her family; and, second, for numerous discussions with her, during which she shared her knowledge and cheery enthusiasm about this project. Dr. C. Martin Wilbur, professor emeritus of Columbia University, announced the Connor Papers to the scholarly community and has maintained an active interest in Jennie Ch'en's autobiography. Others who helped were Dr. Ramon H. Myers, longtime friend and scholar-curator of the East Asian Collection of the Hoover Institution; Prof. Zhang Xian-wen of Nanjing University; Mr. Yan Ru-ping of the Chinese Academy of Social Sciences in Beijing; Prof. Zheng Hui-xin of the Chinese University of Hong Kong; Prof. Wang Ke-wen of St. Michael's College in Colchester, Vermont; Prof. Lai Tse-han of the Academia Sinica in Taipei; Prof. George T. Yü of the University of Illinois; and Mr. Mi Hedu. To each of these people I wish to record my profound thanks.

But it is to my wife, Margaret "Meya" Eastman, that I owe the greatest debt of gratitude and love. I am pleased to dedicate this book to her.

L.E.E.
Urbana, Illinois

INTRODUCTION

The Elusive Manuscript of Chiang Kai-shek's Second Wife, Ch'en Chieh-ju

Lloyd E. Eastman

It has been a strange story, beginning in 1919 when Chiang Kai-shek met the thirteen-year-old Ch'en Chieh-ju (or Jennie Chen, as she will be referred to below).[1] The story continued down to 1990, when Jennie's 425-page memoir of her seven-year-long marriage to Chiang resurfaced after years of being submerged from view.

Jennie's memoir portrays a flesh-and-blood Chiang Kai-shek, a man who, in the historical record, has virtually disappeared behind the legend of a national leader who was more than a mere mortal. Since the 1930s, Kuomintang propagandists and historians have burnished the myth of Chiang Kai-shek as a moral sage and omniscient leader. But Chiang, like so many great world leaders and politicians, was possessed in full measure of all the human drives and frailties. Jennie Chen's memoir reveals this side of Chiang during the 1920s as he scrambled up the greasy pole to power in the Nationalist revolutionary movement. He was, among other things, lustful, ill-tempered, quarrelsome, stubborn, and boundlessly ambitious. He quarreled with Sun Yat-sen, struggled with political rivals, and betrayed one wife, whom he seemingly loved, so that he could make a politically expedient alliance with the now-famed Soong Mei-ling. Later, in the 1960s, Kuomintang leaders in

Taiwan were loath to see these facets of Chiang's personality and career revealed to the world, and Jennie's memoir was suppressed.

Chiang Kai-shek first met Jennie Chen in 1919 when she was thirteen years old and he thirty-two. He was already married to a sturdy, illiterate country girl five years older than he—at the time of their marriage (1901), she was nineteen and he was fourteen. Theirs was not a happy union, although it produced one son, Ching-kuo, and Chiang had soon ceased to live with her. He also had a mistress, Yao I-ch'in,[2] for whom he seems to have felt, at least for a time, genuine affection (and who, later, was largely responsible for rearing his adopted son, Chiang Wei-kuo).

But when he glimpsed the young Jennie, tall, willowy, and looking older than her years, he was smitten with love. Even after he attempted to force himself on her, he pursued her with what can only be called unbecoming persistence. Jennie, however, did not initially reciprocate his ardor, and for two years she avoided him.

Following the death of her father in 1921, however, her mother acceded to Chiang's persistent pleas for permission to marry the daughter, and Jennie—now fifteen years old—acquiesced. She and China's future leader were united in marriage on December 5, 1921, in a civil ceremony, attended by some fifty friends and relatives, in Shanghai's Great Eastern Hotel. Chang Ching-chiang, Chiang Kai-shek's rich Shanghai patron, presided at the ceremony. The marriage was formalized by applying to the marriage certificate a government revenue stamp and the seals of the bride and groom and the officiating officer.[3]

During the ensuing years, Chiang was deeply involved in the work of the revolution. Jennie, now known and accepted as Mme Chiang Kaishek, accompanied him nearly everywhere. When warned that he endangered Jennie by taking her to the war zone with him, Chiang replied, "Where I go, she goes."[4] It has also been asserted that Jennie, who had studied English, frequently served during these years as Chiang's interpreter with English-speaking Russian advisers then in China, including Michael Borodin.[5] If this assertion is correct, then her account of the personalities and events of the Nationalist revolutionary movement, as recorded in her memoir, was probably based on direct participation and observation. But, of the historical reliability of the manuscript, more will be said later.

During the Northern Expedition in 1926–1927, as the Nationalist armies neared the centers of power and finance in Central China,

Chiang's leadership was challenged by Kuomintang leftists and the Communists. Chiang sorely needed allies against this leftist coalition. And help was offered him by Mme H. H. Kung (Soong Ai-ling), who saw Chiang as China's man of destiny. According to Jennie's memoir, Mme Kung proposed that Chiang appoint her brother T. V. Soong as minister of finance, appoint her husband, H. H. Kung, as prime minister, and marry her youngest sister, Mei-ling. In return, she and her brother would withdraw their support from the Wuhan regime and persuade the leading bankers in Shanghai to provide the funds Chiang needed to proceed with the Northern Expedition.[6]

Chiang could hardly contain his delight at this offer. A marriage into the Soong family would give him the prestige that he had hitherto lacked. It would legitimate his leadership of the Kuomintang by linking him with Sun Yat-sen, through Sun's widow, the second Soong daughter.[7] And it would solidify a financial base, Shanghai, from which to resume the military campaign against the northern warlords.

In Jennie Chen's version of these events, Chiang's marriage to Soong Mei-ling was strictly and solely a matter of political opportunism. No romantic sentiment, she insisted, was involved. This sounds like the account of a woman scorned. But Jennie's account of Chiang's motives for marrying Mei-ling was not mere "sour grapes." This has been corroborated by Soong Mei-ling herself, as reported in a private memoir by a prominent American publisher.[8]

With his impending marriage to Soong Mei-ling, Chiang felt that the continued presence of Jennie Chen was an embarrassment. He therefore persuaded Jennie, "for the unification of China," to go to the United States to study for five years, after which he would resume his marriage with Jennie. Jennie and her mother were skeptical, but Chiang took an oath: "I promise to resume my marital relationship with Chieh-ju as husband and wife within five years from today. Should I break my promise and fail to take her back, may the Great Buddha smite me and my Nanking government. And if within ten or twenty years I do not do my duty toward her, then may Buddha topple my government and banish me from China forever."[9]

Shortly thereafter, Jennie sailed on board the SS *President Jackson* for the United States. Arriving en route in Hawaii, she was greeted by a delegation of the local Kuomintang holding aloft a large banner: "Welcome Mme Chiang Kai-shek."[10] After she sailed from China, however, Chiang declared to the newspapers that this person calling herself Mme

Jennie (front row, third from right) probably during a stopover in Hawaii. The banner (partially cut off in the photo) reads: An assembly of Loyal and Upright Chinese Kuomintang compatriots from T'an-(?) welcome Mme Chiang Kai-shek.

Chiang Kai-shek was unknown to him and he certainly was not married to her.

Jennie was shocked and heartbroken by this marital treachery; in New York City, she contemplated suicide. She remained in the United States until 1933; then she returned to Shanghai and resumed her maiden name of Ch'en.

.   .   .

With Chiang Kai-shek's encouragement, Jennie had kept diaries during the years of their marriage.[11] And in the 1950s, "sick and tired of living from hand to mouth,"[12] she decided to use those diaries as the basis of a memoir whose publication, she hoped, would solve her financial difficulties. Such a book could, however, prove immensely embarrassing to Chiang Kai-shek, who was then president of the Republic of China on Taiwan. Ch'en Li-fu, a Kuomintang Party elder then living in New Jersey, learned of her plans in 1959 and implored Jennie to keep her memories to herself: "I hear that you are again listening to people's urgings and intend to publish some kind of book. ... It is my hope that you will, as in the past, maintain your greatness of character, value [your] friendship [for Chiang Kai-shek], and look lightly on material profit. Don't allow evil people to use you."[13]

Jennie ignored this appeal, and by January 1964, she had a completed manuscript in English. Her collaborator was James Lee, a Hong Kong banker who had tutored both Jennie and Chiang in English during the 1920s.[14] With the manuscript completed, James recruited his brother, William Yinson Lee, a retired physician then living in New York City, to employ a literary agent who could find an American publisher for the manuscript. By April, this agent, Lawrence Epps Hill, had obtained an offer from Doubleday, a leading publishing house, to publish the book.[15]

But Jennie's and the Lee brothers' plan to publish the manuscript in the United States collapsed by early January 1965. The reasons are obscure. One problem may have been Jennie's delay in sending Hill, the literary agent, full legal authorization to sign a contract on her behalf. There is also evidence, however, that someone with ties to the Taiwan government intervened to suppress the manuscript.

Ch'en Li-fu and Mme H. H. Kung, both then residing near New York City, threatened Hill with lawsuits if the manuscript were published. Doubleday, allegedly fearing that the manuscript might be libelous, withdrew its offer of publication. And Ch'en Li-fu reportedly offered another publisher $65,000 not to publish the book.[16]

Hill, meanwhile, encountered a different form of obstructionism, albeit probably from much the same source. According to a newspaper account, "Hill has been assaulted and beaten up twice; his hotel room and offices have been broken into three or four times; he has received many suspicious phone calls in the early hours of the morning; he has been threatened with suit by two major New York law firms and he has been investigated by the FBI.[17] Somehow, Hill feels someone is trying to tell him something, and he thinks he knows what it is."[18] Whatever the reasons, Yinson Lee by early 1965 found that no American publisher would touch the manuscript.

Even earlier, however, the Lee brothers, one in Hong Kong and the other in New York, were writing to each other, not about publishing the manuscript but about selling it to agents of Taiwan. On December 31, 1964, James in Hong Kong wrote, "We are going to give Kiang three copies of memoirs and twenty photos."[19] The Kiang mentioned here was Eugene Kiang, a lawyer who represented Chiang Kai-shek's son Chiang Ching-kuo in negotiating with Jennie Chen and James Lee for the manuscript.[20]

Negotiations with Kiang proceeded slowly, however, because the three copies of the manuscript were in New York City, and Kiang was insistent that every existing copy of the manuscript be turned over to him. Finally, in March 1965, Jennie gave Kiang two (or perhaps three) copies of the manuscript.[21] Kiang in turn gave Jennie about US $170,000.[22]

That, presumably, should have been the end of the story. Twenty-and-more years later, however, the manuscript suddenly reappeared.

The preceding account of Jennie's memoir and of the Lee brothers' negotiations with Taiwan's agents is based largely upon a collection of letters between the Lee brothers held by Ginny Connor. This correspondence and other papers are referred to here as the "Connor Papers." Ms. Connor, who was working as a secretary in New York City at the time, has explained how she acquired these papers:

> In 1971 a friend of mine asked me to do some typing for him. He had with him a two-volume manuscript and a number of pictures. An elderly lady from New York City had engaged him to try to have it published. He told me the manuscript was too valuable and far too dangerous to keep in his possession. He wanted me to type some of the pertinent facts for him so that he could return the manuscript and use my notes to approach some publishers.
>
> My friend picked up my typed notes from the first volume and both volumes of the manuscript. I told him I would have the notes from the second volume typed by the end of the week. When he did not come for them I called his house and was told he had died two days earlier. ...[23] Sometime later I was riffling through some boxes and was surprised to find that I had my handwritten notes from the first volume as well as the typed notes from the second. Looking further I found twenty-five to thirty letters written by the Lee brothers.[24]

Also included in the Connor Papers is an article clipped from the *Washington Evening Standard* of September 27, 1967, that briefly related the above story of the suppression of Jennie's "dynamite" manuscript two years earlier. And then the columnist gleefully announced, "Today I can report that the manuscript has not been suppressed, that it is in the hands of an editor and that the chances of publication are favorable. Its appearance would be an event of unusual political interest."[25]

But then, rather like the Loch Ness Monster, the manuscript slipped from view again. Who had submitted the memoir to a publisher in 1967, and why it was not published, remain a mystery.

*   *   *

By the time I got on the trail of Jennie's memoirs in 1989, the suppressed manuscript had made two brief reappearances: first in 1967, and again when Ginny Connor typed her notes in 1971. It seems that at least one copy of the memoir was still floating around somewhere outside of Taiwan's control. Where had it come from?

Eugene Kiang had presumably been led to believe that the three copies that had been in the United States would be surrendered to him at the time he paid off Jennie. From the Lee brothers' correspondence, it is clear that Yinson did indeed send two of these copies to Hong Kong. But what happened to the third copy, held by the literary agent Hill, is uncertain. He had apparently been reluctant to give it up because he had expended sizable sums of cash and considerable effort while working as Jennie's literary agent. Holding on to the manuscript may have been his only means of assuring that he would receive compensation for his services.[26] His may have been the copy floating about.

Another possibility is that the Lee brothers had duplicitously held back a copy even while assuring Kiang that he had received all existing copies of the memoir. That the Lee brothers were not above engaging in a degree of skulduggery is evident in the advice Yinson gave his brother James. In negotiating with the Taiwan representatives, Yinson told James he should "keep something up your sleeve. [We are] accustomed to dealing with honest people; Taiwan is not honest. ... Be smart, and outwit them before you settle." Yinson had been especially anxious that James withhold some of the photos. "They [Taiwan] don't know what pictures you have, so replace the important ones with others that are not important. They are tricky, so we have to be also. Don't be honest with them. It does not pay."[27] Moreover, the Lee brothers had held extravagant ideas about the value of the manuscript, at one time dreaming of obtaining U.S. $1 million for world publication, movie,

TV, and other literary rights to the memoir.[28] With such an attitude and such financial expectations, it would have been astonishing if the Lees had not held back at least one copy of the manuscript.[29]

But did the manuscript still exist in 1989? And if so, where was it located? I had no clue. A year of constant inquiries produced nothing. At a dinner one evening, however, a guest casually mentioned that the manuscript was in the archives of the Hoover Institution in Stanford; that a scholar doing research in Sino-American relations had noticed Jennie's manuscript lying among the papers of Chang Hsin-hai, a deceased Nationalist official and diplomat. How Chang had acquired it will probably never be known; he was not, as far as is known, associated with the preparation of the manuscript. Yet there it lay, uncataloged, in solitary obscurity.[30]

The thrill of discovering the existence of the manuscript has been only slightly diminished by learning that at least one other copy of the manuscript is on the loose. In 1983, one of Jennie's grandsons, Ch'en Chung-jen, published an article announcing that he possessed not only his grandmother's memoir but also her diaries and letters and would publish them shortly.[31] After writing that article, however, he published nothing.

The reason: Taiwan had once again intervened to prevent publication of the manuscript. Three times Taiwan's agents came to Hong Kong to dissuade Ch'en Chung-jen from pursuing his publication plans. These were acrimonious meetings and resolved nothing. Taiwan next refused to grant Mr. Ch'en, a businessman, an entry visa. And then, at just this time, Taiwan agents in California murdered the author Chiang Nan, who had excited Taiwan's ire by writing a biography critical of Chiang Ching-kuo, Chiang Kai-shek's son and the president of the Republic of China. This assassination convinced Ch'en Chung-jen that the better part of valor was to abort his plans to publish the manuscript.[32]

Recently, however, two journals in Taiwan began publishing, in Chinese translation, lengthy, serialized sets of excerpts from Jennie's manuscript. The manuscript published by *Chuan-chi wen-hsueh* (Biographical literature) was sent to the editor of that journal by someone living in "Nan-yang," Southeast Asia, who refused to reveal his or her identity for fear of retribution by the Kuomintang.[33] The second manuscript was published in *Hsin Hsin-wen* (The journalist).[34] From the introduction to this translation, it is clear that the English original is the

Hoover version. Who sent it to *Hsin Hsin-wen* is not revealed. Both of these journals have also published their translations in book form.

Now that Jennie's reminiscences have become widely available, one wonders if it was worth all the fuss. Were the guardians of Chiang Kai-shek's legend correct in fearing that publication of the manuscript would tarnish Chiang's sage image? And is the manuscript of significant historical value?

The answer to the first question is yes. Chiang emerges from Jennie's story as considerably less than sage. Although Jennie was to fall deeply in love with Chiang and wrote of his warmheartedness, she also wrote of his less-endearing qualities. She quoted one of Chiang's closest friends as saying of him, "To be very honest, I must say he is extremely impulsive, opinionated, and too often hot-headed."[35] And an elderly villager, who had known Chiang since childhood, warned the new bride, "He is stubborn, jealous, tactless, bad-tempered, and egotistical."[36]

More damaging to Chiang's sage image, however, was Jennie's account of how the thirty-two-year-old Chiang lured her into a hotel room where he tried, unsuccessfully, to force himself sexually on the thirteen-year-old girl. And soon after their marriage, he infected her with gonorrhea, which left them both sterile. A friend of Chiang's told Jennie that Chiang had been a notorious lecher at one stage of his life. Jennie's depiction of Chiang's treatment of his son, Ching-kuo, and the son's stark terror of the father, also corresponds poorly with the legend of Chiang as a man of transcendent purity and wisdom.

The answer to the second question—is the manuscript of significant historical value?—is more difficult. But the answer is yes, with qualifications. Certainly it is flawed and unreliable. A considerable portion of Jennie's story dwells on matters that are of no historical consequence. Jennie devoted long pages to detailed descriptions of scenery, houses, monasteries, religious ceremonies, and the like. But she tells us disppointingly little—considering the fact that she claimed to be at the center of the political storms during those years—of such factional relationships as those between the Communists and non-Communists, and between Chiang and his principal rivals for power: Wang Ching-wei, Hu Han-min, and Michael Borodin (although her accounts of Chiang's relations with Generals Hsu Ch'ung-chih and Ch'en Chiung-ming, if true, are important).

The manuscript also contains a number of errors, both large and small. It speaks, for instance, of the Blue Shirts secret-service organization set up by Ch'en Kuo-fu in the 1920s. But that organization was not, in fact, instituted until 1932—and not by Ch'en Kuo-fu.[37] Jennie also errs in saying that Chiang was a Shanghai stockbroker for a few months in 1923–1924, whereas it was actually from 1917 to 1922. One could go on ...

Much of Jennie's memoir, moreover, takes the form of quoted dialogue. For Jennie to have had a written record of most of these conversations would patently have been impossible. One can only surmise how accurate her recollections were, forty years after those conversations. Quoting dialogue is a common narrative device in Chinese *yeh-shih*— "wild," or fictionalized, histories—a similarity that instills little confidence in Jennie's story.

Professor Wang Ke-wen, a specialist on the Nationalist revolution in the 1920s, carefully studied Jennie's manuscript and identified numerous other instances where Jennie's reminiscences depart from the known history of the period. [38] He has posed a question—powerful and perhaps devastating to the credibility of the manuscript: If Jennie's account is unreliable when discussing events for which we have independent evidence, how can we accept her scandalizing accounts of her intimate life with Chiang Kai-shek—for which there is, and can be, no corroborating evidence?

Despite the damaging implications of Professor Wang's question, I believe that Jennie's story, especially as it relates to her personal experience, is generally credible, though certainly not in all its details. This conclusion emerges from the following set of considerations:

1. Jennie Chen's memoirs are authentic, in the sense that Jennie had, indeed, been Chiang Kai-shek's wife and that she wrote her memoirs.[39]

2. On the question of reliability, it is important to keep in mind that Jennie was poorly qualified to write a document that could survive, unscathed, the scrutiny of today's professional historians. She was very young at the time of her marriage to Chiang. And she was not highly educated—perhaps, at best, she had the equivalent of a high-school education. It is manifest that she was not familiar with the canons of historical writing. Despite the lack of qualifications, she still thought she could solve her financial problems by writing a memoir intended primarily for an American audience. In writing the memoir, however, she dealt with events on the Chinese political stage that were largely beyond her ken. This led her to commit the errors that Professor Wang picked up so easily.

3. Jennie also wrote of events, however, that she had personally experienced—her courtship, her marriage, her separation from Chiang, and so on. These were events about which she was much more familiar than she was about larger questions of *affaires d'état*. It was presumably these personal experiences about which she was able to write knowledgeably and with relative accuracy.

No doubt Jennie had grounds for grievance against Chiang, having been peremptorily and unceremoniously dismissed as his wife. Nonetheless, her portrayal of Chiang is surprisingly lacking in acrimony.

Shoring up confidence in the veracity of Jennie's reportage of her relationship with Chiang is one piece of corroborating evidence. On its face, Jennie's insistence that Chiang left her to marry Soong Mei-ling purely for politically opportunistic reasons is suspect. But, as noted above (and in note 8), Jennie's story was fully confirmed by Soong Mei-ling herself.

Perhaps Jennie's story *was* sometimes skewed as a result of her personal emotions. And perhaps the passage of time had dimmed her memories. But these are problems inherent in all autobiographical literature.

For all its weaknesses as a historical document, therefore, Jennie's manuscript tells a fascinating and plausible story of one of China's great leaders at a critical time in the nation's history—and of the woman who paid a high price so that he could attain his ambition. It also quotes documents—such as Chiang's letters to her during his mission to Russia in 1924—that appear authentic and of significance. No future biographer of Chiang Kai-shek will be able safely to ignore Jennie's memoir.

╭   ╭   ╭

Jennie stayed in the United States for five years, returning to Shanghai in 1933, where she was sustained by financial payments provided by agents of Chiang Kai-shek, until 1961. Then, with the help of Chou En-lai, she received permission to move to Hong Kong, where she resided in a house purchased for her by Chiang Kai-shek and Chiang Ching-kuo. She died in 1971.

In 1924, while married to Chiang, she adopted a baby girl, whom she named Chiang Yao-kuang. Jennie left the child in the care of her mother when she went to the United States. After returning to Shanghai, both Jennie and the child dropped the surname Chiang and resumed Jennie's maiden name of Ch'en.

In about 1946, Ch'en Yao-kuang married Lu Chiu-chih, who was still living in Shanghai in 1992. Yao-kuang now resides in Hong Kong. She and Lu Chiu-chih have two sons and a daughter. The sons, Ch'en Chung-jen ("James") and Ch'en Hsiao-jen ("George"), are both businessmen in Hong Kong. The daughter, Ch'en Chiu-li (Julia Chan), lives in the United States.

NOTES

1. Jennie in 1919 signed her name as Ch'en Feng, but she was known by friends and family by her "milk name," Ah Feng. Chiang Kai-shek changed her name to Chieh-ju about the time they were engaged in 1921. Most of the materials upon which this introduction is based are in the Ginny Connor Papers, which are generally described in this Introduction. Ms. Connor has deposited copies of this collection in the Butler Library, Columbia University; and in the East Asian Library and Firestone Library of Princeton University. She has also kindly given me a copy. Ms. Connor has been most helpful to me in my work concerning the manuscript. For years Ms. Connor held these papers, constantly feeling concern that she might become the target of a Kuomintang attempt to recover the materials. Fortunately, she retained the papers, which have made my writing this introduction possible.

2. Some writers refer to Ms. Yao as Chiang's second of a total of four wives. According to Chinese custom, they assert, Ms. Yao's status was no different from that of Jennie Chen. Yet Ms. Yao and Chiang never were united in a formal ceremony, as were Jennie Chen and Chiang. Did that make a difference? T'ang Szu-chu, "Szu-wei Chiang-fu-jen te ku-shih" (The story of the four 'Mme Chiangs'), *Hsin Hsin-wen* (The journalist) (Taipei) 256/257 (February 2–15, 1992): 14–15.

3. A translation of the marriage certificate is in the Connor Papers, p. 48, reproduced herein, in "Our Wedding," p. 38.

4. Ch'en Chieh-ju, "My Seven Years as Madame Chiang Kai-shek" (unpub. MS), p. 192 and herein in "Rebellion and Reversal."

5. Wang Yüeh-hsi, "Mao Fu-mei yü Chiang-chia fu-tzu" (Chiang's first wife's relations with her husband and son), *Chuan-chi wen-hsueh* (Biographical literature), no. 322 (March 1989): 124. (Hereafter this source is referred to as *CCWH*.) This source states that Jennie graduated from the Shanghai Russian-language School. In her manuscript, however, Jennie never mentioned having served as a translator of anything more complex than a menu, and it is doubtful that she had sufficient fluency to serve as an interpreter in complex and delicate discussions in either English or Russian.

6. MS, pp. 385–386, and herein in "The Great Intrigue."

7. MS, pp. 306–307, and herein in "The Dinner Party."

8. "Mike" Gardner Cowles, founder and publisher of *Look* magazine, became well acquainted with Mme Chiang during a visit to Chungking in 1942. He recounted a conversation he subsequently had with her: "Her marriage to the Generalissimo, she began, was one of convenience that had been arranged by her mother. As in so many such marriages, the bride and groom scarcely knew one another. On their wedding night, the Generalissimo told her that he did not believe in sexual relations except for the purpose of producing a child. And since he already had a son by a previous marriage and was not interested in having any more children, there would be no sex between them." See *Mike Looks Back: The Memoirs of Gardner Cowles, Founder of Look Magazine* (New York: Gardner Cowles, 1985), p. 90. Because this memoir was privately published and intended primarily for the author's children and grandchildren, it is improbable that the book was written for its sensationalist effect. Cowles also reported (pp. 87–89) a secret romantic liaison that Wendell Willkie had with Mme Chiang during Willkie's highly publicized trip to wartime Chungking.

9. MS, p. 407, and herein in "My Exile." That the punishment invoked by the oath corresponded so closely to the ultimate fate of Chiang and the Nationalist government creates more than a little suspicion that at least this part of Jennie's story is apocryphal.

10. A photograph of this event is in the Chang Ching-chiang file, housed in the No. 2 Historical Archives, Nanjing, and is reproduced in this Introduction.

11. See "Author's Note."

12. Letter, James Lee to Yinson Lee, in Connor Papers, p. 76. After her "divorce," Jennie received financial payments sent to her, indirectly, by Chiang. The first time was when she left China for the United States. In 1937, she received a "big settlement," on the condition that she not make further demands (Connor Papers, p. 88). Soon after arriving in Hong Kong from Shanghai in 1961, she began receiving trimonthly payments of U.S. $500. Conduit for these payments was Tai Chi-t'ao's son Tai An-kuo. The payments terminated around early 1964, presumably after Taiwan learned of Jennie's efforts to publish her manuscript (Connor Papers, pp. 66, 88).

13. Letter, Ch'en Li-fu to Ch'en Chieh-ju, April 4, 1959, in Connor Papers, pp. 47, 49; also see Ch'en Chih-yü, "Chiang Chieh-shih hua-ch'ien mai li-shih" (Chiang Kai-shek pays money to bury history), *Hsin Hsin-wen* 256/257 (February 2–15, 1992): 18. I have altered the quote slightly to increase clarity.

14. Jennie Chen's grandson, Ch'en Hsiao-jen (George Chan), informed me of James Lee's collaboration in writing the book. James Lee, according to Mr. Ch'en, "wielded the brush" (letter dated September 29, 1992). On January 10, 1964, James Lee wrote to his brother Yinson, saying: "You cannot imagine the trouble I have had in putting the 425 pages together. At least it is now in black and white, with all the true facts that had never been revealed due to power poli-

tics" (Connor Papers, p. 55). (James Lee's Chinese name was Shih-min. His brother Yinson's name in Chinese was Yin-sheng.)

I initially thought that James Lee might be the translator of a manuscript that Jennie had prepared. This possibility was suggested by Ginny Connor's report that the friend who had asked her to take notes on the manuscript, Vincent Rouba, saw the Chinese manuscript rolled up in a carpet when he visited Muriel Dexter. However, Ch'en Hsiao-jen's letter to me states that, to the best of his recollection, his grandmother had not prepared a Chinese version.

15. Connor Papers, pp. 45, 62, 64. A search in 1980 of the Doubleday records produced no reference to Jennie's manuscript. This search was prompted by telephone conversations from Illinois, and I am uncertain how thoroughly the search was conducted. However, Ginny Connor in 1992 spoke to Kenneth McCormick, the editor at Doubleday who in 1964 had handled Jennie's manuscript, and he clearly remembered the incident (telephone conversation with Ginny Connor, July 1992).

16. Connor Papers, p. 79.

17. The role of the U.S. government in the suppression of Jennie's manuscript is yet another facet of this mystery. A New York publisher reportedly told a reporter that "officials in Washington *actively* discouraged him" from publishing the manuscript (emphasis added). See *Washington Evening Standard*, September 27, 1967, a clipping from which is in the Connor Papers, between pp. 66 and 67.

18. *San Francisco Chronicle*, April 12, 1965, to be found in Connor Papers, p. 102.

19. Connor Papers, p. 69 (in longhand).

20. Kiang's Chinese name was Chiang I-p'ing. Kiang had also handled many of the arrangements for the marriage between Jennie and Chiang in 1921. See Yü I-ch'i, "Ch'en Chieh-ju Wai-sun Ch'en Chung-jen chih Mi" (The puzzle of Ch'en Chieh-ju's grandson, Ch'en Chung-jen), in *CCWH*, no. 342 (November 1990): 24.

21. On February 26, 1965, Yinson sent a cable to James in Hong Kong as follows: "Two manuscripts [and] photos being mailed [to you] Parcel Post. ... The third copy of manuscript is in Hill's hands. ... Therefore all three copies of manuscript will be accounted for, as well as the photos, that Jennie wants returned" (Connor Papers, p. 85). Whether Yinson ever got the third copy of the manuscript back from Hill is unclear.

22. Yinson was expecting 10 percent of what Jennie received. After Jennie was paid off, the amount of payment that Yinson expected to receive was U.S. $17,000. Ergo, total payment to Jennie should have been $170,000. See Connor Papers, pp. 90, 114, 116.

23. Ms. Connor has not suggested that Mr. Rouba's death was other than natural.

24. Connor Papers, Introductory matter. Ms. Connor revealed further details about her acquisition of these papers in a telephone conversation with me on July 26, 1991. The manuscript and letters had been in the possession of Muriel Dexter, who was a close friend of Yinson Lee and who provided Yinson with a roof over his head during at least the period of the negotiations discussed here. Yinson died in late March or April 1965, and Ms. Dexter doubtless inherited the manuscript. Ms. Dexter was, of course, the "elderly lady" who was now trying to get the manuscript published. The friend she engaged to help her was Vincent Rouba.

25. Connor Papers, between pp. 66 and 67. The article appeared in the *Washington Evening Standard*, September 27, 1967, on p. 7, in the column "Jeremy Campbell in Washington." See also the clipping from the *Washington, D.C. Examiner*, November 22–26, 1967, in *CCWH*, in section of photographs.

26. Connor Papers, pp. 64, 81.

27. Connor Papers, pp. 72–73.

28. Connor Papers, pp. 64, 72–73.

29. That James Lee intended to withhold copies of the memoir from Taiwan's agents is suggested in a letter he wrote to Yinson shortly before the settlement with Taiwan: "I'll let you have a copy of [the] memoir and a set of photos in due course, but for the present, do not fail to return those that are now in your possession" (Connor Papers, p. 83).

There may, however, be more than one copy of the manuscript in the United States. The suspicion lingers that Muriel Dexter, the "elderly lady" mentioned in the Connor Papers, may have retained a copy held by James Lee. Ginny Connor, who has been involved for many years in the mystery of the manuscript, is of the opinion that Ms. Dexter retained not only the photographs but also the Chinese original of the manuscript. But Ms. Dexter, if she is still alive, is incommunicado, perhaps still living in fear of Kuomintang retribution.

30. The memoir, under the authorship of Ch'en Chieh-ju and entitled "My Seven Years as Madame Chiang Kai-shek," was, and continues to be, housed in the Hoover Institution Archives, Box 16 of the Chang Hsin-hai Collection.

Prof. T'ang Te-kang (Tong Te-kong) offers some informed speculations, but nothing more, regarding how Chang Hsin-hai acquired the manuscript. See T'ang's preface to the Chinese text, in *Ch'en Chieh-ju Hui-I-lu* (The memoir of Ch'en Chieh-ju) (Taipei: Chuan-chi wen-hsueh Press, 1992), pp. 21–22.

31. Ch'en Chung-jen, "Wo-te Wai-p'o Ch'en Chieh-ju" (My grandmother, Ch'en Chieh-ju), in *CCWH* 342 (November 1990): 22.

32. Letter, Ch'en Hsiao-jen to Eastman, September 29, 1992.

33. *CCWH*, January 1992.

34. Part 1 is in *Hsin Hsin-wen* 256/257 (February 2/15, 1992).

35. The friend was Chang Ching-chiang. See MS, p. 60, and herein in "Matchmaking and Courtship."

36. MS, p. 100, and herein in "Honeymoon."

37. Jennie was doubtless confusing the Blue Shirts with a similar organization created by Ch'en Li-fu, also at Chiang Kai-shek's behest, in 1928. Ch'en Li-fu was the younger brother of Ch'en Kuo-fu. See Howard L. Boorman, ed., *Biographical Dictionary of Republican China*, Vol. 1 (New York: Columbia University Press, 1967), p. 107.

38. Wang Ke-wen, "P'o-hsi 'Ch'en Chieh-ju Hui-i-lu' te Mi-hsin yü Shih-shih" (The secret bitterness and historical truth of Ch'en Chieh-ju's memoirs), in *Ch'en Chieh-ju Hui-i-lu* (Taipei: Hsin-hsin-wen Wen-hua Shih-yeh Publishers, 1992), pp. 259–279.

39. Chiang himself referred to Jennie in his diary. See ibid., p. 278. Chiang Wei-kuo, Chiang Kai-shek's younger son, speaking to the Legislative Yuan in early 1992, also affirmed that he knew Ch'en Chieh-ju and did not deny that she had been married to his father. He doubted, however, for two reasons, that Jennie had written this memoir: First, the tone of the work does not at all resemble the Ch'en Chieh-ju he knew, who was very kindly, loving, and intelligent. Second, he first met her, not in Shanghai when he was six years old, but in Canton when he was nine years old. See "Chiang Wei-kuo: 'Ch'en Chieh-ju Hui-yi-lu' Nei-jung k'o-i wu-mieh" (The contents of Ch'en Chieh-ju's memoirs are deliberately malicious), *Kuo-ji Jih-pao* (International daily) (Los Angeles), April 16, 1992. (I am indebted to Prof. Wang for bringing this, and other information, to my attention.)

The preceding paragraph speaks to the point that Jennie was married to, or at least lived with, Chiang Kai-shek in the 1920s. That it was she who wrote the memoirs, at least in collaboration with James Lee, and that she was intimately involved in the attempt to publish them are fully verified by the correspondence between James and Yinson Lee (see the Connor Papers). The Lee brothers' correspondence has a separate history from the manuscript and is, therefore, an independent source of verification. I do not think Chiang Wei-kuo's attempt to cast doubts on the authenticity of the memoir is at all persuasive.

Finally, a body of scholars knowledgeable about this period and the manuscript—including Wang Ke-wen, Zhang Xian-wen, and Yan Ru-ping—accept the authenticity, if not the reliability, of Jennie's reminiscences.

AUTHOR'S NOTE

I am in a unique position to record, to the best of my ability, an account of my married life with Chiang Kai-shek at the time of his rise to power—a period that has never been correctly recorded even by modern historians. This is chiefly due to the suppression of the true facts of General Chiang's and my life during this period.

There is one account of my life, however, contained in a widely read, two-volume Chinese book entitled *Chin-ling Ch'un-meng*, meaning "Spring dreams of Nanking," by T'ang Jen. It is, unfortunately, as false as it is misleading. It is because of this that I am moved to publish my own memoirs.

My memoirs will reveal an important eight-year period that has been widely whispered about, but never told. Here I will clear up the mystery regarding my true identity. Even today, responsible journalists write that I was a Eurasian, an ex-singsong girl, a concubine, a nurse, a Cantonese, an adventuress, or even an imposter. The material for my memoirs is taken from my diaries, which Kai-shek encouraged me to keep.

Among the many letters that have come to me recently is one from Mr. Ch'en Li-fu, the junior member of the C. C. clique of the Kuomintang. He is one of many politicians still living who are familiar with my background. His letter reads: "I beg you not to publish your memoirs. Your sacrifice for the unification of China, and your silence all these years, make you a grand person and a loyal citizen. But should your book be published, it will only injure the generalissimo and the Kuomintang. So, do remain constant as you have always been."

Contrary to Mr. Ch'en's contention, I do not believe my memoirs will injure anyone. In fact, they will serve as an authentic record, showing our happy married life and how an ordinary man may, with persistence and favorable opportunities, rise to become the undisputed leader of a nation.

Jennie Ch'en Chieh-ju

Chiang Kai-shek's Secret Past

1

A Young Girl in Shanghai

My family background was similar to that of most Shanghaiese. My father, Ch'en Hsueh-feng, was a native of Chen-hai, commonly called Ningpo, a land renowned for its bamboo. He was a paper merchant dealing in a wide range of handmade native products. My mother was from the family of Wu, of Soochow. She was a very gentle and kindly lady, loved by all our friends, relatives, and neighbors. Mother stood out because she was literate and could explain the Chinese classics and write beautiful calligraphy. Many friends and relatives took advantage of her talent, asking her to write letters for them, to read letters they had received, or to explain some literary phrase. She was always willing to help everyone.

This was a time when conservative Chinese took seriously the old saying, Only the untalented woman is virtuous. Women should, therefore, be kept illiterate, and most girls, therefore, received no education at all. Their main job was to live in semiseclusion, to be virtuous and obedient daughters, and learn to make the finest of embroidery.

So, when Mother was young, there were hardly any public schools for girls. Most places of learning had been established by scholars seeking to squeeze out a living, by local gentry, or by several families who combined to hire a tutor for their children. High schools or colleges were established on very much the same principles. There were many of these in the cities, but they were for boys only.

The Chinese Empire was almost completely indifferent to the education of girls. Nonetheless, there were not a few girls who managed to
pick up a smattering of Chinese characters so that they could read and
write. Such was my mother's case.

In fairness, I must say that there were some Christian Mission
Schools for the education of girls. But these were mostly for Westernized Chinese, orphaned children, and children who were willing to
change their faith. During my childhood, it was the rarest thing to find
an elderly woman who was able to read and write or even sign her own
name. Most of the men, however, except laborers, were literate. To be a
literate woman, therefore, was a great exception, and it is little wonder
that my mother was beloved and admired by all who knew her.

When China became a republic in 1912, I was six years old. And despite the fact that the establishment of the republic marked the beginning of China's modernization, the centuries-old customs died hard.
Women all over China, therefore, continued to live in a sphere different
from men—a sphere that, though it must of necessity have touched
that of men at some points, was kept as separate as possible. My parents
were conservatives and sticklers for tradition. Therefore, according to
the practice of the ancients, I did not, as a young girl, occupy the same
room or eat with my father or with my young brother, Ah-bun. My
clothes and those of my mother were not mixed with those of my father
and brother. Nor did we sit and talk together in idle chatter.

In these modern days, such customs may seem absurd. Of course, in
some more Westernized homes, such customs were observed more in
the breach than in the practice. Generally, however, conservative
Chinese of the better class strictly observed such orthodox rules.

The many restrictive customs affecting women were based on the
idea that they occupied a lower plane than men. As heaven is to earth,
so was man to woman; man was the superior, woman the inferior. In
my upbringing, I was taught to be absolutely submissive to my father
and my mother. It seemed natural to me because I am by nature shy,
sensitive, and docile. Whatever they said was the law, for they were my
elders, more experienced and wiser than I.

As I entered my teens, my mother, following tradition and as part of
my upbringing, spoke to me in confidence about the great importance
of a maiden's virginity. "A man," she explained, "will always try to
have sexual intercourse with a young girl. So beware! You must understand that there are three kinds of men. The first type will want it, but

his moral concepts will tell him it is wrong and he may desist. The second type will try, time and again, to inveigle a girl into submitting. The girl who is weak-minded will foolishly submit—to her unending remorse. The third kind will trick a girl into a compromising situation and take advantage of the situation to rape her.

"Now, the girl who cannot protect that three-inch spot of her body, and who lightly gives in to a man's passion, deserves all the scorn and contempt that society will heap upon her. She has no one to blame but herself. Besides, in sexual intercourse, there is a possibility of the girl's becoming pregnant and giving birth to an illegitimate child. This is not only a disgrace to the child but is equally disgraceful to the mother and her whole family.

"Therefore, protect your virginity with a firm mind, my dear daughter, for it is by far the most precious thing in a girl's life. It is a symbol of chastity.

"The hymen is the mucous membrane that partly closes the orifice of the vagina and therefore protects the womb. It should only be broken by the husband on the wedding night. The bridegroom will regard the hymen as a very important thing because it will prove to him whether his bride is virtuous or a girl of easy virtue.

"So, it is of the utmost importance that a girl should be pure minded and never allow a man to maul her or to be familiar with her, so as to avoid any possibility of becoming his victim."

I naturally took this advice to heart and never forgot Mother's words. Fortunately I had plenty of common sense, and I regarded the sex act as wicked for any girl unless she was married.

∕ ∕ ∕

In 1918, the Chinese Republic was already six years old, and the emancipation of women was an established fact. Modern schools for girls sprang up all over Shanghai. Thus, women of China had a chance to assert their rights and acquire a good education. In my case, Mother placed me, after extensive inquiries, in the Ai-kuo Girls' School on Haining Road. This school had been established by the famous revolutionist Ts'ai Yuan-p'ei. Here I diligently studied so that I might acquire a good Chinese education, as did my mother.

I was then nearing thirteen years old, tall and lanky, but well formed. Most people thought I was at least eighteen. Although I had a smooth complexion and sharp features, my mouth was large, with prominent teeth, and my jawbones were rather heavy. My teacher, Miss Hsu, seeing that I had an inferiority complex, said that these distinctive features added to, rather than detracted from, my good looks. I wore thick, heavy bangs, which almost covered my eyebrows, and my hair hung in a long plait down my back.

My only bosom friend was Miss Chu Yi-min, who lived in the same kind of house as ours, next door, on Tibet Road, and I used to go to her place for chats and to do my homework. Although Yi-min was only five years older than I, I admired her immensely. She seemed so worldly wise, always dressed beautifully, and to know the answers to all my inquiries.

Father and Mother used to upbraid me for staying at Yi'min's rather than at home. One late afternoon, when my mother came to Yi'min's to look for me, she saw that my friend and I were engrossed in my homework and not idling away our time. It happened that that day's lesson was particularly difficult and I needed Yi'min's help. Mother apologized to Yi'min, saying: "It's a shame for Ah Feng to trouble you every day like this. I am sure she disturbs you and takes up too much of your precious time!"

"I'm only too glad to coach Ah Feng," replied Yi-min. "She is a very intelligent girl and eager to learn. I have to tell her only once and she understands quickly. We are good friends, so don't say she is taking up my time." She added, "Please sit down and have some tea, good Auntie Ch'en."

Mother was grateful to know that I was under such a good influence, and from that time on, she allowed me to go out alone without worrying that I would stray.

I abruptly learned the truth of the Chinese proverb, Favorable situations are never constant, when Yi-min married old Mr. Chang Ching-chiang. Mr. Chang lived in an expensive house at the west part of Nanking Road. For weeks I was disspirited, weeping in private, thinking I had lost my chum. Yi-min told me that Old Mr. Chang had been a widower. His wife had died in America, leaving him with a family of five teenage daughters. She assured me that her husband was a kindly man, and that he would welcome me as a regular visitor to their home. I jumped at this offer and visited Yi-min regularly.

To me, it was a special event when Yi-min's five stepdaughters arrived in Shanghai from America. The Chang household that day was astir with excitement. Five lovely daughters, all well dressed, intelli-

Jennie (center) with her close friend Chu Yi-min (Mrs. Chang Ching-chiang, on the right) and one of Chang Ching-chiang's five daughters (on the left).

gent, and charming, came to live with their father and stepmother. These were no ordinary daughters. They had been educated first in France and later in America. To me, they appeared to be the very epitome of modernity. I was especially impressed by their free and easy dispositions, their gracious manners, and chic costumes. They were stunning! So different from the ordinary run of Shanghai girls.

Yi-min, conscious of being the new stepmother, set out to win their goodwill and affection. But I could see it was no easy task. The five daughters were too self-willed, too attached and devoted to their beloved mother, who had died in an accident in New York the previous year. To expect them to shift their affection to a strange woman who had usurped their mother's place was out of the question. It goes without saying that there existed an undercurrent of resentment. Outwardly, however, they displayed no unfriendliness. Because all concerned were people of education, each kept her personal feelings well controlled, and on the surface they appeared to be one happy family.

The five girls all had English names, and their five personalities were as far apart as the antipodes. Their ages ranged from twelve to twenty-two.

Therese, the eldest, was slender and plain looking and wore thick glasses. She was very sincere and kindly; those who did not know her might think she was a schoolteacher because she dressed mostly in somber colors and wore no jewelry. Yvonne, twenty, was modest, with a protruding chin, but very efficient in playing the part of the little mother in the home, which she managed very well. Suzanne, eighteen, had a roundish, smooth face, with nice roundish eyes and a cute nose. She was stylish, talkative, and fond of dancing. Georgette, sixteen, was the prettiest of all the sisters and the most dignified. She behaved like a princess and took her art of painting very seriously. Helen, twelve, was, like Georgette, interested in art. Being the youngest, she had a thirst for knowledge, was studious, and was regarded as the smartest of all the sisters.

Although none of the girls was blessed with remarkable beauty, their charm, modernity, kindly dispositions, and education made them very popular. Therese seemed to me the most congenial, and we quickly became fast friends.

Since the girls had not completed their schooling in America, Old Mr. Chang made arrangements for Therese to teach at the McTyre Girls' School on Edinburgh Road, while Yvonne managed the household. Suzanne, Georgette, and Helen attended school. To brush up on their Chinese studies, an old Chinese tutor, Mr. Yang, was engaged to give Chinese lessons to the girls after school. Yi-min thought that because I was more advanced than the girls in Chinese, it would be nice if I joined the class to give the girls some encouragement. I quickly and gratefully accepted this offer, for I knew I could learn much about Western manners from these modern young ladies.

From conversations with Therese and Yi-min, I gradually became acquainted with old Mr. Chang Ching-chiang's background. Hailing from Chekiang province, he had become a wealthy merchant in Paris, selling all kinds of valuable curios. In 1909, Dr. Sun Yat-sen took refuge in France after the failure of one of his revolutionary attempts to oust the Manchu viceroy from Canton. Having no money when he arrived in Paris, he approached Chang Ching-chiang, who listened to Dr. Sun tell of his revolutionary ambitions. He was so fascinated by Dr. Sun's patriotic story that he then and there donated half his fortune to the revolutionary cause. For Dr. Sun, this was like spring water to a thirsty soul. Thereafter, he regarded Chang Ching-chiang as a true patriot and made him his honorary adviser.

When World War I broke out, Old Mr. Chang removed not only the remaining part of his curio collection to New York but also his wife and family. In the years that followed, he left his wife and daughters in New York while he returned to Shanghai to speculate in gold bar exchange. Whenever Dr. Sun came to the "Paris of the Far East," he never failed to pay his respects to Chang Ching-chiang and to talk about his latest revolutionary activities.

One day during the school holidays in the summer of 1919, when I was studying with the Chang sisters, Dr. Sun Yat-sen arrived at the Chang home. He was accompanied by two men. One was a Mr. Tai Chit'ao; the other was a Mr. Chiang Kai-shek.

When they came into the drawing room, Old Mr. Chang introduced Yi-min and us girls to the famous leader. Then pointing to me, he added: "This is our friend Jennie Ch'en. She not only has a good knowledge of Chinese but can also read and write fluent English. You may test her. Talk to her!"

I was embarrassed by this sudden compliment and blushed.

"What are you doing to help our country?" asked Dr. Sun, while his eyes focused piercingly on me.

"I'm only a schoolgirl," I muttered softly. "But I hope I shall one day be useful to our country."

"The young are to be respected," exclaimed Dr. Sun smilingly. "While you are young, you must think of ways and means to serve our country. Every Chinese must do his or her duty. We revolutionaries cannot do the work alone. 'One pillar cannot support the whole roof,' " he said, quoting an old proverb. "We are doing all we can to unify China so that she will become a dominant power in the near fugure." He turned to Chang Ching-chiang and said, "She is a very intelligent girl and a good example of our revolutionary womanhood."

The two other male guests present grinned with broad smiles on their faces to show their approval of what their leader had said. But their noisy laughter made me squirm. After pleasant amenities, we girls beat a hasty retreat into the inner rooms.

For three hours the men talked in the drawing room about politics; Yi-min and I helped the servants in the kitchen prepare afternoon refreshments and wine for the guests. From scattered conversation, we girls could gather that Dr. Sun was talking about a revolutionary campaign by a General Ch'en Chiung-ming.

It seemed that Dr. Sun had succeeded in persuading General Ch'en Chiung-ming, who was stationed in Fukien, to throw in his lot with the revolutionaries in an effort to carry the fight back to Canton and oust the warlord there. Dr. Sun's plan was to use Canton as a base for military operations. It was to discuss the financial angles of this campaign that had brought Dr. Sun to consult the wealthy Mr. Chang Ching-chiang.

2

The Pursuit

About six o'clock Dr. Sun and the men had departed, so I bade Yi-min good-bye and walked out of the house to go home to dinner. There, at the front gate, standing like a sentinel, was one of the two men who had come with Dr. Sun. The man's face was flushed from the wine he had drunk, and he looked so very red. He came forward to ask why I was leaving so early and where I was going.

His questions startled me, for the man had only been perfunctorily introduced to me and was practically a stranger. So I blushed and forced myself to answer curtly, "It's getting late. I am going home."

"Are you not pleased that our leader singled you out to pay you a compliment?"

On the spur of the moment, I did not know what he meant, and I looked at him inquiringly. He was a man of average height, somewhat wiry in frame, with shaven head, strong, jutting jaws, prominent chin, and short, straight nose. When he spoke, he grunted and revealed extra-long teeth, dark, penetrating eyes, and sensuous lips. He looked at me lecherously and explained: "Our leader is Dr. Sun Yat-sen. He paid you a very nice compliment. Don't you remember?"

I shook my head and ignored the question.

"Where do you live?" he asked anxiously. I thought it was none of his business, so I purposely told him a wrong number: "Eighty-eight Tibet Road." Actually my house number was 33 Tibet Road.

"Then I will take you home!" he said determinedly.

"No, no," I protested excitedly. Then he stood in front to bar my way. Seeing this, I stopped short and said: "You must not walk with me.

9

My parents are very strict and will scold me for walking with a stranger in the street." Suddenly I became panicky and made a dash to get away from him.

Seeing my nervousness, he stepped aside to allow me to pass. I hurried along and could vaguely feel his gaze and what was on his mind. I rushed home without looking back at him.

The following week, when mother went out shopping, she left the front door wide open so that I could have more light, as I was doing some work on our sewing machine in the front room. I was deeply engrossed in my work when the red-faced man passed by my house and looked in. When he saw me, he became highly excited, as if he could not believe his eyes. Without asking permission, he rushed in and called me by my name, Ah Feng! Then, without another word, he dashed out to look at my house number. When he came in again, he said in a loud, chiding voice: "How can you be so cruel? You gave me the wrong house number, and I have been looking for you for days. Up and down this street I have walked a thousand times looking into each and every house, eagerly searching for you until I was exhausted. I have never experienced such a strenuous time. I was only sustained by the thought of finding you. Why, oh why, did you give me the wrong number?"

"Because I didn't want you to come here," I pouted.

"Don't you want to see me?" he asked smilingly.

"No," I said rather rudely. "Why should I?"

"Well, I have found you at last, and I do not want to lose you again."

For a moment I felt deeply contrite and asked, "What do you want to see me for?"

"Don't you know I like you very, very much? The first time I saw you at Mr. Chang's, my soul leaped halfway up to heaven. Ever since then, I've been unable to get you out of my mind. I think of you all day and dream of you at night!"

Hearing this kind of talk, I felt embarrassed and even ashamed, for no one had ever said such words to me before. I was not flattered. In fact, I wanted to run inside to hide.

Fortunately, Mother came home at this crucial moment from shopping, carrying her many small bundles of commodities. She was surprised to find a strange man in the house.

I did not say anything, and Mother asked the intruder, "May I know what business brings you here?"

With much politeness, the stranger stood at attention, clicked his heels, smiled, and bowed respectfully. "My name is Chiang Kai-shek and I am a friend of Mr. and Mrs. Chang Ching-chiang," he said diffidently. "I merely dropped in to pay my respects and to visit your daughter, Ah Feng."

As I heard this, I felt very embarrassed and tried to assure Mother that I had nothing to do with this man's visit. "I don't know him. I only saw him once at Yi-min's place," I protested. Then I blushed and ran inside to the next room to hide.

I could hear Mother's voice saying: "My daughter is only a child. She is thirteen and tall for her age. She is very studious, and I would not like to have anything distract her mind from her studies. If you have something to say, you may speak to her father at the shop."

But the man was persistent and refused to leave. He said, "I admire your daughter very, very much and would like to be her friend."

"I presume you have studied the Confucian Classics?" asked Mother.

"Yes, I have. Indeed, I have."

"In that case, you should be deeply versed in the Confucian doctrine," said Mother candidly. "Even in these modern days, no respectable man who has any regard for propriety, honor, or decorum would ever think of running after a young girl of thirteen without the approval of her parents. I, as her mother, and I can safely speak on behalf of her father, definitely disapprove of your friendship."

The stranger was terribly mortified and left our house sheepishly. After that, he dared not come to our home again.

The very next day I called at the house of Chang and said to Yi-min: "Oh, Yi-min, that Chiang Kai-shek man called on me at my house yesterday. It was so embarrassing! Mother did not treat him very courteously, I'm afraid. Do you think him a good man or a bad man?"

"Men are neither good nor bad. Men are only strong or weak," she answered authoritatively.

"Then what do you think? Is he strong?"

"I would call him strong in a way, but I do know he is madly in love with you."

I blushed and pouted. "Don't say that! I don't want anyone to be in love with me. I am thin and skinny and tall and I don't believe anyone will love me."

"You are very wrong, my dearest," said Yi-min gently. "There is a saying, Every man to his taste, and that man certainly knows women." Yi-min laughingly added: "You are a lovely girl; so virginal and so innocent! You happen to be his ideal type."

It startled me to hear those words, and I thought she was teasing me. I felt goose pimples all over my body.

"It's refreshing to meet a virginal beauty such as you—full of innocence," continued Yi-min, "and I quite understand the man's feelings. Do you know he was astonished to see your young, sweet face, your aureole of black hair, your willow-arching brows, your smiling mouth, and lovely white teeth?"

I turned red, for the compliment did not please me. In fact, it made me tremble in terror and shame, as if I were assailed by unclean thoughts. I managed to stammer in protest: "I don't like him! He is very rude! He displays his long canine teeth in a wolfish grin. He eyes me in such a strange way; his eyes shine like fire; they seem like a cat's eyes watching a mouse. And I feel like a mouse before him," I said nervously.

"He fell in love with you at first sight!" said Yi-min smilingly. "This is the first time you have been courted, so it is only natural that you feel nervous. But in this modern day and age, a lovely girl like you must not be so afraid of men. You are to say the least, too old-fashioned; you must get out of your shell."

Her words struck me between the eyes, and I felt enlightened. I told myself: Why should I be so old-fashioned? I must not feel so nervous and blush in the presence of men. I must learn to be calm, steady, and broad-minded. After all, male and female can be friends, as in the West. I must have poise and get out of my shell, as Yi-min advised.

✓   ✓   ✓

In the days that followed, Chiang Kai-shek became a frequent visitor to Chang Ching-chiang's, but I avoided him entirely and made it a point not to see him at all. But with both of us being regular guests in the same house, this was easier said than done.

One afternoon, Yi-min was coaching me with my lessons when the doorbell rang. It happened that we were the only ones in the house, so she told me to open the door. The visitor was Chiang Kai-shek. So, when I opened the door, I said coldly: "Mr. Chang Ching-chiang has gone to a business meeting. He will not be back for an hour."

"Then I'll wait," he said airily.

Reluctantly I let him enter. Before I could turn to leave, he blocked my way and said contritely: "May I be allowed to say a few words to you? I am very sorry to have caused you so much embarrassment the other day. I hope your mother did not scold you too severely on my account. I know it was wrong of me to force my attention on you, but you must know that I could not help it. I was restless and agitated. I really adore you tremendously. To tell you the truth, I have never admired any other girl as much as I admire you. You must believe me. Won't you allow me to be your friend?" I stood there feeling a chill course down my spine and goose pimples all over my body. I could not reply.

"What can I do to atone for the wrong I have done you?" he asked in a tender voice. "You have merely to say the word, and I will do it. Don't you trust me? Don't you want my friendship?"

I stood there, flustered and nervous. "I don't want anything from you," I managed to utter abruptly. "Why should I accept anything from you, a complete stranger? You may as well go into the sitting room and wait for Mr. Chang. He will be back in an hour."

He stood there and advised: "You must not be so old-fashioned. After all, I am no stranger. I am a good friend of Mr. Chang Ching-chiang, and you know it. Chinese women have been emancipated and are the true equals of men. Why should you feel so embarrassed to talk to a man? I will not eat you. You must learn to be more open-minded."

I was silent for a minute and realized that what he said was true. How silly of me to be so shy and nervous! Yi-min or Therese would never be so shy, so why should I?

"You must have someone to love you and help you in your studies," he murmured kindly. "And I offer you once more my loyal and lasting friendship. Please don't turn me down and make me unhappy, will you?"

I still stood there unable to say a word. I felt tongue-tied. I had been brought up according to strict Confucian morality. And I felt, therefore, that for a maiden merely to have a conversation with a man, and a strange man at that, was very, very wrong. Mother would never approve of it.

"We modern Chinese are outspoken and do not hide our feelings," he advised, looking at me with his dark, flashing eyes. "Being friends, we must be frank, so I hope you will give me your answer and say that you will be my very good friend, won't you?"

At this I felt a little bewildered and did not know what to say. I could not work up enough courage to utter the words, I accept your friendship. In fact, I stood there as if paralyzed.

"Now that you know how I feel," he continued, "I would like you to say yes and accept my friendship. I am a revolutionary and usually do things in a clear-cut manner. I consider your shyness to be only false modesty, and it does not become a charming girl like you to be so old-fashioned."

"What do you mean, false modesty?" I stammered, feeling a little annoyed.

"I asked you a question and you should give me your answer directly and spontaneously, yes or no. Why don't you talk? Are you afraid of me?"

"Certainly not," I retorted, trying to cover up my shyness. "I'm afraid of no one." Then I decided that I would make the best of a bad bargain. Since he loved to chat and wanted to be friends, I decided to be a good, attentive listener and at the same time accept his friendship. I motioned him into the drawing room.

For the first time we sat down opposite one another. I kept him at arm's length. He seemed very polite and anxious to win my friendship. At last he said: "To celebrate our friendship, I will invite you to lunch tomorrow at 12:30 P.M. Meet me at St. George's Restaurant on Jessfield Road, opposite the Bubblingwell Monastery." He looked at me earnestly and urged, "Will you give me 'face' and come?"

I gave the matter thought, and at last I said, "Yes, I will meet you there."

"It's a promise," he said earnestly. "Don't make a fool of me again!"

We met at St. George's the following day. And throughout lunch, he bombarded me with a stream of questions for which I had few answers. He was so excited and spoke so loudly in his Ningpo dialect that I had to tell him to lower his voice several times. He asked me about my likes and dislikes, what work I would like to take up after I graduate from school, whether I liked to travel, whether I knew about modern Chinese history, whether I knew about the leaders of the revolution, and a hundred and one other things. When he saw that I was disinclined to talk, he told me about himself.

Sitting there, I tried to figure out this thin, wiry man, with flashing eyes and long white teeth. He was certainly filled with high ambition. He was a revolutionary, having studied in Japan at a military academy. But most of what he said went over my youthful head, for I was ashamed to admit that I did not know half of what he was talking about. I merely became a good listener. He spoke of his closest friend, Ch'en Ch'i-mei, who had been assassinated for his opposition to Yuan Shih-k'ai; of Dr. Sun Yat-sen, whom he had first met in Japan; and of General Ch'en Chiung-ming, who had offered him a position as military adviser at Changchow. These and a jumble of other names did not impress me, so when coffee was served and the bill paid, we rose to leave the restaurant.

When we left St. George's, I fully expected to go straight home. But Chiang Kai-shek said to me casually, "I'll take you to visit my sister."

I hesitated, then shook my head and answered, "I must go home now to do my homework."

"Oh, come on," he urged. "The homework can wait. My sister is a very kind lady and you will like her. She lives not far from here."

Not to be rude, I reluctantly obeyed and said, "You lead the way," for I did not want to walk beside him, it being improper for a young girl to walk with a strange man in the street. All along Bubblingwell Road I followed, ten paces behind him. Vaguely I felt misgivings. I knew it was wrong of me to be going out with a stranger. I trailed along for several blocks and could see him turning his head to see if I was following him.

Finally, we came to a place called the Burlington Hotel, and there he stopped. This place had a picturesque entrance with a lot of greenery in the driveway. He waved his arm for me to come closer and said: "My sister lives on the second floor of this building. Follow me."

"But this is a foreign hotel," I protested.

"Yes, this is where she lives. It's a very nice place, and you will like it. Come!"

We entered the lobby and climbed a wide staircase, which was thickly carpeted. On reaching the landing, a white-uniformed attendant came forward, and after whispering something that I could not hear distinctly, he ushered us to a room down the spacious hallway.

On entering the room, I was surprised to see it was a large bedroom with a wide, foreign bed at one side and a dressing table at the other. The large French windows had long snowy-white lace curtains. Everything looked so white and clean. I walked around the room curiously, looking into the bathroom and the closet, then turning toward him, I asked: "Where is your sister? I do not see her here!"

I was just in time to see him turn the key to lock the door on the inside. I suddenly became frightened. In fact, I was petrified. "Why do you lock the door?" I blurted.

"Don't be alarmed. I want to talk to you and tell you a secret," he confided coming toward me, all smiles. "Ah Feng, I'm really lonely. You are the only person who can make me happy, but your coldness makes me unhappy." He snatched up my hand and kneaded my fingers greedily.

"You've lied to me and I demand that you open that door!" I said angrily.

His face dropped, and I could see he was on the verge of flaring up. I controlled my temper and exclaimed irritably, "Is this the way you trick young girls?"

He ignored my words and made an effort to embrace me. I took one step backward and demanded vehemently: "Open that door at once! I want to go home."

But he stood there and grinned awkwardly. "Oh, don't be like that," he urged. "I am madly in love with you."

I didn't want to hear any more, so I quickly ran past him and tried to pull open the door. To stop me, he showed an uncontrollable temper. He seized me with both his arms in manic frenzy. Then he threw his arms around me and forcefully kissed my cheek and then my mouth. But I fought like a tigress. I kicked and lashed out with all my strength to strike at him.

Seeing my fury, he let me loose and I became hysterical. "If you don't open that door at once, I shall scream for help!" Then I began to shout at the top of my voice. He sheepishly opened the door and I made one dash down the hallway and out of the hotel.

All the way home I felt badly shaken. I was too ashamed to tell anyone about my harrowing experience. Feeling tired and sick, I told Mother I had a headache and wanted to rest. Lying on my bed, I wept and asked myself a thousand times: Why did that man brazenly lie to me? Oh, why did he take me to a hotel room and lock the door?

I knew there could be only one explanation, and fortunately I had thwarted his evil designs. I had escaped from being raped! I had trusted the man, but he had played me a filthy trick. For that, I loathed him and made up my mind never to speak to him again. I wanted to blot out this terrible experience from my brain.

⸗ ⸗ ⸗

That night I felt sick and feverish and lay on my bed staring into space. My maidenly pride was deeply wounded, and all night I tossed about, unable to sleep. I thought I could never live down such an insult. I made up my mind that I would never forgive that wicked man. He was insufferable! He was hateful! The more I thought of him, the more I loathed him. Whatever hoped-for friendship or goodwill had existed between us was now completely shattered. Never, never, never, would I talk to him again!

At the first glimmer of gray dawn, which appeared through the window, I fell into a deep slumber. When I awoke, Mother was feeling my forehead and asking how I felt. "It is already late morning," she said, "and I am glad you have no fever. What is it my child? You look so worried." She looked at me intently.

I kissed her cheek with a smile and said I would get up. Of course, I had decided that I would not divulge anything to her, for it would only cause her endless worry. "I must have caught a chill," I lied. "I feel much better now. I'll be down in a minute to help you in the kitchen; please let me first wash and get dressed."

"Where's Ah Bun?" I asked, as I came into the kitchen. I tried to appear as casual as possible.

"He's gone to the shop with father. A large shipment of paper arrived from Loyang last night, so they are terribly busy."

Just then the telephone rang. When I went to answer it, I found it was Chiang Kai-shek. "Is that you, Ah Feng?" he asked.

"What do you want?" I snapped bluntly.

"I hope you are not angry with me. Now listen to what I want to say. I admire you more and more," he confessed shamelessly. "You are a very clever and intelligent girl. I cannot get you out of my mind. I love you dearly. Please ..."

Although miserably annoyed, I tried to be calm so that Mother could not hear. I asked gruffly, "What do you want?"

"I want to see you and ask your forgiveness."

My mind was in a whirl, and I kept glumly silent.

"I want to see you today. What are you doing this morning?"

"I have no time to see you," I snapped and immediately hung up the receiver. "Damned nuisance!" I said under my breath. Then I hurried back to the kitchen to help mother prepare my breakfast.

While I sat eating at the table, I thought of that man's ungentlemanly behavior. He was certainly brazen to phone me. It was true that many a girl would like to have the love of a persistent man, but not me. Indeed, he was distasteful. Even if there had been any chance of some sort of friendship between us, he had certainly talked himself out of it. I was sure that I would never again act in defiance of my own self-respect and decency and give him the opportunity to maul me the way he had tried to do. There was no doubt of the sincerity of his protestations of love. His adoring looks, his self-abasement, and his eagerness to win my goodwill had shown that. But I decided it would be dangerous to accept any more invitations from him or even to see him, for he might misinterpret that as giving him encouragement. And I had no intention of doing that.

For a few days, I did not go to visit Yi-min's so as to avoid that nuisance of a man. But I had no peace. Day after day, he would keep phoning me, once or twice a day without fail. Our conversations followed a common, tedious pattern: "When can I see you? Don't be so cruel to me!" he would plead. "I want to ask you to forgive me for what happened. It will never happen again, I promise. Only say you will see me again." Or: "I apologize humbly for my bad behavior. You must be broad-minded and forgive me. Will you do that? Will you tell me that you are not angry with me?"

Refusing to talk, I would bang the receiver and hang up on him. But sure enough, he would phone and phone again.

In my heart, I felt a mixture of bewilderment and anger. How can I get rid of that pest? I asked myself a dozen times. Sometimes, when no one was around, I would break down and weep. Only then could my pent-up grief over this persecution find release.

In my young life I had never been placed in such a predicament. At home we were always outspoken; Father and Mother spoke their minds freely and fearlessly. But today I was weighed down with this dark secret and dared not express myself truthfully for fear of upsetting my parents. I told myself repeatedly that I must fight my own battle.

The following week, Chiang Kai-shek changed his tactics in order not to repeat his failure. Like a spoiled boy, he had decided that he must win what he wanted at any cost.

The more I rebuffed him, the more desirable I seemed to become. One day he sent a special messenger with a letter to me. Boldly written on the envelope were the words "A reply awaited." The letter read:

Dear Ah Feng,

The Chinese Revolution is yet to be completed. But I, a revolutionary, feel down-hearted and am unable to devote my full energy to our country. All day long I look to you to give me the necessary comfort and encouragement to ease my unhappy mind. I only want you to promise me one thing, and then I shall find strength again to work hard for the revolution. If you will promise to forgive me and let us meet again, then whatever in the future I contribute to our nation will indirectly be accomplished by you. You have, I am sure, a deep love for China and will not want selfishly to deny one of her revolutionaries a little happiness. Your continued refusal to talk to me, or to see me, will diminish this revolutionary's morale and spirit. I cannot rest until I receive your reply. I lay my heart at the hem of your skirt. Say that you will forgive me and talk to me again very soon. Let me see you today!

Chiang Kai-shek

Rereading the letter, I felt that there was danger ahead of me and I began to worry. This unwavering determination to lay his heart at the hem of my skirt was something strange. I had to make up my mind. Why was Providence so cruel as to put this unwelcome suitor across my path? What could I do to avoid him? I could not entirely ignore the letter because the messenger was waiting, and I realized that he would refuse to leave without an answer. But if I replied, I would be giving in to him.

Since I first met this man, he had, within a very short time, placed me in two tight spots. The first time was when he came to my house uninvited; the second time was at the Burlington Hotel. This was my third predicament! It made my head ache just to think what I should do. After thinking for a while, I made up my mind, took up my pen and wrote a simple, short line:

Your letter received. Don't annoy me by telephoning or writing, and you shall, in time, be forgiven.

Chen-feng

I sealed the envelope and hurriedly gave it to the messenger with a tip. When he had gone, I sat at the table to do some studying, but try as I might, I could not concentrate. I walked the floor trying to think of a way to stop this man from persecuting me. The more I thought about my problem, the more I worried. I thought I should confide the matter to Yi-min and Therese for advice, but on second thought I didn't. For a week I stayed home and dared not venture out. Of course, the telephone rang continuously, but I told Mother not to answer it, explaining that some of my schoolmates wanted me to go out to play, which was a waste of time.

As the weeks passed into months, I began to feel quite relieved that I had rid myself of that unpleasant pursuer. I studied diligently for my Chinese and English lessons and also in my spare time read about the lives of famous Chinese women. I was particularly interested in the biographies of the *One Hundred Famous Chinese Beauties*. After finishing this book, I wanted to study more modern Chinese women, but could find only a few books on these. What was available, however, inspired my girlish imagination, especially Tsai Chin-fa, known as the Fabulous Concubine; the woman revolutionary Ch'iu Chin, and Princess Der Ling, the author of *Two Years in the Forbidden City*. These women were well educated and had made a name for themselves. I laughed and wept with them in their many bitter trials and unique experiences.

Since English was widely spoken in Shanghai, I envied the Chang girls their excellent command of that language. With Therese's help, I progressed quickly, especially by reading aloud the many English periodicals and magazines that kept me informed of life in foreign countries. I also took an interest in modern Chinese history and especially about Dr. Sun because I had met him. I admired his commitment to his revolutionary activities. Seeing my interest, Yi-min told me that Dr. Sun was trying to inject new blood into his revolutionary party, the T'ung-meng-hui.* To do that, the old name of the society was now changed to Kuomingtang, meaning the Nationalist Party. This news

---

*Jennie errs here. The T'ung-meng-hui was reorganized into the Kuomintang (Nationalist Party) in 1913; subsequently, the Komingtang (Revolutionary Party) temporarily replaced the Kuomintang. Jennie was probably referring to the Komingtang here. —L.E.E.

gave me the incentive to study more deeply into Dr. Sun Yat-sen's background.

⁕   ⁕   ⁕

The saddest day of all my fifteen years was on September 7, 1921, when Father suddenly died of a heart attack. For some time he had suffered from palpitations. But Mother, brother Bun, and I never thought for a moment that he was getting worse, because he had never once complained about his condition.

After hours of wailing and grieving, Mother had some men from our paper shop and our neighbor, Aunt the Third, help us in our hour of sorrow. Our front room was cleared of furniture. There were a hundred and one things to do. Death notices were sent out to relatives and friends. And according to custom, we had to be very punctilious in our observance of death. We mourners, especially son and daughter, had to be clothed in white. Father was dressed in his best long silk gown and short black-satin jacket, with skullcap and a pair of cloth-soled shoes. Leather soles were taboo, and regarded as bad luck. The body, having been dressed, was placed in the front room, feet toward the front door, there to lie in state for twelve hours or more, until the coffin arrived. This enabled relatives and friends to come and pay their last respects.

Brother Bun and I had the arduous duty throughout this period of kneeling on the floor at the side of the bier, as befitted filial children. Brother Bun went unshorn and I had to let down my hair and discard my earrings and other jewelry. Mother, being the wife of the deceased, remained in her room. The only ceremony required of her was to put an extra coverlet over the remains before the encoffining ceremony. At the foot of the bier, a narrow side table was placed to serve as an altar, upon which were set an incense burner, with incense burning, and a pair of candles on pewter stands. Relatives and friends who came would, according to custom, bow and kneel before this altar. Some brought incense, candles, and joss paper to burn as an offering to the departed.

Two large blue-white globular lanterns were hung up outside the front door, one on each side. These bore our family name, "Ch'en," in blue and black characters. A folded white drape hung over the doorway with a large white rosette at the center top to signify that the house was in mourning. Those days in the republic, many old customs had been greatly modified. We did not have to suffer the many discomforts that were demanded by the orthodox creed. For instance, Brother and I only wore white calico gowns instead of sackcloth. And we did not wail as loudly when visitors came to bow before father's remains. We simply bowed silently in return when visitors bowed in paying their respects to father.

Many relatives and friends came and usually only stayed for a few minutes before departing. Yi-min and Therese, however, stayed on to comfort Mother in her room, and whenever I could, I stole a minute or two to go in and talk to them. On the whole, however, I had to stay at the side of the bier with brother Bun throughout the day because visitors were coming and going intermittently.

I experienced a great shock during the afternoon, however, when I looked up to find a visitor who was standing before the altar at the foot of the bier, lighting two candles and a bunch of incense sticks that he had brought. It was, of course, Chiang Kai-shek. His clothing showed that he was in deep mourning. As I discreetly looked at him, I felt my heart flutter. He respectfully placed the burning incense sticks and candles in place and then deeply and reverently knelt down, three times, on the cushion before him in deep respect to Father's remains. As he arose, I watched him and experienced a rather strange, uneasy feeling. He stood there with a sorrowful expression. When I saw him paying homage to my dear father, my prejudice and anger against him quickly disappeared. He then bowed to me and then to brother Bun. We reciprocated the honor by bowing to him in return.

Just then, Yi-min and Therese came out and escorted him into the inner room to see Mother so that he could express his sympathy to her. I purposely stayed outside beside the bier and did not talk to him.

Being in deep mourning, I did not go out of the house for more than fifty days. According to custom, seven times seven days is the minimum period to observe the formal mourning rites. During these forty-nine days, Mother, according to custom, invited 108 Buddhist bonzes to perform the High Confession Mass in our front room. This was necessary so that Father's soul could ford the abyss of suffering. A group of Taoist priests was also engaged for nineteen days to offer up prayers for absolution from punishment and purification from retribution. To venture out before these rites were ended was believed to bring bad luck on any household visited [by death].

Being in mourning, I had to have my entire wardrobe remade. My new gowns consisted mostly of gray calico or pale-blue linen with white piping. Silks and satins of any kind were taboo. My shoes were of white cotton cloth, with flat heels, and at the side of my hair behind my right ear was placed a white velvet flower. I wore no rouge or makeup.

During this sad period, Yi-min and Therese came to visit me every other day. "You look good in mourning colors," said Therese to me. "If you walk down the street, I am sure people will turn their heads to give you the once over. You look so attractive."

"Don't tease me," I pouted.

"Only certain people can wear severe plain clothes and look elegant in them," agreed Yi-min. "We have a saying, 'Simplicity is the key to attractiveness.' Would you be angry if I told you something?" asked Yi-min softly.

"No," I answered in surprise. "What is it?"

"Well, Chiang Kai-shek has been asking about you, not just once, but repeatedly. He wants to be your friend. He loves you madly."

I kept silent and blushed. I was surprised to discover that I did not feel as annoyed at him as before. Ever since I had seen him at the foot of Father's bier, looking so forlorn and unshaven, and so very humble and respectful in burning incense and lighting candles, I felt a change of heart. His humility somewhat dispelled my strong dislike for him. I had thought to myself: A man's grievous mourning for the father of a girl he admired meant something. It expressed his deep sincerity and great regard for me. But a girl does not talk about men. So I told Yi-min abruptly, "I'm in mourning, and I don't want to hear any more about that man!"

But she persisted with the same line of talk, and I exclaimed impatiently. "Oh, Yi-min! You of all people! Don't joke with me. I'm only a teenage student without any talent or ability. How can anyone love me?"

"He does really love you, and madly," giggled Therese teasingly. I blushed and could feel my heart thump. I remained silent, and Therese tilted her head and laughed, "What is your opinion of Chiang Kai-shek?"

"I know nothing about him. Why should he be in love with me! I am tall and plain and not so pretty as you, Suzanne, Georgette, or Helen."

"He's always asking about you. He used to visit us only once in a blue moon, but now he calls daily," said Yi-min.

"I don't believe you," I said impatiently.

"Well, come and see for yourself. He used to have many girlfriends. But after meeting you at our house, other girls no longer interest him. What he wants is to see you, to be close to you, to be your devoted friend. He told me to tell you so."

I couldn't help feeling deeply embarrassed, so I simply replied: "Shanghai is full of lovely girls. He will meet the right one soon."

But Therese said boisterously: "It seems that the warriors of the Kuomintang are really romantic. They all have good taste and pick the loveliest of girls. All their ladies are talented and beautiful. They provide moral support, helping the heroes to strive on to ever-greater achievements. Now I hope that you and Chiang Kai-shek will make a match. He is really crazy about you. He told me so many times."

3

Matchmaking and Courtship

The following week, Yi-min called again and asked me to go into Mother's bedroom for a chat. This was not unusual, since she was my bosom friend. We sat on Mother's bed, and after beating around the bush, she said: "Ah Feng, please don't be angry with me. But Father asked me to tell you that Chiang Kai-shek is madly in love and has been pestering him to act as matchmaker. He wants to get engaged to you. He is indeed a love-sick man. So, do be merciful and consider his proposal. If you will agree, he can send a professional matchmaker to speak to your mother about it. If you refuse, he will get sick and die of a broken heart."

I blushed and answered, "I have told you many times that I don't want to marry. Why do you keep talking about it?"

"I know, but Father sent me," confessed Yi-min. "You needn't marry now," she advised seriously. "You can first get engaged and after six months or a year, then you can decide on marriage. But don't make me lose face before Father."

"No, no, no!" I cried impatiently. "I don't want to get engaged or get married."

"Marriage is a natural need of every human being," Yi-min told me. "To go against nature is a serious thing. Every girl has to marry sooner or later. My mother married when she was fourteen. Now you are fifteen!"

"Oh, Yin-min, please stop it! Stop it!" I pleaded.

"I will, but before I do, I must tell you what Father told me to say to you." He said: "Chiang Kai-shek is his sworn brother. He, Ch'en Ch'i-mei, and Chiang Kai-shek have dedicated their lives to the Chinese revolution, to work for the unification of our country. He is a good, honest man. Since he loves you madly, even to the point of sickness, you might as well get engaged to him first and marry later. As a man, our father feels that Chiang Kai-shek has a great future; he is one of the budding heroes of the Kuomintang. It is not easy to get a man to fall at the hem of your skirt. Your refusal will be a direct spurn, an insult, a loss of face, to Father."

I refused to answer Yi-min, and she went straight home. We both felt strained and embarrassed.

The following week, old Mr. Chang Ching-chiang sent Yi-min again. But this time it was to see Mother. After pleasant amenities, she broached the subject of my marriage to Chiang Kai-shek. She said that she did not want to come, but Father had insisted because most young girls of the old school would say no to an offer of marriage, even if they wanted to marry.

"I've seen Mr. Chiang," said Mother, "and I know he is a close friend of your husband. But what kind of work does he do?"

"He is a revolutionary," replied Yi-min.

"But what are his prospects?" asked Mother.

"He has a great future," exclaimed Yi-min spontaneously. "Father and Dr. Sun are recommending him to be adviser and strategist in General Ch'en Chiung-ming's army. His prospects are unlimited. Father wishes me to assure you that it will be an ideal marriage and hopes that you will give your consent. Any refusal, naturally, would be a loss of face to the House of Chang."

The last words conveyed a veiled threat, and it sounded like a warning. But Mother had a mind of her own. There was no use talking hot air. To cut the conversation short, she said: "Dear Yi-min, I appreciate Mr. Chang's effort to play the part of the Man in the Moon. Still, I will have to give consideration to the matter. My daughter is only fifteen. So, as a mother, I will have to follow the proper channels and make the traditional investigations before considering any favorable answer. You may rest assured that I shall give the matter much careful thought. In the meantime, convey my thanks to Mr. Chang for taking an interest in this matter."

, , ,

In the weeks that followed, mother engaged a professional investigator to make inquiries regarding Chiang Kai-shek. This was a common practice and was regarded as an essential preliminary step before any promise of marriage could be made. Its purpose was to trace the ancestral line to see if there had been any insanity or criminal record in the family.

The case of Chiang Kai-shek was comparatively easy because he came from our own Chekiang province, where his home was almost adjacent to our own county of Ningpo. The investigator's report revealed, among other details of Mr. Chiang's background, that for the past four years, he had been living in Shanghai and was unemployed.*

To marry an unemployed man with a wife and a concubine, and without visible means of support, was out of the question. So, after weighing the investigator's report, Mother decided that the matter of marriage should be closed once and for all.

But later, completely unexpectedly, old Mr. Chang Ching chiang called at our house to talk to Mother. She regarded this visit as a great honor, for Mr. Chang, after all, was a great personage.

After the usual amenities, Mr. Chang got down to business and explained the purpose of his visit. He assured mother that Chiang Kai-shek's first wife, Miss Mao, had become a devout Buddhist and had renounced the world. After all, he told Mother, that marriage had been arranged by his [Chiang Kai-shek's] mother. Although a son had been born to the union, there was no love between husband and wife. The concubine, Miss Yao I-ch'in, who lived in Soochow, had recently accepted a settlement of $5,000 to relinquish any and all claims on Kai-shek. Old Mr. Chang thereupon produced an agreement of separation signed by Miss Yao. "So you see," said Mr. Chang, "that the question of wife and concubine should not constitute a problem.

"My wife, Yi-min, and your daughter are very close friends, and we love Ah Feng very much. Chiang Kai-shek is also my very good friend,

---

*Jennie, at this point in her manuscript, recorded the investigator's report, which is of little or no interest, historical or otherwise. I have deleted it here. —L.E.E.

and he is infatuated with your daughter. He has asked me to act as matchmaker. He is most persistent and will not take no for an answer. So that is why I have come to ask you to allow him to be your daughter's suitor."

"Will you please tell me candidly what kind of a man is this Chiang Kai-shek?" asked Mother.

Old Mr. Chang answered, "He is a man with a good heart, and as a revolutionary he has absolute devotion. I feel sure he will make your daughter a good husband, Mrs. Ch'en. But to be very honest, I must say he is extremely impulsive, opinionated, and too often hot-headed. His only fault is that he takes risks unnecessarily. He is a junior member of our group, and we like his quality of absolute loyalty. But we do not always follow his opinions or suggestions. We, as revolutionaries, cannot afford to be hot-headed or impulsive. We must at all times remain calm and self-possessed.

"Dr. Sun, who is always wary of, and distant toward, all strangers, did not pay much attention to Chiang Kai-shek in the early days," continued Old Mr. Chang. "To get nearer to our leader, Chiang Kai-shek became a most devoted follower of Ch'en Ch'i-mei."

"Did Dr. Sun then become very friendly with Chiang Kai-shek?" asked Mother.

"Not immediately," answered Old Mr. Chang. "Despite his loyalty to Ch'en Ch'i-mei, our leader could not be so easily won over. But to show how resourceful Chiang Kai-shek is, he begged Ch'en Ch'i-mei and me to become his sworn brothers. Since we had pledged our lives to the revolution, the three of us went through a ceremony, swearing an oath to live and die together for our country. Ch'en Ch'i-mei and I are two of Dr. Sun's most entrusted followers. But this sworn brotherhood with Chiang Kai-shek did not alter our leader's attitude. This indifference continued even up to the time when Ch'en Ch'i-mei was assassinated. But Chiang Kai-shek is a resourceful man, and I admire him for it. Seeing that Dr. Sun was still cold toward him, Chiang took the bull by the horns and wrote to Dr. Sun, saying that he had served Ch'en Ch'i-mei with unswerving devotion and loyalty. And he was now ready to serve Dr. Sun with that same devotion and loyalty, if he were allowed to do so. But, he complained, Dr. Sun was always cold and indifferent toward him and did not offer any signs of friendship, as Ch'en Ch'i-mei had done. It takes two to make a bargain, he explained, and he hoped that Dr. Sun would in the future be friendlier toward him and regard him as a devoted follower. This candid letter had an effect, for soon Dr. Sun sent for him to talk over various aspects of the revolution."

"That is very interesting," exclaimed Mother, deeply impressed. "Indeed the man is very resourceful and certainly has great persistence, a quality that makes a great leader."

"That is true," agreed Old Mr. Chang. "Today we lack good, honest leaders, and if he continues in his revolutionary ardor, he will no doubt have a bright future. So, in answer to your inquiry, I have tried to be very fair. I have told you not just the good things about him in order to deceive you, but I have also mentioned his weaknesses. As you know, I have daughters of my own, and when I make inquiries about my prospective sons-in-law, I will also want to have honest answers like these I have given you."

Then mother asked about Chiang Kai-shek's future prospects. Old Mr. Chang was enthusiastic and waxed eloquent. He assured her that a very good job awaited Kai-shek in General Ch'en Chiung-ming's army at any time he wanted it.

"Revolutionaries are supported by our organization," he told Mother, "so do not worry about money or jobs. I am only anxious for Kai-shek's peace of mind, which he now seems to have lost. I want him to concentrate on the revolutionary work that Dr. Sun and I have mapped out for him in General Ch'en Chiung-ming's campaign. Kai-shek is so utterly infatuated with your daughter that he has no mind for anything else. Yes, indeed," he mused thoughtfully, "your daughter has become a really strong influence over him. I am sure that, after your daughter and he are married, his mind will be at rest and even his bad temper will gradually change for the better. I can predict your daughter will be able to help him achieve great things for our country, if only you will give your consent."

Old Mr. Chang's talk with Mother had the desired effect, for Mother had a deep sense of patriotism. She now thought more kindly toward Chiang Kai-shek, as he was a warrior fighting for China. But she did not promise Old Mr. Chang anything. Seeing that Mother's feelings toward Chiang Kai-shek had now moderated, friends and relatives became very meddlesome in trying to persuade me to marry Kai-shek: "This is a good chance for matrimony! He is a very fine man who adores you madly. What more could a girl wish?"

With the best intentions in the world, Yi-min and Therese too started carping at me, every time we met, to accept him. I knew they were merely doing Old Mr. Chang's bidding because the other sisters also hinted pointedly about marriage. I became terribly tense and thought I'd go mad.

For days I was glum and silent. Mother came into my bedroom one night and asked: "What is it, Ah Feng? What are you brooding about?"

I could not answer and simply shook my head.

"Yi-min and Therese assure me that Mr. Chiang is a very good man and will make you a fine husband. What do you think of him?" She looked at me and added, "Only say something!"

"I don't want to marry," I said abruptly.

"He is a brave warrior and is so fond of you," urged Mother. "If you marry him, both of you will be very happy."

When Mother started harping in this way, it hit close to home and it made me ever so self-conscious. All this talk was like the gathering of storm clouds, and I often ran from the room to choke back a flood of sobs. Smarting under the lash of the repeated hints, I finally gave up and left the entire matter in Mother's hands. I could no longer make up my own mind. I felt hemmed in and became hopelessly confused.

"A boy thinks of marriage when he grows up, and a girl yearns to be wed at adolescence." This was a common Chinese adage, and Mother repeated it like a barrage at me. Her advice may have been perfectly sound, but I had no way of judging anymore. As a result, I allowed her to make whatever decision she wished about my marriage.

Then came the day that Mother had arranged for me to meet and become acquainted with Chiang Kai-shek. He was very polite and attentive and insisted that we go together to the House of Chang to meet Dr. Sun, who was there on a visit. On our arrival at Old Mr. Chang's, Yi-min and Kai-shek insisted that I go into the drawing room to pay my respects to this great leader. When, as a result of shyness, I stubbornly declined, Kai-shek took me by the arm and practically dragged me along. I felt very nervous and blushed terribly, deeply conscious of the glances of the other guests present. There were five other men besides Dr. Sun. Kai-shek introduced me and said: "This is the Miss Ch'en I told you about." Then turning to me, he ordered, "Pay your respects to our leader."

I bowed my head and kept my eyes on the floor.

"She is a very fine girl, but so young," exclaimed Dr. Sun in a jovial voice. "Didn't I meet her once before?" Without waiting for an answer, he continued, "Have you decided on the date of the wedding?"

"Not yet," answered Kai-shek.

"Marry by all means if you are in love, and I wish you both great happiness. But do it as soon as possible, for we have many important things to do for our revolution." Turning to me, he asked, "Are you ready to dedicate your life to work for our revolution?"

For a minute I was at a loss for words but forced myself to say yes.

This was the first time I had a close look at this famous leader and noticed his wide, square forehead, heavy brow, graying hair, and the wrinkles around his eyes. He was wearing a "Chungshan" uniform of creamy Shantung silk, the jacket of which buttoned from the collar, right down the center, with mother-of-pearl buttons.

While Dr. Sun smiled at me kindly, I could feel the impact of the eyes of all those present in the room, for I knew they were scrutinizing me from head to foot. I kept my eyes on Dr. Sun's tan shoes.

When Dr. Sun started to talk about other things, I walked over to Yi-min, and she took my hand to give me courage. Dr. Sun was such a colorful personality and so respected by all revolutionaries that people in his presence usually whispered or spoke in undertones. Then Yi-min and I left the room to prepare refreshments. I shall never forget that moment. As I walked out, I could visualize the people watching me with undisguised curiosity.

After Dr. Sun and the guests had left, Kai-shek took me into Old Mr. Chang's library. We were alone and he held my hand and said: "Now you can't get out of it. You know I love you very, very much. I want you to be my loving wife, to share my dreams for the future. Won't you promise to marry me?"

It would have been brazen for me to say yes, so I merely stood there, unable to answer. I blushed, and I could feel my cheeks burning.

"Without you, my life is empty," he told me in a voice filled with sadness. "There's just nothing left for me unless you say yes. I'll not take no for an answer. Now, say you will marry me. Please say it."

I became tongue-tied and turned my head away without answering.

Thinking I was too shy because of our surroundings, Kai-shek took me by taxi to the French Park, in Frenchtown. We sat on a garden bench, and he talked and talked about himself. Suddenly he said: "I do not know what you have heard about my former wife and concubine, but I want to explain that my marriage with my first wife, Miss Mao Fu-mei, was a blind marriage, arranged by my mother. I had never seen my wife's face before the wedding ceremony, and after marriage we did not get on well together. In our unhappy married life, she gave birth to only one son; then she became a devout Buddhist and practiced celibacy.

"In 1916, after my closest friend and mentor, Ch'en Ch'i-mei, was assassinated, the assassins hunted high and low for me. With the help of my friend Feng Chieh-wen we secretly took refuge in Soochow. There we stayed at his old haunt, the Soochow Pleasure Garden, where he introduced me to a singsong girl named Yao Shih [Yao I-ch'in]. She was a petite beauty and very charming, and we became very good friends. But her friendliness aroused the bitter jealousy of her wealthy patron, an old Mr. Pang, who warned her time and again to give me up. One night when this Mr. Pang was giving a dinner there, he asked Yao Shih, point-blank, before his many guests, whether she would give up her friendship with that pauper Chiang Kai-shek. He purposely timed his question to the exact moment when the large round platter of piping-hot sharkfins was served on the table. When Yao Shih said no, he told her: 'I've spent thousands of dollars on you and your house, yet you make me lose face repeatedly. Since you prefer this penniless revolutionary to me, then wear this hat!' So saying, he took up the platter of sharkfins with both hands and suddenly dumped the entire contents over her head. The boiling liquid disfigured her face and ruined her career.

"This so-called Sharkfin Hat Incident caused a terrible scandal all over Soochow. To avoid further embarrassment, and in gratitude for her favor, I took Yao Shih away from the Pleasure Garden and made her my concubine. But now, both my wife and concubine have agreed to accept monetary settlements in return for relinquishing all claims on me as a husband. By mutual agreement, our relationship is that of sisters and brother. Your mother has investigated this matter and knows that what I say is true." He looked at me tenderly, and added: "Now, I will tell you what is in my heart. Please listen carefully: If you will marry me, you will be my one and only legal wife according to our republican law."

I sat there in silence and was tongue-tied. Seeing my nervousness, he exclaimed: "I swear to you:

> Oceans may evaporate,
> Mountains may crumble,
> But my love for you
> Will never change.

He sat closer to me and asked: "Do you believe me? Do be kind and say you believe me!"

But try as I might, I could not answer. Then he took from his pocket a jackknife. Pulling open the shining blade, he said: "If you do not believe that I love you most devotedly, I will prove it to you in another way. See! Just say the word, and I will cut off one of my fingers with this knife to show that I am very serious. Now, just say the word!" He moved his open palm with its outspread fingers toward me. I was stunned by his action and grabbed his hand to protect it.

"With my blood," he continued, "I will write you a pledge of my undying love."

"Please, please put away that knife. I believe you. Only put it away!" I managed to stutter, very much frightened and deeply touched. His willingness to sacrifice a finger just to prove the sincerity of his love filled me with a feeling of indescribable sympathy. Besides, his "Oceans may evaporate and mountains may crumble" oath was unique; I had never heard such words spoken to me before. Hearing them flattered my vanity—and, then and there, I gave him my heart. From then on, I let my mother take over and make the decision of marriage for me, for I was too shy and embarrassed to talk about it.

In the days that followed, I should have been very much frustrated again when I learned that Kai-shek's unshaven face and forlorn appearance at my father's funeral was not solely due to his sorrow over my father's death. His deep mourning was due to the death of his own mother, Mama Huang, who had passed away on June 14, five months before. Although this discovery brought back to me a sense of frustration, the die had been cast, and I simply allowed the matter to pass. Mother and old Mr. Chang Ching-chiang, however, enthusiastically discussed arrangements for my wedding.

Since both Kai-shek and I were still in mourning, the first thing to be done before our marriage could take place was to streamline our period of mourning. In imperial days, the death of either parent required a mourning period of three years. A government official would retire from office in order to mourn in seclusion. Since the establishment of the republic, however, this ancient custom had been modified. One hundred days of mourning was considered adequate for the funeral and sacrifices. The chief mourners, such as sons and daughters, still observed part of the old custom. Men did not shave or cut their hair and women wore no makeup from the day of their bereavement until forty-nine days had passed. This was considered an adequate period to complete the proper mourning rites.

Kai-shek and I considered ourselves modern, so on December 2, 1921, our mourning periods were brought to an end. The ceremonies were simple: A tray of foodstuffs, candles and incense, wine, and joss paper were offered to the deceased. After we performed the appropriate obeisances, a string of firecrackers was set off, and we discarded our plain-cloth mourning clothes for silk and colored clothing.

Mother had great respect for old Mr. Chang Ching-chiang. On his insistence she agreed that the wedding be done in proper style. So an engagement took place in which presents were exchanged, and elaborate red papers were filled with the dates of our births and other particulars. This made Kai-shek and me irrevocably one.

The day after our engagement, Kai-shek and I, following Western custom, spent the day shopping and visiting. He was so kind, considerate, and courteous that the day became for me a memorable one. During that late afternoon, we sat at the chocolate shop on Nanking Road having some refreshments. Kai-shek said to me: "Your name Ah Feng should be used solely by your mother, for it is your 'milk name.' According to Chinese etiquette, it is improper for your friends to use it. So, I have chosen for you a new name, which I think perfectly fits your personality. The name is Chieh-ju, meaning 'pure and unblemished by the world.' To me, you are pure and unblemished. Do you like it? Here it is!" He unwrapped a photograph of himself with my new name boldly written on the left of his three-quarter-length picture and signed with his name. He looked quite handsome in his uniform.

"It sounds very nice and thank you also for this photo. When shall I begin to use my new name?" I asked as I studied the calligraphy attentively.

"From now on, my sweet Chieh-ju," he said. "Let me be the first to call you by that name. To tell you the truth, I thought of that name on the first day we met at Mr. Chang Ching-chiang's. To me you are as pure and virginal as an angel—you are like pure-white jade."

So from that time on, I adopted the name Chieh-ju for formal use by all my friends. Only Mother and a few very intimate friends continued to call me Ah-feng.

4

Our Wedding

Our wedding took place very quietly on December 5, 1921, in the large Reception Hall of the Great Eastern Hotel, located in the Wing On Building in Shanghai. This was one of the more popular places where official ceremonies were held.

Due to the fact that this was a period of modernization in China, we agreed to dispense with much of the tedious ceremonies required by strict Chinese etiquette. We called ours a semi-Westernized wedding. Kai-shek's gift to me was a postcard-sized Kodak camera. My gift to him was a gold Waltham pocket watch with a gold chain.

Instead of white or red, my wedding dress was a very pale pink satin with silver and gold embroidery. And in my hair, I wore pearl ornaments. Kai-shek wore a dark-blue long gown with a black satin *ma-kua* (short top-jacket).

The spacious hall was made festive by the hangings of large red-silk drapes decorated with colorful embroideries. Four huge red lanterns with long ornamental tassels hung across the hall's entrance, symbolizing a wedding. Many large painted-gauze lamps were suspended from the hall's ceiling, and from the center hung a kingfisher-bird ornamental chandelier in rich colors. Pots of flowers and palms were placed here and there.

The ceremony was to be in two parts. The first consisted of the stamping of the marriage certificate, which would authenticate the modern form of marriage. That was to take place at the main table at one end of the room. The second part was the symbolic worship of Heaven, Earth, and our Ancestors at the altar at the opposite end of the hall.

The main table was covered with a heavy red-silk cloth, upon which were placed a modern Chinese marriage certificate, several vermillion-ink pads, and several ivory personal seals. The only table decorations were two vases of flowers at either end of the table.

On the opposite side of the hall stood another long table for the second part of the streamlined Chinese-style wedding. On the table was placed a large pewter incense urn, which was flanked by a pair of large matching candlesticks. The candlesticks held large red candles, and on the table were arranged a number of plates full of fruit, pieces of sugarcane, and various highly decorated cakes and condiments piled high like pagodas. A large embroidered picture, in gold on a red-satin background, bore the Chinese characters Double Happiness.

At three o'clock, the ceremony began. At the center of the main table sat old Mr. Chang Ching-chiang as officiator. At his left stood Mr. Tai Chi-t'ao, witness for the bridegroom. And on his right sat my mother, Mrs. Ch'en Wu-shih, witness for the bride.

Kai-shek and I stood in front of this principal table facing the officiator. At my side were Therese Chang and Lily Lin, dressed in pastel blue, acting as my bridesmaids. At Kai-shek's side stood Mr. Lam Yip-ming, who acted as master of ceremonies, and Mr. Feng Chieh-wen, who acted as the matchmaker.* Almost fifty friends and relatives sat on both sides of the hall to witness the happy proceedings.

I felt very nervous, and my eyes were glued to the floor, as becomes a Chinese bride. According to custom, a bride must not appear to be too happy, which would be considered brazen, nor can she stare at the guests, which would be considered rude. Nothing could induce me to look up, and I remained mute.

Suddenly the sonorous voice of the master of the ceremonies announced, "The officiator will address the bridegroom and bride." Then old Mr. Chang Ching-chiang rose with awkwardness from his chair and made a short speech pronouncing us to be married and wished the bridegroom and bride good fortune and happiness.

When he finished, the master of ceremony announced, "The bridegroom will stamp his seal on the marriage certificate." Accordingly, Kai-shek stepped forward, took up from the table his ivory seal, inked it on the vermillion-ink pad, and stamped his seal on the marriage certificate.

---

*The wedding certificate states that there were two matchmakers, the second being Chen Hock-choi. —L.E.E.

The master of ceremonies called again, "The bride will now use her seal to stamp the marriage certificate." The master of ceremonies then called to the remainder of those participating in the ceremony to place the imprint of their seals onto the allotted spaces.

The master of ceremonies announced, "The bridegroom and bride will now thank the officiator by bowing to him three times." Accordingly, Kai-shek and I bowed our heads in unison three times.

The master of ceremonies announced, "The bridegroom and bride will now pay their respects to the guests by bowing to them one time." This done, the first part of the ceremony was completed.

The second part of the ceremony began when the master of ceremonies asked Kai-shek and me to go to the other end of the room to bow to the altar. An elderly matron of honor in a royal-blue dress came to attend upon me. She was a professional and a really useful lady. As the master of ceremonies commanded, Kai-shek and I went to the other end of the long room, where we knelt before the altar three times in symbolic worship of Heaven, Earth, and our Ancestors.

This done, the master of ceremonies said, "The bridegroom and bride will be seated." We sat at a square table covered with red and were each given a silver cup of wine. The master of ceremonies announced, "The bridegroom and bride will drink wine." After we sipped from the silver cups, we exchanged cups and sipped again. This was done three times while the matron of honor chanted three "wishes": "May the bridegroom and bride live till their hairs are gray." "May the bridegroom sing and the bride harmonize." "May the bridegroom and bride have many children."

At this point a long string of firecrackers was discharged outside, causing a deafening noise. The children especially became excited over the detonation. This completed the second part of the ceremony.

Whenever I looked up to steal a glance at Kai-shek, I could see he had a preoccupied and uncomfortable look about him, appearing to be happy and proud, but a little impatient. I knew instinctively his main thought was to get the ceremony over with. But he was polite and wore a smiling countenance.

In the meantime, lavish preparations were in progress for the wedding feast. This is a must at Chinese weddings. While waiting for the dinner, it was customary for the guests to visit the bridal chamber, where close friends, usually men, would play rather bad jokes on the bride or try to make the bridegroom drunk by challenging him to drink

WEDDING CERTIFICATE

(Note government revenue stamp at center top)

(Groom) Chekiang Province, Feng Fa County citizen,
   Chiang Kai-Shek
 (Born) 15th day, 9th Moon, Ting-Ki Year at (hour 4 A.M.)
   [October 31, 1887]
(Bride) Chekiang Province, Chin Hai County citizen, Chen Che-Ju
 (Born) 10th day, 3rd Moon, Ping-Wu Year at (hour 10:30 P.M.)
   [February 4, 1906]

   Through the introduction of
   MESSRS FENG KAI-MIN AND CHEN HOCK-CHOI
   it is decided that on December 5th this year at 3 P.M. at the
   GREAT EASTERN HOTEL AUDITORIUM a marriage ceremony will be performed.
   It is respectfully requested that
    MR. CHANG CHING-KIANG
   will officiate in marrying this couple.
   The Hall is full of guests to witness this ceremony. It is
   wished that the couple will live until their hair is gray and
   the union will be blessed with many children. This certificate is proof of this marriage.

Persons married:	Chiang Kai-Shek	(authenticated by seal)	Chiang Chung-Ching
	Chen Che-Ju	"	Chen Che-Ju
Officer officiating:	Chang Ching-Kiang	"	Chang Jen-Kit
Match-Makers:	Feng Kai-Min	"	Feng Kai-Min
	Chen Hock-Choi	"	Chen Hock-Choi
Representing grooms's father:	Tai Chi-Tao	"	Tai Chin-Hsen
(Bride's Mother):	Chen Wu Shih	"	Wu Chiao-Yung

NATIONALIST 10TH YEAR, DEC 5TH (1921)

large amounts of liquor. If the bride refused to do the bidding of the male friends, she would have to pay a forfeit of fifty pounds of candy, a dozen bottles of brandy, or the like.

Since Kai-shek's home was in the village of Hsi-k'ou, and our room at 44 Rue Vallon in Shanghai, in Frenchtown, was not ready, Kai-shek had ordered a suite of rooms, No. 127, in the Great Eastern Hotel, as our bridal chamber. The room was furnished with modern European furniture and a brass double bed. The room, however, was made to look luxurious, like a beautiful boudoir, with red scrolls and drape hangings. The brass bedstead was hung with pink silk curtains, which were heavily embroidered with dragons and phoenixes. The bed cover and pillows were all of matching design. There were four satin-covered, padded quilts folded lengthwise in the traditional manner at the far side of the bed.

Hustled by the guests and supported by the matrons of honor, I was then taken to the bridal chamber. The women guests all crowded in to see my dress, and many of them made remarks about my appearance and jewelry. Seated on a chair in the middle of the excited throng, I had to submit to being examined all over. In fact, every move I made was the subject of casual comment. My four trunks of trousseau, stacked at one side of the room, all passed under review, while I looked on in silence, trying not to laugh or cry. This was an inescapable ordeal for a Chinese bride.

Meanwhile, Kai-shek was entertaining his male friends in another room, while children of the guests ran from room to room, all excited, noisy, and nosy.

My ordeal was very trying, but I considered myself lucky because after the revolution customs had changed. I consoled myself with the thought that my lot was easier than that of brides before me. My female critics, however, seemed inconsiderate and even sarcastic in their remarks. Yet I had to suppress all my feelings and not show any outward emotions. So I followed the old custom and appeared humble and demure. I tried to be tactful and not take offense at the jokes played on me.

While the guests were enjoying the feast in the ceremonial hall, five tables in all, I sat in the bridal chamber, attended by the matron of honor. A tray of food for Kai-shek and me was brought to my chamber. But I had no appetite to eat. I simply picked at my food while Kai-shek took perfunctory gulps and rushed to the ceremonial hall again to supervise and entertain the guests.

When we were alone, the matron of honor said to me in a sweet, confidential tone: "This is your wedding night and you must be brave. If the bridegroom touches your body, you must not resist him. In fact, you must do everything to cooperate and allow him to do what he wishes. Do you understand what I mean?"

I kept silent and said nothing, but I could feel my heart thumping in my breast.

At midnight, when the wedding party came to an end and it was time to retire, the matron of honor, as her parting advice, said to me: "Remember what I have told you. Don't resist the bridegroom; let him have his way. I have set the bed and spread a small sheet there. You will find the hand towels and lubricant near the pillows. Now don't be afraid! Congratulations! May you have a hundred sons and grandsons!"

Turning to Kai-shek, she said cheerily, "Congratulations and good night, Mr. Bridegroom."

I sat there in the room and said nothing while Kai-shek personally locked the door. He took me in his arms, and I could feel my heart thudding against my breast. I stood there like a clinging vine, defenselessly, with eyes half-closed, and waited. He murmured in a jovial tone of happiness: "You are now my dear wife, my only love in the world! Oh, darling, darling, I shall never love any other woman except you, and that is a solemn promise."

He kissed me passionately and pressed himself against me and whispered: "I have never wanted anything in the world more than you, my sweet one. You are the answer to all my hopes, to all my dreams, and the only girl there will ever be for me. I swear, I shall love you always. Won't you believe me?"

I nodded and said I believed him. Then he pressed himself against me passionately and held me tight. I yielded to his desire.

The following day, Kai-shek and I spent the whole day in our room, even taking our meals in the room. He was so very happy and passionate, smiling all day and behaving like a young boy, joking and teasing me. I could never have imagined him to be so romantic and was quite overwhelmed by his gusts of passion. While we were lying on the bed, he suddenly broke out in laughter. So I asked him, "Why are you laughing so much?"

"Because I am very happy to have had my first wish realized."

"What do you mean by your first wish realized?" I asked curiously.

"I'll tell you a secret," he told me confidentially. "When my mother died, I was extremely unhappy, for I had achieved nothing noteworthy that could repay her kindness. In my misery I took stock of my life and I asked myself what was my ambition in life. I churned the matter over in my mind for days. At last I decided that, above all, I wanted three things. Each day I prayed that they would be granted me."

"What were they?" I asked.

And he confessed: "First: to win you to be my wife. Second: to win the confidence of our leader, Dr. Sun Yat-sen, so that I will eventually become his heir. Third: to become China's greatest military leader and unify the whole of the nation under one government." He looked at me lovingly and added: "Now, you know why I am so deliriously happy. Having achieved my first wish, my mind is at peace, and that is why I am laughing. With you at my side, I can devote my energies to achieving my two other wishes. Oh, my darling, darling! You must work shoulder-to-shoulder with me and help me realize my ambitions. Will you do that?"

"But I am inexperienced and ignorant!" I answered. "In what way can I help? What can I do?"

"Never mind that!" he said tenderly. "Just love me and never leave me. You are the only one that can give me a big lift spiritually. For without you, I feel miserably down and out!"

"If you really mean that," I countered seriously, "I will, of course, do my utmost to help you. That, I promise."

He pulled me to him and caressed me until it hurt. "You are my only love," he murmured. "You are so perfect, yes, so perfect."

I was curious to know why he wished to get closer to Dr. Sun Yat-sen and asked naïvely, "Why do you want to win the confidence of Dr. Sun?"

"Because he is the greatest Chinese of this century. You have seen his wide, square forehead." He touched my brow and forehead to emphasize what he meant. "He has a wonderful brain. If I get my wish, I will one day make him the patron saint of our Chinese Republic."

"But when I studied the history of the revolution, I read that Yang Ch'ü-yün of Hong Kong is said to be recognized as the patron saint of the Chinese Republic. Is that not so? How can there be two patron saints!"*

---

*On Yang Ch'ü-yun, see Chün-tu Hsueh, "Sun Yat-sen, Yang Ch'ü-yun, and the Early Revolutionary Movement in China," in *Revolutionary Leaders of Modern China*, ed.

"You are too naive, my sweet one," He held me tight and answered: "Yang Ch'ü-yün was a pioneer only. He did much for the movement, and Dr. Sun was his secretary for a year before Yang was assassinated. But I believe Dr. Sun should be the patron saint of our Chinese Republic, and that is definite.

                              ʼ   ʼ   ʼ

On the third day, according to Chinese tradition, Kai-shek and I went to visit Mother, taking with us the customary load of gifts, and to pay respects to my family's ancestral tablets. This visit was called "Small Full Moon." After Kai-shek and I had done obeisance to the departed, we turned to the living. We invited Mother to sit comfortably in an armchair. Both Kai-shek and I then kowtowed to her. She, in turn, gave us each a red envelope for doing her this honor. My uncle, aunt, and other guests who were present were also shown our respect. We bowed to them individually and this ended the first part of the ceremony.

Kai-shek was then invited to sit down to a feast that was called "Invitation to a New Son-in-law Banquet." We planned to leave for Kai-shek's ancestral home at Hsi-k'ou the next day and had, therefore, given up our rooms at the Great Eastern Hotel. So we left Mother's early so that we could supervise the packing and storage of our many things. Despite the help of Kai-shek's two very efficient male servants, Ah Shun and Sui-Chang, there was still much for Kai-shek and me to do. I also had to make out a shopping list for the many things we had to buy to take to the village, both as gifts and for our own use. Kai-shek also ordered fifty catties of candy and fifty catties of biscuits to take with us.

Now that I was married, my outlook on life seemed greatly broadened, and I felt like a new person. Although only fifteen* years old, I had become a woman. I was surprised to find that my shyness had somewhat disappeared. And when I told Kai-shek I truly loved him, I uttered the words without blushing. This I would never have admitted before marriage, for it would have been considered brazen of me under the old school of thought.

Chün-tu Hsueh (New York: Oxford University Press, 1971), pp. 102–122, and Harold Z. Schiffrin, *Sun Yat-sen and the Origins of the Chinese Revolution* (Berkeley: University of California Press, 1968), pp. 46–47, 68–70, et passim. —L.E.E.

*Actually, she was sixteen years of age at this time. —L.E.E.

❦ 5

Honeymoon

On the fourth day after our marriage, together with our two servant boys, Kai-shek and I took the river steamer *Ningshai*, bound for Ningpo. Because this was my first trip on a large and modern ship, I was thrilled beyond words. Everything seemed immaculately clean, both in the saloon and in the cabin. The trip itself was uneventful, except that I did notice how jarring and unpleasant were the loud voices of the Ningpo passengers. They monopolized the entire saloon and shouted at the top of their voices when they talked. And they talked incessantly. It was very unpleasant.

"Do they have to talk so loudly?" I asked Kai-shek as we walked around the deck.

"Have you not heard the saying?" he answered laughingly. "When Ningpo people talk, it sounds like a quarrel; when they quarrel, it sounds like cannon firing."

"But my father is from Ningpo, and I never did hear him shout like that!" I said. "So it cannot be characteristic of all Ningpo people, and only of the common class."

"You are right as usual," smiled Kai-shek, and he squeezed my arm.

At 6 A.M. the following morning the steamer arrived at the port of Ningpo, and we went ashore, leaving the two servant boys to attend to our baggage, twenty pieces in all. As we disembarked, two rickshaws were awaiting to take us directly along the waterfront to the large wooden junk bound for Feng-hua County. I saw that the large junk was the ocean-going type, very solid and spacious and crowded with people.

43

Men and women, mostly peasants, carrying their children or bamboo baskets, were all anxious and excited to get on board. They wore the usual kind of blue-broadcloth two-piece tunic. At 8 A.M. sharp, the junk pulled away from the wharf.

What seemed most strange to me was the junk's compartments. The first-class saloon was situated at the very bottom of the hold. It was reached by a narrow wooden staircase. It was nicely furnished with the traditional blackwood furniture, had framed pictures on the walls, and was illuminated by an acetylene lamp hung from the center of the ceiling. The chief fault was that there was no proper ventilation, so it was very stuffy. I sat with Kai-shek at a square blackwood table where a waiter served us green tea, but the stale air made me miserable.

The floor above the saloon was called second class, the difference being only in the furniture, which was made of coarse, plain wood. But the air in this compartment was much better. The upper uncovered flat deck was without any furniture except wooden planks and was loaded with cargo. It was the third-class level, and I thought it to be the best part of the junk, despite the crowd of noisy passengers and stacks of cargo. At least I could inhale deeply the fresh air there and enjoy the beautiful scenery.

After sitting in the first-class saloon for a while, I told Kai-shek that I would rather sit on the upper deck. He, therefore, ordered Ah Shun to place two cane chairs there for him and for me. As we rose to leave, some old friends detained Kai-shek in conversation, so I left them to talk while I ascended to the deck by myself. Although the upper deck was crowded to capacity, Ah Shun managed to squeeze in our two cane chairs, sandwiched between the peasant passengers, who regarded it as an honor. In fact, sitting there, I caused quite a stir. They stared and smiled at me and I could see by their looks that I was, in some respects, well favored but regarded as a curiosity. Everything I wore was freely discussed among them. The men squatting near my feet looked sturdy and muscular, and the women had ruddy cheeks and well-formed features. To them, I was a city lady and something strange and different.

Our junk traveled southwest upriver, and my whole attention was on the charming vistas around me. I could see the high peaks and rolling mountains standing out distinctly against a clear blue sky, and the water seemed like a sheet of glass. I thought to myself: The scenery of Chekiang is justly celebrated and most picturesque. Almost completely devoted to agriculture, the plains were all covered with emerald-green plants. Here and there were groves and groves of luxuriant bamboo.

At 11 A.M. our junk docked at Feng-hua County. When Kai-shek and I disembarked, two cane sedan chairs, enclosed ones, were already awaiting us. Our destination was Hsi-k'ou village: The journey would take four long hours on foot. Kai-shek was in a very happy mood and explained apologetically to me that we had no time to visit the town of Feng-hua, but we would do it at some other time. I thought this was most considerate of him.

He then pointed out: "Feng-hua is situated on the Feng-hua River at the foot of that Tiger-Killing Mountain. We are now in the East of Chekiang. We will travel southwest to the highland and will pass vast fertile plains and more hills until we reach Wu-ling."

Standing there I could see the stream of peasants carrying on their shoulder-poles stacks of bamboo ware such as bamboo sieves, bamboo blinds, bamboo cages, and baskets to be taken on board [the junk], destination Ningpo and Shanghai.

"This is bamboo country," I remarked.

"But we also produce tea, rice, fish, and salt in great abundance," he said. "Now let us go."

Kai-shek's sedan chair led the way, and my chair followed immediately behind. Ah Shun and Sui-Chang followed my chair on foot, with coolies carrying our baggage and several extra chair bearers, called relievers, who were to relieve our chair coolies when they got tired. This was my first experience in a sedan chair, for Shanghai is built entirely on a plain so there is no need for such conveyances, except rickshaws. As I was being thus borne, raised to the level of the shoulders of the coolies who carried me along, I felt some misgivings. I thought that the infliction of such painful labor upon two human beings was quite feudal. It was so cruel and out of place under the Chinese republican flag. I could feel their physical pain as if it was inflicted on me myself. I winced many times and thought of getting off and walking, but I did not want to upset Kai-shek's arrangements.

As they trotted on and on, they found it necessary to shout in a sing-song voice a ditty all their own. The singing relieved their strain, and I was amused to hear their humorous words: "Who told you to be poor? Buck up and bear it! Buck up and bear it!" And, "Here we turn a corner! Watch your step and don't crack your head!"

Being carried in a sedan chair is really very uncomfortable, especially with the tossing, up-and-down motion that reminded me of a ship on a choppy sea or something just as unpleasant. I had to sit very straight and steady so as to make the chair bearers' burden easier. Despite this, I was well compensated by the magnificent vistas of rural life that unrolled before us. We passed attractive villages with all the beauty of sylvan scenery. There were overhanging trees, gnarled pine trees, thousands of years old, sparkling valleys, shining hillsides, cool, gurgling streamlets, a profusion of lovely wildflowers, and many kinds of pretty birds that I had never seen before. All these contributed to make my journey enjoyable indeed, although I felt rather hungry.

The day was one of those bright ones, and our chair coolies carried us uphill along narrow, precipitous paths and downhill over unpaved, beaten-earth tracks with great ease. When I was passing the narrow, precipitous paths, I closed my eyes, for one slip of my bearers' feet would plunge me a thousand feet into the valley below. I really felt nervous. Despite the charming scenery, my thoughts wandered several times to Miss Mao, Kai-shek's first wife. I wondered what kind of reception was in store for me. I asked myself, Will she be jealous of me? I made up my mind to be nice to her and to respect her in every way, to the best of my ability. As I made this decision, I felt a certain tranquility come over me.

It was a little after 3:30 P.M. when we arrived at Hsi-k'ou, Kai-shek's picturesque village. Our chairs came to a stop and were lowered to the ground so that we could get off. It had taken four-and-one-half hours to travel about thirty miles.

As I alighted from my chair, I saw that we were at the entrance to a rather large old-fashioned house, whose main entrance faced a sparkling shallow stream with flowing crystal-clear water.

At the tall, wide doorway stood a rather short, gentle lady whom Kai-shek introduced as Fu-mei, his first wife. She was plain-looking, with a squarish face. I bowed respectfully to her and she reciprocated by returning the bow and said sweetly: "I welcome you! It is our very lucky day to have you come home. May you bring great prosperity to this household." So saying, she took hold of my left hand and led me into the house, which was of the traditional architecture, consisting of an antechamber, a medium-sized courtyard, and a large, square reception hall with an altar placed against the wall. At both wings of this structure were other rooms.

Crossing the courtyard, Miss Mao pointed to the left side of the building and said to me: "Your bedroom is there. Mine is on the right. You go in, freshen up, and change your clothes. There will soon be many guests coming to see the bride. Try to hurry. I'll go and get things ready."

I thanked her and went into the spacious bedroom, which had a four-post double brass bed and Westernized teakwood furniture. As I looked around, Ah Shun and Sui-Chang brought in my suitcases and bags. I quickly freshened up and changed into more formal clothes.

When I came into the hall again, I saw Kai-shek supervising the un-packing of the baggage and parcels while Fu-mei stood at the altar light-ing a bunch of candles and incense sticks and placing them in the two pewter urns. When she had done this, she clapped her hands and bowed her head before the wooden ancestral tablet very reverently. I watched her in deep admiration and could see that she was a devout woman. Ah Shun and Sui-Chang had quickly placed some foodstuffs on plates and set them on the altar. This done, Ah Shun put two mats on the floor at the foot of the altar. Fu-mei, turning to Kai-shek and me, said, "Every-thing is ready for you both to worship our ancestors."

Kai-shek and I knelt three times in unison before the ancestral shrine at the upper center of the main room. Then we repeated the same obei-sance before Mama Huang's large portrait. This ended the first part of the ceremony in making my marriage legal in the eyes of the Hsi-k'ou villagers. I had worshipped my husband's ancestors!

The second part of the ceremony consisted of my paying respects in-dividually to Kai-shek's elder brother and his wife, two sisters and other relatives, village elders, and other friends who had suddenly arrived as if from nowhere. Then I took it upon myself to invite Fu-mei to take an upper seat, and when she sat down, I bowed my head to her three times and offered her a cup of tea. This was my ceremonious greeting to her. Kai-shek merely looked on and smiled, nodding his head in happy ap-proval. As I performed my duties as a bride, all eyes were fixed on me until the ceremony was completed according to Chinese custom.

Then a crowd of curious neighbors came straggling into the house until the place was crowded, all anxiously wishing to see the bride from Shanghai. The ordeal here was much harder than on my wedding day in Shanghai, for here, the villagers were much more particular, conserva-tive, and demanding about proper form than any of the modernized

Jennie.

people in Shanghai. They stared, criticized, giggled, or laughed as they pleased.

Fu-mei seemed to be in a flutter of excitement over the house being so crowded with uninvited guests, and she tried her best to make everyone happy. What may seem rudeness to a city dweller was not felt as such in a Chinese village. These simple people live much closer to one another and, with their peasant outlook on life, never consider it impolite or inquisitive to invade one's privacy. Their idea is, Your business is my business, and it is regarded as an honor to have people come. Come one, come all, is their slogan on all festive occasions.

The ceremonies being over, I had to stand at one side of the hall to be admired by the crowd. The old saying is, See the new, not the old, so the staring eyes looked at my hair, pearl ornaments, silk dress, shoes, earrings, bracelets, and rings. All these excited a great deal of wonder and comment. I was relieved, however, to find that I met with their approval, and when Fu-mei asked me to bow to the crowd to show my respects to them, my mere action of bowing caused a ring of merry laughter. And they chatted away, saying the bride was really so very gentle, well mannered, and pretty.

Since the uninvited guests showed no desire to leave, Kai-shek ordered the servants Ah Shun and Sui-Chang to spread a large sheet of paper on the floor. Then the fifty catties of candy and fifty catties of biscuits, which we had brought from Shanghai, were emptied upon it as the bride's gift to the villagers. When this was announced, there followed a free-for-all. Finally, the crowd, armed with the gifts and politely escorted by Kai-shek, left the house content and happy.

That night a feast was served to Kai-shek's relatives and close friends—all in all, five tables for fifty people. This was regarded as a belated wedding feast, and according to custom, Kai-shek and I had to pay our respects, moving from table to table, to the seated guests. We urged them to drink to their fullest capacity and not stand on ceremony.

All ate heartily and enjoyed themselves. When Kai-shek and I stood before the first table to urge the guests to drink, an old man with a flowing white beard who looked like Confucius rose and said to me: "You look like a sensible girl, and I can see that you will make your husband happy. My advice to you is, have patience with the bridegroom. I have known him since boyhood. As a boy I called him 'Jui-t'ai,' and I refuse to call him anything else, for I cannot follow all his new names. He is stubborn, jealous, tactless, bad-tempered, and egotistical. So, if you can use your patience and tact to change his fiery temper and bad ways, you will do the Chiang ancestors a real service. So do try to change him and make him a better man."

I was shocked and embarrassed to hear this unexpected outburst. Kai-shek, standing by my side, however, merely giggled sheepishly, patted the old man's arm gently, and urged him to sit down and drink more wine.

r   r   r

In the late afternoon on the second day after my arrival, as the sun was setting, Kai-shek asked me to accompany him for an outing on a bamboo raft, which was in front of our doorway, to sail a mile down the crystal-clear river. Because the freshwater stream was only five feet deep, the bottom could be seen clearly, and oval-shaped pebbles lined the riverbed. Our raft was made of ten thick bamboo poles, eighteen feet long, bound together by cane strips, and reinforced at several sections. With two cane chairs placed side by side, and a small table in front of us, our "barge" glided over the smooth surface while our boatman dipped his long bamboo shaft in to the river bottom to deftly push forward. But Kai-shek gave instructions to the boatman to push backward toward the left, for he wanted to show me his favorite spot. It was a pile of jutting boulders; he pointed at it and explained: "That spot is called Wen-Chang Kuo. It is a promontory. When you stand up there, you can see in the distance the rolling mountain tops that surround this locality. One can also see at one's feet that there is water on three sides, and underneath the rock a stream drips springwater, making a gurgling sound like music. It is a most inspiring spot, and I love it."

Because they were so close to the water, trees and shrubs grew profusely in the crannies of the rocks. Then Kai-shek added: "Whenever I have time, I come here to meditate. One of these days I hope to build a house here, where you and I can admire the surrounding landscape and, at the same time, listen to the gurgling spring."

"I hope you will get your wish," I said, and I silently prayed that his wish would come true.

As our raft glided on, the scenery was indeed serene and restful. Kai-shek held my hand and kneaded my fingers to express his ardent love. On the bank to our right were a number of one-story, rather delapidated houses and some huts, which made up the village of Hsi-k'ou, numbering about fifty homes. A curious crowd of villagers in their somber blue costumes loitered around after their day's work, laughing and staring at us. Some children jumped and gesticulated, pointing and audibly commenting on our strange city looks. To the left of us, bordering the bank as far as the eye could see, stood a verdant bamboo grove. I had never before seen such tall and sturdy bamboo trees. With the gentle breeze, the leaves rustled, making a very weird sound. This typical Chinese country scene was spoiled only by a poor imitation of a foreign bridge, cracked and made of white cement, straddling the stream. Our raft glided on, under the bridge.

We could see in the distance another raft similar to ours with a shaggy old fisherman fishing with several jet-black cormorants. He sat there meditatively smoking his piccolo-length pipe. As we neared him, he looked up to greet us with a few perfunctory words. He had six birds, with yellow, hooked beaks, perching on the raft. The whole scene was so picturesque! This method of fishing intrigued me. Kai-shek, noticing my interest, told our boatman to anchor there a moment for my benefit so that I could see what was going on. I watched the tame cormorants perching there untied, and they looked up at us unafraid. The fisherman placed a slender cane ring over the cormorant's neck and pushed it firmly to the end of the gullet. This was to prevent the cormorant from swallowing its catches. One by one, as the harnesses were placed into position, the cormorants splashed and dived away underwater. By the time they had caught many small fish and could not manage any more, they swam back to their raft, with their necks distended, to be relieved. The fisherman took the bird in hand and gently squeezed its *ayus* (food-pouch). This caused the bird to disgorge the fish into a waiting wooden bucket until the *ayus* was empty. The fisherman then removed the cane ring from the bird's neck, gave it a fish as a reward, which was quickly swallowed. After a short rest, the cormorant was ready to be off again, but not until the fisherman gave the "go" signal.

"How many fish can a cormorant catch a day?" I asked.

"Each bird can catch up to a couple of hundred," the man answered. "The best catch," he added, "is at night when a lantern shines on the barge. The bright light attracts the fish, and they are easy prey for my birds."

As we sailed away, I said to Kai-shek: "This is my first experience in seeing cormorants fishing, and I think it is most interesting. Do tell me some more about them. Can they catch big fish also?"

"Some birds are more expert than others," he replied, "but they rarely fail to secure their prey. Sometimes, however, when they catch a big fish or an eel and cannot manage to swallow it, two or three of the cormorants will go to its aid."

"That is true brotherly love," I said happily.

"Of course this method of fishing is very ancient," he continued.

"The cormorant is most admirably adapted for swimming because it has ducklike feet. Yet it is among the very few web-footed birds capable of perching on a tree branch, which it does with great ease. There are quite a number of species of cormorants distributed over different parts of China, as in Chekiang here, Foochow in Fukien, and the North River in Canton. They are closely allied to pelicans in conformation and habits. Being voracious feeders, they dive with great force, and swim underwater, as you have seen. Few fish can escape them. They are called the hungriest birds in the world."

By degrees, the excitement of my marriage passed, and the initial strangeness wore away. I began to talk a little more freely, especially with Fu-mei, until, by the end of the first week, things settled down into a routine. I soon felt sufficiently at home to assume my share of the household duties and to help Fu-mei whenever I could. Brought up in a conservative family, I naturally was used to household chores. I always assumed a modest and respectful demeanor, especially to Fu-mei, who was ever so kind and thoughtful to me. The two of us got on wonderfully well, and we liked one another immensely.

Our daily life would start at daylight, for Kai-shek was an easly riser. Naturally, I could not stay in bed after he had risen, so I, too, rose from bed to wait on him and make myself useful. He usually walked into the reception hall, breathing deeply the sweet fresh air for some minutes. He would then sit perfectly still with closed eyes and folded legs, back erect and straight, in meditation. This was in order to acquire good health and a relaxed mind. After half an hour of this, he would either read or write a few letters or make a record of events in his diary. During these hours before breakfast, which was at 8 A.M., we seldom chatted.

Kai-shek had several favorite books, but the one he studied each morning was *The Art of War* by Sun Tzu. He read and reread it when alone and only put it down when I came into the reception hall. Curious, I asked what the book was about. He explained that it contained Sun Tzu's advice regarding strategy in war. The author, he told me, lived over two thousand years ago and was a Shantung man. He had not only helped the King of Fu to conquer the Kingdom of Chu but also helped to subdue other neighboring states. It was written in simple language and had been handed down through the centuries as a military textbook.

Daily breakfast consisted of plain rice gruel (à la Nipponese) mixed with one fresh egg and a pinch of salt. Lunch at twelve noon consisted of two bowls of rice and four dishes of meat and vegetables—cooked in Ningpo style. Sometimes, for good measure, he would also eat a steamed freshwater fish or some steamed chicken soup. After lunch, he usually took a nap on a sofa or in the bed for an hour. In the afternoon, when he did not chat with relatives, villagers, or mechants, he would insist that I accompany him on a stroll. We went to Wen-Chang Kuo promontory or in the hills or climbed a nearby mountain. On our return at 4 or 5 P.M., he usually took a small bowl of bird's nest soup with rock sugar. It looked something like white jelly but was thought to be very nutritious. Dinner was served at 7 P.M. We usually retired at 10 P.M. because there was hardly any nightlife in Hsi-k'ou.

One day, as Fu-mei and I were sitting in the reception hall folding a batch of joss paper, which was symbolic of silver sycee taels, she asked anxiously, "Have you seen my son, Ching-kuo, who lives in Shanghai?"

"Not yet," I answered. "But I will do so when we get back to the city."

"He is eleven years old and, like his father, has an adventurous spirit. He hates to stay home and longs to travel. He is a good boy," she said meditatively, "and very sensible, but terribly afraid of his father. I cannot help but worry about him being all alone and so far away." She sighed and wiped away a tear. "He is my chief worry."

"There is no need for you to worry about him unnecessarily," I said in a effort to comfort her. "I promise I shall do my utmost to help him in every way possible when I return to Shanghai. Will you promise me you will not worry about him?"

"You shall have my deep gratitude if you will help me," she cried gratefully, and I could see her eyes welling with tears. "I know you are a very kind person and will help him all you can."

"That, I promise," I pledged sincerely and made up my mind I would do it.

At that moment, I thought of the old man who looked like Confucius at the wedding dinner. Since I was curious to know who he was, I asked: "What was that old man with the flowing white beard at the wedding dinner? He spoke so tactlessly in his outburst to Kai-shek that night."

"He is old Uncle Mao, our neighboring-village elder. His bitterness goes back to the old days when he boxed Kai-shek's ears. It came about this way, and I was indirectly involved." She paused a minute meditatively and continued: "I was twenty years old and Kai-shek was only sixteen in 1902 when we were married. Old Mama Huang was anxious to have a grandson, and that's why she arranged our blind marriage. As a bridegroom, Kai-shek was invited to my mother's home for the first time to attend a formal 'Invitation to a New Son-in-Law Banquet.' That was on the third day after marriage. Instead of being very polite and ceremonious, do you know what Kai-shek did?"

"No," I answered curiously.

"Amidst the ceremony, Kai-shek saw some boys outside my mother's house playing a game of shuttlecock. So, like an overgrown kid, he ran out to join them. This was a terrible faux pas on such a formal occasion, causing consternation to the host and guests. When the feast was finally ready to be served, Old Mr. Mao went out to call Kai-shek to come in. But he kept on playing, ignoring the old man. Exasperated, Old Mr. Mao caught hold of Kai-shek, boxed his ears, and literally dragged him into the house. This, of course, caused a scandal and a terrible disgrace to Mama Huang. So, instead of scolding her son, she gave Old Mr. Mao a sizzling tongue-lashing that the old man can never forget. Now, every time he sees Kai-shek, he invariably retaliates from force of habit."

"What made you take up Buddhism?" I asked.

"It is a long story, but I will tell you what I have never told anyone before," she said confidentially. "For the first two months after my marriage to Kai-shek, we were young and very happy. He insisted on taking me out on his outdoor trips each day. He had no job and no heart for studying, but had a strange obsession for the solitude of the mountains, the sounds of roaring waterfalls, the singing of wild birds, the serenity of the temples, and rides on the raft down the stream to watch cormorant fishing—just as you did the other night. But Old Mama Huang soon put a stop to all that. She blamed me bitterly for being a disturbing influence on her son and accused me of aiding and abetting him in his idleness. She even said I was leading him astray. One day when we returned from an outing, she called me to her bedroom, scolded me, and said: 'I haven't enough rice to feed idle mouths. You are a shameless hussy to gallivant all over the mountains and monasteries with a man. Have you no shame? It ill becomes a young married woman like you, and it must stop. From today on, I forbid you to waste any more of my son's time unless you can guarantee his future prospects. If you cannot give that guarantee, then stop ruining him!' After that, I refused to go out with Kai-shek anymore. Even when he begged me to go, I refused. I am only a simple, countrified woman; how can I guarantee his future prospects?''

"I am sorry to hear that," I said sympathetically.

"But trouble did not end there," continued Fu-mei thoughtfully. "Things became intolerable whenever Kai-shek and I talked or laughed in the house. Our mere conversation irked Mama Huang terribly, and she cursed me for talking. In order not to cause any more unpleasantness, therefore, I kept quiet and seldom spoke. More and more I avoided any direct conversation openly with him in the house. That was not easy, however, especially when he asked me questions and expected my answers. The situation went from bad to worse, and Kai-shek soon became impatient with me. I dared not say one word to defend myself, even when he scolded me, for, as you know, the villagers in their narrow-mindedness would accuse me of being an unfilial and disobedient daughter-in-law. And you know what that means in an isolated village such as ours! The strain gradually caused a split between Kai-shek and me. All I could do was to weep secretly over my utter helplessness, and for a long period I suffered from melancholy. To escape the intolerable woe, which seemed to have enveloped me, I more and more turned to Lord Buddha for consolation. Now, after so many years, I have found a profound peace of mind in Buddhism and enjoy contentment in my ascetic life. But I am so very happy that Kai-shek has found happiness with you."

I looked at Fu-mei and marveled at her self-imposed sacrifice and wonderful temperament. She was really a good and virtuous woman, and I respected her as a loving sister.

The following day, Kai-shek, his brother, Fu-mei, and I, together with a few relatives and our two boy servants, went on a visit to Mama Huang's grave so that I could pay my respects to her remains as a new daughter-in-law. In the old days, only male members visited the grave. But since women's emancipation, Kai-shek insisted that I and Fu-mei also go. We took with us four cane baskets containing many platters of cooked foodstuffs, tea, wine, incense, candles, and dozens of strings of gold and silver joss paper that Fu-mei and I had folded into shapes of "nugget taels." These were to be offered to the deceased. Kai-shek had also asked a contractor to make an estimate of the cost of having a Chinese headstone built in front of Mama Huang's mound. Before we left the house, he told me: "The grave is now only a rough pile of earth, but I plan to build a low, two-foot-high, balustrade around it. For the head-stone, I will ask Dr. Sun to personally write the inscription. That will give me much prestige." He glowed with happiness, for the mere thought of this made him so very proud that he swaggered when he walked.

Our little group set out from the house, taking the right side of the road, and we trotted on and on, passing old village homes and then stretches of farmland until we came to a mountain road. On the road-side we soon reached a small picturesque pavilion. Kai-shek pointed it out to me, saying that it was built by order of Mama Huang as a resting place for weary travelers. I went in and rested my tired bones for a min-ute. I could see the foresight of Mama Huang, who so wisely and kindly had provided for the comfort of weary visitors.

Then we plodded on, up the slope, until we came to a comparatively level piece of ground with many tall trees growing. There I could see a mound of earth piled six feet high, marked in front by a small stone tab-let that merely read: "Mother Chiang's Grave." Fu-mei ordered the two servant boys to unpack the foodstuffs and place them before the grave, while she went ahead to light incense sticks and candles.

As a rule, most Chinese people are very superstitious about graves, for they believe that the dead in the next world require the same com-forts and necessities as the living. This is due to a common belief that a man possesses a trinity of souls. After death, one soul goes into the an-cestral tablet that is enshrined on the family altar, where it receives the worship of his descendants; the second soul inhabits the grave; and the third goes into the netherworld to receive rewards or punishments be-fore finally returning to the upper world. It was, consequently, the filial duty of all male descendants of the deceased to pay annual visits, called "Sweeping of the Tomb." Offerings were burnt at the grave; the articles used, made of paper, represented such things as houses, boats, clothes, sedan chairs, joss paper, and every conceivable object. It was seriously believed that nearly all the ills to which the flesh was heir, such as sick-ness, bad luck, calamity, and death, were inflicted by the spirits of rest-less souls.

Having had all the offerings laid out before the grave, Fu-mei gave me a signal. Kai-shek and I then knelt down three times and bowed our heads nine times in deep respect before Mama Huang's mound. When we had finished, Fu-mei and the others followed suit to pay their respects.

The ceremony over, the foodstuffs were divided up and served. We all enjoyed an outdoor picnic.

Kai-shek walked around the grounds with the contractor, and they discussed ways and means of having the grave built.

6

The Dragon's Pulse

Altogether, I stayed in Hsi-k'ou village for ten days. My last outing was a trip to the famous Shih-Tao Monastery, which Kai-shek regarded as his favorite institution. This monastery, named after the Shih-Tao Mountain, is about six miles away and is inhabited entirely by Buddhist monks. It acquired its fame because a Ming emperor had visited it in A.D. 1518 and left an imperial edict there to commemorate the occasion. This was considered a rare honor.

Our sedan chairs ascended a lofty peak, and we could feel the cool air, which was even more exhilarating than that of the village. We quickly felt refreshed, and Kai-shek shouted to us to inhale deeply.

Now on the summit, we could in the distance see the glorious temple nestled among shrubbery. The bright sun's rays struck the structure's curved eaves, and the tall dark-green trees and hedges caught the reflected light and sparkled like jade and emeralds.

The path leading to the monastery was lined with wildflowers, graceful ferns, and other plants. We entered the temple gate, and I was surprised to see that the monks who greeted us wore their hair long, right down to their shoulders. They wore an inch-wide brass band around their forehead to keep their hair in place, framing their faces. I had never seen this type of monk before, except on the stage or in paintings. Now, seeing them in real life, my curiosity was aroused. In answer to my inquiry, Kai-shek explained: "These long-haired monks are athletes who specialize in feats of strength and are masters of the art of defense. That is why they don't shave their heads like the others."

Upon entering the monastery, I could see that it was constructed in the traditional style of Chinese architecture. As we stood in the ante-room, I was greatly impressed by the Four Heavenly Kings, which were much larger than any I had ever seen, at least thirty feet high and ten feet wide, two on each side, in sitting positions. In the center of this room stood a finely carved wooden altar, enclosed with glass. It contained an imperial edict issued by the Ming Emperor Cheng-te, who had stayed at this monastery during his Kiangnan journey four hundred years ago.

At this point we were met by a number of black-clad, shaven-headed monks. Kai-shek introduced Fu-mei and me as his "sisters," and the monks all bowed to us, murmuring, "Omi tofu."

After crossing the square courtyard, we were conducted to the majestic main hall. We went in to offer incense before the three huge golden images of Buddha. Having burned the incense, lit the candles, and filled the lamps with peanut oil, Fu-mei and I knelt down to pay our respects to Buddha. In the meantime, Kai-shek wandered over to the corner of the room where a young priest, seated at a desk, had charge of the little pieces of yellow paper with oracular statements printed thereon. These were for people who wanted to know what their earthly future would be. To get one of these little papers, one had to first shake the cylindrical bamboo holder until a stick bearing a number fell out. That number represented the number of the message.

Kai-shek's message read, "The pine tree stretches its head to heaven." This was a good omen and indicated a bright future.

Fu-mei's read, "Straw covering genuine pearls." This could be interpreted as precious qualities hidden away unappreciated.

My slip read, "The sapling caught in a typhoon." This indicated danger, suffering, or even tragedy. Feeling disappointed, I crumbled up my paper. Although Kai-shek wanted to read it, I refused to let him do so.

We were then taken into a side chamber, where we saw the life-sized Eighteen Lo-Hans, also known as Arhats. These were the disciples of Buddha. They were arranged nine on each side; in the center was enshrined a chubby-faced, benign-looking diety called "God of Contentment." He smiled on us as we entered.

Here Fu-mei and I again offered incense, but we did not kneel. We merely "chin-chinned" the saints with both our hands.

Kai-shek then led us outdoors to roam the vast grounds surrounding the monastery, which he dearly loved. We looked around, admiring the sylvan beauty, and before we realized it, we were standing in front of a small building. Here a monk was shut up in a cagelike cell, by his own wish, Kai-shek said. He was to be immured for five years. The door leading into this cell was locked with a padlock. Two strips of paper, serving as "seals," covered with writing, were pasted crosswise so that the door could not be opened without the paper strips' being broken. The monk's hair and beard were quite long, and although his face was gaunt and pale, he seemed to enjoy good health. He looked serene and contented, sitting at a table reading the sutras. Looking through the small window through which he communicated with the outer world, we could see the scanty furniture of the little room. Bed boards stretched across two stools and covered with matting served as the bunk upon which he slept. On the right side stood a little table with a teapot and a cup. Nearby was a little altar on which stood a small porcelain image of Kuan Yin, the Goddess of Mercy, and a stack of books.

"This self-imprisoned monk," Kai-shek told us, "came from Hangchow. He originally was a merchant but became a monk after his young wife, whom he dearly loved, eloped with another man. The reason for imprisoning himself was to show that he had given up his whole life to chant sutras to Buddha."

Seeing my surprise, Kai-shek explained that it was not unusual for Buddhist priests to undergo voluntary confinement in this way. After five years seclusion, the hermit would emerge with long, unkempt locks and flowing beard to go out into the world on a praying expedition as a "holy" man.

Kai-shek then led us back to the monastery to meet the abbot Tai Shih and to have lunch. We retraced our steps and, finally having reached the courtyard, looked at the ten-foot-high wooden fish that was suspended from the eaves. Kai-shek explained that this fish was hollow and over a thousand years old. It was still used as a drum, in conjunction with the temple bell, to summon the monks to prayers. Of course it was very much worn and splintered in many parts where it had been struck for so many centuries.

We then made our way to a side room that looked like a library, with the walls lined with many volumes of prayer books. At the upper center of the room stood the venerable Abbot Tai Shih, a very old, bearded monk, of whom Kai-shek was very fond and whom he regarded as a mentor. On being introduced by Kai-shek, Fu-mei and I bowed to him most reverently. He returned the greeting with his fingers outstretched and hands clasped together. He then pointed with much ceremony to the well-laid table, covered with many delicacies all made from beans, beancurd, and vegetables. He asked us to make ourselves at home. Then he left us and retired to an inner chamber. So Kai-shek, Fu-mei, and I sat there at our ease to enjoy a meatless but delicious luncheon.

The reason why Fu-mei accompanied me on this trip was that, according to the ancient ordinances of Buddhism, one woman alone was prohibited from entering this sacred building. She must be accompanied by a companion of the same sex. Since Kai-shek was anxious for me to see this monastery, he had to ask Fu-mei too. And how glad I was that she had come along!

At two o'clock, when the afternoon service began, we heard the sonorous tone of the gong and then the wooden drum being struck. We proceeded to the Main Hall, where we stood on one side to watch the rows of Buddhist monks, with their shaven heads and long, flowing gray robes, facing each other in two lines, droning out alternate verses of sutras and praising Buddha. On the right of the altar was a monk who occasionally struck a drum and a gong, while another kept time with a stick beating a small, round hollow instrument made of wood. This instrument was also called a wooden fish. Abbot Tai Shih stood in front of the altar, with a red cloth draped over his left shoulder and wearing a lotus-shaped embroidered hat, and prostrated himself occasionally before Buddha. At one part of the service, he took from the altar a small cup containing sacred water and, after praying for some time, carried the cup outside and sprinkled its contents slowly over a square stone near the temple door. This was regarded as a libation to dismembered spirits. Then he snapped his fingers three times and, forming ring after ring with his fingers, did other quick symbolic movements with both hands. After a while he turned around and proceeded once more to his place before the altar. There he resumed his prayers and prostrations while the priests chanted their sutras in a singsong voice. Toward the end of the service, the monks, still chanting, walked in procession round and round the interior of the temple while Abbot Tai Shih manipulated his heavy string of beads, which he held in his hand.

The evening was on the wane, and as the prayers came to an end, Kai-shek, Fu-mei, and I said farewell to Abbot Tai Shih and his monks and rode our palanquins back to Hsi-k'ou.

The monastery, quaint surroundings, and, indeed, the excellence of the food itself were for me a most enjoyable experience. And Kai-shek, having been in one of his jocular moods, and with his natural wit and humor, had made our visit a memorable one.

、　、　、

Our holiday at Hsi-k'ou did Kai-shek a world of good. He seemed much relaxed and in an exceptionally happy mood. Each day he wanted to show me more and more of the wonderful scenery in and round Hsi-k'ou. But it would have taken many weeks to make all the long treks he envisioned.

"If you see nothing else, you must see my favorite waterfall, and that's an order!" he exclaimed joyously. He half pulled and half dragged me to go with him.

"Wait," I laughed, "let me first dress and put on a pair of low-heeled shoes, and then I will outwalk you!"

From the house we duly set out on foot, just the two of us, and we walked and walked. We passed numerous green fields, ascended a slope, and thence higher and higher, passing shady bamboo groves and large pine trees. Finally we came to a series of hill knobs.

"I frequently visit this place whenever I come to Hsi-k'ou," Kai-shek told me. "Look how attractive the scenery is." We stopped for a few minutes to catch our breath. "The best time to see these hills is early morning after a refreshing shower. People call this scene Clear Sky After Rain."

Indeed, the landscape was charming. There were so many varieties of trees and plants that I quite understood why the outdoors appealed to him so intensely. Here was nature at its loveliest, appealing to the pure instincts of man.

After a short rest, we climbed higher still, until we arrived at the top of a mountain. He explained: "This is called Szu-ming Mountain. The name is derived from that large square boulder over there, which reflects light on its four sides. It is perfectly square—without benefit of man's chisel!" Then he walked over to a precipice and told me: "From this spot where I stand, there is a spring underneath that issues forth the water that forms my favorite waterfall. It flows ten thousand feet below. You cannot see it from here, but I'll take you to see it later. But come here first!"

I could never have guessed that Kai-shek would be so enthusiastic about a mere waterfall. I looked at his slight, wiry figure, his eager eyes full of delight, and saw the buoyancy in his movements. He behaved like an overgrown boy.

"This spot," he explained, "is called the Dragon's Pulse and is regarded as a sacred spot. Come! Stand here with me! It will give us good luck!" I moved closer to him and he took me in his arms and whispered: "On this Dragon Pulse I stand with you. I now swear, once again, that I shall love you forever. You, too, must swear that you will love me always. Now swear and let the dragon hear your oath!"

"I shall love you as long as you love me—but not a moment longer," I told him teasingly.

"That means forever and ever," he said seriously.

He crushed me in his arms and caressed me long and tenderly. Then we walked, hand-in-hand, toward the West and descended the mountain, heading southwest. Little by little, we trod over rocks and dirt paths, winding our way through wooded glens and over a bridge spanning a deep ravine. Then we came to a rocky hillside where the magnificent waterfall fell from above like a long white bridal veil, roaring its wonderful springwater down into a large pool.

The sight was indeed enthralling. No wonder Kai-shek loved this spot so very much. Kai-shek held my hand tight and led me to a jutting rock at the side of the pool. I sat there and he sat close to me. I could feel the cloudy mist of water spraying us, but we did not care. We wanted to be part of the waterfall. We both sat there holding hands while listening to the lovely music of the churning waters and watching the sunlight break through the falling spray.

Now I began to understand Kai-shek's fondness for the countryside, where he loved to linger and spend the whole day communing with nature. There he enjoyed the delicious sense of coolness of pure springwater, the verdure and woodland beauty, richness of foliage, and the fragrant pines, the singing of birds, and the sound of dancing waters.

Sitting there holding hands and watching the waterfall was most exhilarating, and I thought to myself: Nature in her pristine garb is like balm to Kai-shek's hungry soul. No wonder he loves it so, but alas and alack, Mama Huang did not realize this.

My thoughts were interrupted when Kai-shek kissed my ear and said: "I'm glad you love this waterfall as much as I do. I've sat here at this very spot many hundreds of times though the years, but I can truly say that today is my happiest because I have you at my side," he said cheerily. He meditated a while and added: "Isn't it strange? Such a wonderful sight as this can also mean nothing to me when I am unhappy."

"What do you mean?" I asked looking into his eyes.

"It's all one's mental outlook," he answered brushing his chin against my ear. "I remember the day when you ran away from me at the Burlington Hotel. I was so very miserable. I longed to see you again to explain matters but knew you would never forgive me. In my dejection I had no heart to do anything. The future seemed bleak and hopeless. I took stock of myself and felt as if I was caught in a rut from which I could not escape. In all my life I had never felt such desolation." He looked at the waterfall and murmured: "Yes, I came back here for comfort. But even this marvelous scene meant nothing to me. I sat here for hours asking myself what I could do to win your forgiveness. This wonderful roaring crystal water, the singing of the birds, the dragonfly alighting on my shoulder, simply meant nothing. That is how I felt during those days without you. I asked myself repeatedly, If I cannot win even the first of my three ardent wishes, how can I have heart and courage to achieve the other two? It was only after the death of my mother that I learned of your sad bereavement. That gave me courage to pay homage to the father of the girl I loved so deeply. And you were so good and kind to forgive me. Oh my darling wife! Before this waterfall I swear to you once again, I shall love you forever."

7

Two "Sons"

On the morning of my ninth day in Hsi-k'ou, Kai-shek received the long-awaited telegram from Dr. Sun Yat-sen asking him to proceed to Canton as soon as convenient to take up a position under General Ch'en Chiung-ming. Kai-shek wanted to take the opportunity to go by one of the larger steamers that traveled from Shanghai via Hongkong, and we found that the earliest departure was the SS *President Taft*, sailing from Shanghai at the end of the month. This gave us more than twelve days to prepare for our trip.

After bidding a tearful adieu to Fu-mei, I left Hsi-k'ou with Kai-shek for Feng-hua County and thence by a large wooden junk to Ningpo. Arriving at this ancient and famous port, I made it a point to take note of the scenery, much of which I had missed on my previous trip. It was a bright afternoon, and the entrance to the river was exceedingly picturesque. On one side I could see a steep hill, on the summit of which stood the famous Tin Tung Monastery. A short distance toward the sea I could see a lighthouse, with its white tower and numerous windows glistening in the bright sunshine. Inside the mouth of the river, opposite the village, was my native Chen-hai. I could see a large fleet of junks lying at anchor there, ready to brave the dangers of the ocean. A group of other junks had just arrived from their perilous wanderings over the choppy seas. Gliding up the winding river, our junk finally brought us to the riverbank outside the Chinese city of Ningpo.

With an hour's wait before we could catch the coastal steamer for Shanghai, Kai-shek and I went ashore and wandered through the narrow streets to see Ningpo. It was a typical Chinese town, with granite-paved streets that were fairly clean. After walking some distance, we came to one of the city gates, a small, low archway. We passed through and immediately found ourselves in a bustling street with shops on both sides. So this was Ningpo's main street! Many shops sold pretty silk embroideries, all kinds of silks, bamboo ware, and the gold wood carvings for which the city is famous. Having seen the better part of the town, we then went to our steamer bound for Shanghai.

Back in Shanghai, Kai-shek thought it would be more convenient for us to stay at the Great Eastern Hotel than to move to our rooms at Rue Vallon in Frenchtown, especially when we were scheduled to leave so soon for Canton via Hongkong.

He shaved and, dressed elaborately in his new blue-silk long gown, took me out. This was the beginning of a new phase of my life. We went out to dinner at restaurants, saw a moving picture at the Olympic Theater on Bubblingwell Road, and visited many revolutionary friends, all of whom called us an ideal couple. I felt embarrassed at the lavish compliments they showered on me, but Kai-shek wallowed in it, saying that he had found the right girl in me and confessed that I suited his temperament perfectly. "You see," he would say to me, "my impressions of you are shared by all my friends. I never lie to you, do I? I am a good judge of people and that is why I married you."

On the fourth morning after we got back to Shanghai, the hotel boy knocked at our door and ushered into our room a lad who looked like a countrified schoolboy.

"Father!" he exclaimed to Kai-shek and then stood at one side with respectful demeanor. Kai-shek gave him one stare and gruffly said, pointing to me: "This is your new mother! Pay your respects to her!"

The boy came over and nervously looked at me and said, "Mother!" As he spoke he bowed from his waist in a ninety-degree angle.

"He is my son, Ching-kuo," said Kai-shek.

Although I was overwhelmed at having such a big son, I thought it was very nice of the boy to have bowed to me so courteously. "So you are Ching-kuo," I asked in a very friendly voice, and at once I thought of Fu-mei and my promise to her. "Please sit down and tell me how you are." I pointed to a nearby chair, but I was surprised to see he refused to sit.

Although young, the boy had closely cropped hair, a square, heavy face that somewhat resembled his mother's, a high forehead, large mouth, and prominent buckteeth. He seemed a well-behaved, quiet, and docile lad, but far too nervous and ill at ease.

Kai-shek was impatient and glared at the boy. The embarrassing situation was only saved by the timely entrance of a hotel servant who told Kai-shek that he was wanted on the telephone. When Kai-shek left the room, I went over to Ching-kuo and led him by the hand to a chair.

"You must not be so ceremonious," I told him kindly. "Sit down and relax. I want you to feel at home whenever you come to see me. Now, tell me about yourself. I am interested in everything you do. I promised your mother I'd look after you."

But the boy only trembled more and said nothing.

"I was in Hsi-k'ou village for ten days," I said, trying to break the ice, but the boy refused to relax. He sat there as if frozen. "I saw your mother and she is very anxious about you. Have you written to her lately?"

He shook his head. That was one thing I hated in children, and I wanted to scream and say, Don't shake your head as if you are dumb. Say yes or no! But since the boy was so nervous, I did not want to make things worse for him. I merely smiled and advised him: "You must write to your dear mother at least once a week to tell her that you are well. Your mother worries about you. Do you know that? Will you write to her? Make a practice to write home regularly. Do you know your mother worries about you being alone in a big city like Shanghai? She told me to look after you, and I promised her that I would do so. Should there be anything I can do to help you, no matter what it is, please don't fail to let me know. Will you do that?"

Ching-kuo still sat there without a word. He listened to me attentively enough but merely blinked his thick eyelids and moved his heavy jaws and swallowed hard.

"Will you?" I persisted. He then merely nodded again with a blank expression.

I looked at his slight, boyish figure, swarthy face, and small, darting eyes and knew his silence was not due to rudeness or ignorance but to an extreme shyness, bordering on fear.

To ease matters, I went over to my dressing table, took out $40. I wrapped $20 in red paper and placed $20 on the table.

"Here is a red packet for you," I said as I handed it to him. He rose politely, bowed, and took it hesitantly. "Thank you," he said and bowed. Then he quickly resumed his seat.

"Where are you staying?" I asked.

"At Uncle Ch'en Kuo-fu's in Frenchtown."

"Are you comfortable there?"

"Yes, I am."

"Don't forget what I just said," I reminded him. "If there is anything in the world I can do to help you, please don't fail to let me know. Will you do that? I really mean it."

"Yes, I will."

"Have you enough clothes and shoes?"

"Yes, I have enough, thank you."

I felt so pleased that the boy had finally calmed his fears that I took up the $20 on the table and said: "That red packet I gave you just now is to celebrate our first meeting. It is a Shanghai custom. But here is another $20, which is for you to buy something that you really, really like. It will save me time if you will go and get it for me. Will you do that?"

For the first time the lad giggled awkwardly and said with embarrassment: "There's no need. You are very kind to me. I cannot accept so much." He refused to accept the money.

"Nonsense. Take it," I insisted and simply stuck the money in his pocket.

Now that the boy had become much more relaxed, we bagan to converse normally and even animatedly about his school and his friends. Unfortunately, Kai-shek came back into the room, and Ching-kuo rose quickly from his seat to stand respectfully at attention. I could see he had once more resumed his tenseness. He simply shut up like a clam.

I rang for the hotel boy and ordered lunch. The three of us enjoyed a fine repast in our room, but I could see that Ching-kuo felt terribly ill at ease and did not enjoy his food. It was only years later that I learned what had instilled in him this terrible fear.

That night before Ching-kuo left, I made him shake hands with his father, and they appeared much friendlier. And when we were alone, I tried to be tactful and said to Kai-shek: "Ching-kuo is a fine boy and is very sensitive. At heart he loves you very much. I think, in the future, you should not speak so harshly to him. You may not realize it, but your loud voice frightens him."

"I don't want to pamper him in any way," he answered me abruptly. "Boys must learn their place and their duty."

"But you can show him a little affection and devotion. As it is, the lad shakes with nervousness in your presence. It makes him think that you don't care at all for him."

"Pamper him and make him lose his fatherly respect for me? Oh, no, no! A small boy must learn to be filial, responsible, and respectful. He must learn discipline. The worst thing for a boy is to be spoiled by his parents. When I was a boy, I was very playful and mischievous. Although my mother was strict, I would never take advice and wanted my own way. So, many a time the neighborhood boys would ill-treat me, beat me up, and even boycott me from their games. This was because I did not know discipline and comradeship. I don't want Ching-kuo to be spoiled and have to suffer as I did. He must learn discipline."

"I agree with you there," I said earnestly. "But as it is now, the boy is lonely. He needs your love. Instead you seem to inspire terror in his young heart. For my sake, please don't be overly stern with him. Try to talk softer to him, instead of in your loud, strained voice. When you talk so gruffly, he thinks you are angry with him, which I know you are not. Why don't you talk to him in the same tone of voice as you talk to me? Won't you do that? For me?"

He was silent for a while, weighing my words. Then he came over to embrace me and said smilingly: "All right! All right! I'll try to do what you say. but see that you don't spoil him!" He patted my cheek and caressed me tenderly.

"Are you happy now?" he asked.

"Very happy!" I answered.

If anyone had told me that within a month of my marriage I would be a mother to two sons, I would never have believed it, even in my wildest dreams. So, imagine my surprise when my "official" matchmaker, Mr. Feng Chieh-wen, called unexpectedly from Soochow and brought along a little boy of six to see Kai-shek and me. He was a sweet-looking lad with a long, thin face, delicate features, narrow, dark eyes, and a very fair complexion. But he was very, very delicate and frail.

Kai-shek picked up the child, fondled him most affectionately, and, pointing to me, told him in childish tones: "This is your new mother. Say to her, Good Mother!"

"Good Mother," muttered the child shyly and obediently.

"What a nice little boy! Who is he and what's his name?" I asked in surprise.

"He is your second son! His name is Wei-kuo. Do you like him? I'll tell you all about him later."

"What a sweet child!" I said and patted his tiny, thin cheek. He was so pathetically thin that he captivated me from the start.

Although Mr. Feng had acted as Kai-shek's and my official matchmaker at our wedding, he was a complete stranger to me. It was customary, however, to have a matchmaker at a wedding, even as a figurehead, since no marriage could be complete without a go-between. He seemed rather handsome and debonair in his European suit, and his chatter and laughter at first was pleasant and friendly. But it only took an hour for me to size him up as a born gusher and scandalmonger. He was a man of thirty-five and so talkative that his conversation knew no bounds; he tended to say the first things that came into his head without thinking. His appreciative gushing about me was more embarrassing than pleasing, and I wished he would stop.

I studied this young man for a while, and hearing his loud chatter with Kai-shek about his latest romantic exploits, I realized it was purely habitual boasting. His real attention was always on something else and never on just one subject.

Before finishing one subject with Kai-shek, he turned to me, smiled ravishingly, and said I was too beautiful, too good, and too young for an old reprobate like Kai-shek. "So you're going to Canton?" he asked.

"Yes," answered Kai-shek good-humoredly, "at the end of the month."

"Canton is better than Shanghai and I long to get back." Looking at me, he added: "Do you know that Canton is my native city? When did you say you were leaving?"

"At the end of this month," repeated Kai-shek.

"Oh, how beautiful!" He eyed me fully in the face. "Just the right age for Kai-shek. He loves them young!" His eyes then wandered over to little Wei-kuo and then to Kai-shek. "Isn't he cute and healthy?" he asked. "Miss Yao has done a good job. She has kept him for three months. Now she wants me to take him to Hsi-k'ou for Miss Mao to look after for an equal period. But why don't you take him to Canton instead? It will save me a trip to Hsi-k'ou."

"It will be rather awkward for us to take him just now, since things are so uncertain in Canton," said Kai-shek. "You first take him to the village tomorrow morning: Ah Shun will accompany you. For the time being, at least, I think it will be better to keep the old arrangement. The boy can stay here with us for one night, and you can leave for Feng-hua tomorrow morning. Will that suit you?" Kai-shek went over to the chest of drawers and took out some bank notes. In handing the money to him, he said: "This is for your fares and expenses. I'll write to you as soon as I get to Canton. I'll also try to get you a job there."

Feng Chieh-wen pocketed the money and, without batting an eye, looked at me and exclaimed: "Canton has all the advantages of Shanghai. It is the most progressive city in China and is the place where all the famous revolutionaries come from. So, at last you're going to Canton! I can't believe it."

"Not until the end of this month. We plan to go to Soochow first," said Kai-shek.

"Soochow is interesting but not so fascinating as Canton," mused Feng Chgieh-wen. Again his roaming eyes looked at me with a vivacious smile.

"I will take Wei-kuo back to Miss Mao in Hsi-k'ou tomorrow. I only brought him here since the boy insisted on seeing his father and new mother!" Abruptly he changed the subject and said to me: "I am glad that Kai-shek has at last found his ideal in you. You deserve each other. Just look at him!" He pointed at Kai-shek and laughed: "He blooms with contentment and henceforth will not be sowing his wild oats as he did a year ago. Now he will learn how to settle down and not scatter his seeds all over Shanghai. But be sure to keep an eye on him! He's very tricky!"

"You talk too much nonsense!" exclaimed Kai-shek impatiently.

"How many times did I go with you on your nightly trips to the Sing-song Girl Houses? The magnets that drew you there were the sexy girls. I never once encouraged you. In fact, I attempted to dissuade you from going many times, but you insisted, remember?"

"Shut up!" shouted Kai-shek.

But the gusher continued: "You were certainly a suave and knowing lover. You had an uncontrollable urge for liquor and girls! Some of your affairs caused shocked gossip among your pals. Your changes of bedmates were so frequent that it was shocking. You certainly were promiscuous; you were not very particular in your choices. Ha, ha, ha!"

I was certainly stunned to hear this line of talk and did not wish to listen to any more. Taking little Wei-kuo by the hand, I said: "I am going into the hall to telephone. Come!" and I quickly left the room.

After lunch Feng Chieh-wen left to do some errands and promised to come back early the next morning to take Ah Shun and Wei-kuo by steamer to Feng-hua, via Ningpo.

According to custom, I gave a red envelope containing $20 to little Wei-kuo as a "first meeting" gift. The child was so pleased that, little by little, his shyness began to wear away. He looked fondly at me and started to ask innumerable questions. When I gave him some cookies and sweets, he smiled and said thank you without any prompting. Then he ran in and out of the room just like any normal, playful boy would do. The strangeness of the place delighted him.

When Kai-shek told him to do something, such as close the door, ring the bell, or pick up the newspaper from the floor, little Wei-kuo did it obediently and thought it was lots of fun. He was such a sweet child, very intelligent, and most curious. Seeing things on the table, he would ask what they were and what they were used for. He would not stop his inquiry until the object was explained to him.

I thought this was all to the good and tried to explain to him to the best of my ability all his questions, but Kai-shek jokingly said to me, "I can see you will soon spoil him!"

Then out of the clear blue sky, little Wei-kuo said to me, "Yao Ma Ma told me to watch you and Papa and tell her what you say and what you do everyday!"

I felt rather shocked at this innocent admission and told Kai-shek: "From the mouth of a child comes truth!"

Kai-shek burst out laughing and said, "That is Yao Ma Ma all over."

That night the three of us slept together. I put Wei-kuo in our old-fashioned brass bed near the wall, and I slept in the middle. While the child slept soundly, I asked Kai-shek who was this Feng Chieh-wen and why he tolerated such abuse.

"You are not the only one who dislikes him. In fact, he is hated by most of my friends for his wagging tongue," he told me. "But he is useful in many ways. He has many good contacts and can read and write English. Many a time he has acted as my interpreter in my contacts with foreign friends."

"Is he reliable?" I asked.

"Fairly so," said Kai-shek.

"But how can you entrust little Wei-kuo to him?" I asked.

"There's no need to worry about that. Ah Shun will go with them. Chieh-wen knows Hsi-k'ou very well. He's been there lots of times and knows most of my relatives. I know you were embarrassed today, but it will not happen again."

"Wei-kuo said that Yao Ma Ma wanted to know what we did and said. Will we go to visit her on our Soochow trip?"

"Certainly not! I would not want to embarrass you in her presence. As you know, I made a settlement with her before you and I were married."

I felt grateful to be spared that ordeal, and my mind wandered back to Feng Chieh-wen. I thought, how could Kai-shek tolerate such a scandalmonger as a friend, while he was so fanatically correct on other things? Will the child be safe with such an irresponsible man? Then Kai-shek began to tell me in a low, confidential tone the story of how Wei-kuo came into his life. He explained: "A few months ago when I was at our headquarters, 44 Rue Vallon, the doorbell rang, not only once, but several times. I opened the door, and lo and behold! Standing there was a Japanese lady holding a small boy by the hand. Our recognition was mutual, for she was an old friend that I had known in Tokyo. I invited her to come into the drawing room.

"'How are you, Ai-Ko San?' I asked. 'And when did you arrive in Shanghai? Please come in and I will call Tai Chi-t'ao to come down to see you. He is living upstairs on the second floor. Wait till he sees you! He will be so happily surprised!'

"The woman bowed low in Japanese fashion and said: 'This little boy is Tao Chi-t'ao's flesh and blood. Do you think he looks like his father?'

"She sat on the proffered seat, and feeling very excited, I dashed up the stairs, two and three steps at a time, shouting at the top of my voice: 'Chi-t'ao! Chi-t'ao! Guess who's here? Ai-Ko San is here looking for you. She has brought you your son! Ha, ha! A son is looking for his papa!' My shouts of joy resounded though the house.

"I was shocked to see Tai Chi-t'ao turn pale. The name Ai-Ko San upset him. Beckoning to me to go quietly into his room, he closed the door and said in an undertone: 'That page of my escapade in Japan is a closed book. I had my supreme moment and that's that. I don't want to be reminded of the past. I cannot resume my relationship with Ai-Ko San as I now have a wife and children of my own. I don't want to see her or the boy, so please invent an excuse to get rid of her for me as quickly as possible. Tell her I am not here—anything—only get rid of her. Tell her you don't know my address or where to find me.'

"You can imagine how awkward I felt. So I asked him: 'Are you sure you don't want your own child? He's quite a nice little boy!'

"Tai Chi-t'ao waved his hand impatiently and scowled: 'I have a family of my own: boys, girls, and wife! What do I want Ai-Ko's son for? That phase of my life is closed. Do you understand? Get rid of her! Get rid of her fast!'

"I descended the stairs crestfallen and tried to think of what excuse I could give Ai-Ko San. I knew her to be a good sort, for in the old days, she was always gentle, gracious, and kind. I tried not to hurt her feelings, so coming into the room, I said to her: 'Ai-Ko San! I am really very sorry. Chi-t'ao is not in, and I am not sure when he will come back. Would you like to leave a message for him?'

"I could see Ai-Ko San drop her jaw and she almost wept. She kept silent for a while and then murmured as if to herself: 'I made a mistake in coming to Shanghai. I trusted that man's sweet words and honeyed phrases and thought he truly loved me. That is why I suffered so many hardships to make this trip, to show him his little boy. I thought we could resume our old relationship where we had left off. He did promise me that when he left Japan. Now I know my dreams for a happy reunion were only a tragic delusion. I blame myself for being a deluded fool.' She broke down and wept.

"Then I said to her: 'Ai-Ko San. Please don't blame yourself. Things will turn out favorably if you will only have patience.'

"'Patience?' She gave me a mirthless laugh and then wept hysterically. 'Don't deceive yourself and deceive me, Chiang Kai-shek. If he refuses to see his own flesh and blood, it means that he doesn't want us anymore. But he shouldn't forget his revolutionary days in Japan. When he was poor, I gave him my gold bracelets and gold neck chain to help him, and this is all the thanks I get. It was entirely my fault for trusting a faithless man, and now I can weep over my folly.'

"She looked out of the window to hide her tears, and then made up her mind, saying: 'Tell him, Mr. Chiang, for me, that if he does not want his own flesh and blood, neither do I.' She kissed the lad perfunctorily and made a dash toward the door. She opened it and ran down the street.

"Naturally, I was taken aback by her sudden action and rushed out after her. 'Come back! Come back!' I shouted, but it was no use. She ran so fast that when she turned the corner on Avenue Joffre, I lost track of her. I stood on the street not knowing what to do, and I did not know where to look for her. So that's the story of this little boy. As he had no father and no mother, I adopted the child as my own and gave him the name Wei-kuo. I also arranged with Fu-mei and Yao Shih each to look after the lad for three months and that is why the boy is going to Hsi-k'ou tomorrow morning."

I looked at Kai-shek and said: "But the child is so thin and weak! You must tell Fu-mei to give him plenty of milk and eggs."

"Yes, that I will do. Now that you have two sons," said Kai-shek jokingly, "how do you feel?"

"Well, it does seem strange that a bride of one month can suddenly have two sons." I looked at this dear little orphan lying beside me and felt much pity. He was sleeping so peacefully. How anyone could callously discard such a cute little child was beyond my understanding.

8

Soochow

*T*he following morning, Feng Chieh-wen and Ah Shun took Wei-kuo to Hsi-k'ou. At the same time, Kai-shek and I left by train for Soochow, which was only about fifty-three miles west of Shanghai, on the Nanking-Shanghai Railway. It was a very interesting journey, passing small towns, cypress trees, green fields, and many, many grave mounds. Kai-shek told me that this trip was the second part of our honeymoon. He wanted me to see this famous old city with him.

We registered at the Railway Hotel, which was outside the city gate. And after taking lunch and a short rest, we went sightseeing by rickshaws.

The principal streets inside the walled city were too narrow for anything but donkeys and rickshaws, and I was surprised to see so many canals intersect the rich and beautiful city. Indeed, I thought the nickname "the Venice of the Far East" was most apt. Scholars of the past have also called Soochow "the Athens of China." The Chinese expressed their admiration for one of the oldest and most famous cities in the country in the familiar quotation "Above is Heaven; below is Soochow."

Kai-shek explained that the history of the city dates back more than 2,500 years. It was in 525 B.C. that the prince of the feudal Kingdom of Wu ordered this city to be built to serve as his capital. So the city was built with eight water gates, like heaven, and square like the earth. Inside there were two inner enclosures, the larger one enclosing the Forbidden City, for the palaces and yamens, and the smaller enclosure for the personal use of the prime minister and other important officials.

"Down through the centuries there were many restorations, notably in 1662, under the Manchu Emperor K'ang-hsi," explained Kai-shek. "A Manchu garrison was quartered here and the town refortified. The walls as they stand today have frequently been repaired but are much the same as in 1662."

To me, Soochow was a fascinating city. One could see tall pagodas left and right. There were five of them inside the city, and three crowned the nearby hills. The pagodas of Soochow were intimately connected with the city's history and were characteristic landmarks.

Our rickshaws drove us to see the most famous Great Pagoda, near the city wall. A prominent landmark, it could be seen all over Soochow. Kai-shek and I climbed its nine stories, 250 feet high, and I marveled at its beautiful proportions. Sixty feet in diameter at the base, it was 45 feet at the top, each story being proportionately shorter, each balcony narrower, each door and window smaller. The massive construction was 700 years old. As we climbed to the upper stories, we could see the surrounding countryside: beautiful hills and lakes, the latter connected by innumerable small canals. To the east, I could see the level plain, broken only by the many graves that surrounded the prosperous villages.

"There are five million people living within this radius," said Kai-shek as he pointed his finger to the stretches of land at our feet.

"Marvelous," I exclaimed. "I never imagined Soochow to be so beautiful and so interesting."

Our next trip was to visit the Tiger Hill Pagoda, often called China's "leaning tower." Kai-shek seemed very anxious to explain to me the history of this ancient edifice. He said it was first built in A.D. 601, burned down in 1428, and the present structure was restored about 1440. It was a majestic-looking pagoda, although it leaned slightly. I admired its beautiful lines, although it needed a coat of paint or, at least, a face wash.

Then, arm-in-arm, we sauntered nearer to the hillside to look at a spot called the "Pool of the Sword." Kai-shek exuberantly explained: "The actual purpose of our visit is to show you this pool. To me it has a special significance. Two thousand years ago, the Great Emperor Ch'in made this spot famous when he came here and stood at this very spot. He believed that the King of Wu's Sword of Victory was buried with him in his grave here. He therefore ordered his men to dig up this ground in the hope of finding it. The workmen dug deep and furiously but failed to find the treasured sword. Disappointed, they left. Now this pool of water fills that excavation, which was once believed to be the grave."

"But why was this sword so special, and why has this place a special significance to you?" I asked curiously.

"That is a good question!" answered Kai-shek. "In those days, Soochow, as you know, was called the Kingdom of Wu. And the tale goes that when the sword was being forged for the king, the metal would not fuse. The sword maker's wife watched her husband's failure, day after day. She knew that according to the traditions of his trade, when an important operation of this kind was in progress, a sacrifice to the fire god was necessary. To help her husband succeed, she secretly cut the arteries of her arm and drained her blood into the molten metal. She died, of course, but with the help of her selflessness, the casting was immediately perfected."

"Wasn't the wife foolish to sacrifice her life for merely a sword?" I asked.

"Oh, no," answered Kai-shek in shocked surprise. "Her great deed lives in the minds of all people down through the ages. Her sacrifice was not for the sword alone. The sword was merely symbolic. It was for a greater purpose. Her sacrifice was to help her husband achieve his ambition!"

"To die merely to perfect a sword!" I said glumly. "Self-slaughter is against the canons of filial piety." Then I quoted from the Confucian Classics: "Flesh, blood, and body are inherited from parents. Do not destroy them!"

"In a sense, that is true," agreed Kai-shek, "but often one's love is measured by the size of the sacrifice one is willing to undertake. We are revolutionaries, and we cannot adhere too strictly to Confucian dictums."

"You said this place has for you a great significance. What do you mean by that?" I asked.

"The Great Emperor Ch'in conquered the Warring States and unified China under the Great Ch'in Dynasty," he told me in a patient tone. "I admire the strength and spirit greatly, and my ardent wish is to one day emulate him. I hope to destroy the warlords and unify China under one government so that our country will become very powerful among the family of nations. That is precisely why I came here, to stand at the very spot where he once stood—and with you, the one I truly love. You may call it sentimental, but it is nevertheless my ambition."

"But the name of the Great Emperor Ch'in was expurgated from Chinese history for two thousand years!" I argued. "How can you admire such a cruel tyrant? Don't you remember he buried over 400 scholars alive?" I looked at him with vague eyes and a sarcastic smile. The words flowed from my mouth without thinking, and I marveled at myself for being so argumentative, for I had never wished to argue with him before. Why was this? I asked myself. Subconsciously, I knew the answer. Ever since Feng Chieh-wen had so brazenly exposed Kai-shek's past debaucheries, the shock had changed me. Kai-shek's sterling qualities had, in my mind, been tarnished by that revelation. And now, instead of agreeing with him, I found myself arguing, simply to even the score.

But Kai-shek could read my mind like a book. We walked on and on, and when we found a cozy spot in the shadow of the Tiger Pagoda, he made me sit down comfortably on a stone seat and said in all seriousness: "I never did have a chance to tell you why I went wild in Shanghai after Ch'en Ch'i-mei's death. After you hear my story, I'm sure you will forgive me. The shock of his death threw me off balance, and I did not care if I lived or died. For you to understand my story clearly, I must go back to the autumn of 1915, when I returned to Shanghai from Japan. At that time, Yuan Shih-k'ai was planning to destroy our republican form of government to make himself emperor of China. My old friend Ch'en Ch'i-mei and I discussed with other revolutionaries ways and means to show our protest by an uprising. On the strength of having the support of some sailors on the gunboat *Chao Ho*, Ch'en Ch'i-mei, after long discussion, drew up a plan to raid and take over the Shanghai Garrison Headquarters.

"Our first move was to eliminate the garrison commander so as to weaken the government. This we did on November 10, 1915. Our group used bombs and pistols in our attack on him. He was instantly killed. With this enemy leader gone, we immediately started a general uprising.

"We decided to take over the cruiser *Chao Ho*. The sailors secretly supplied us all the information we needed. Thirty of our men sailed in a boat to seize the cruiser by a surprise attack. Simultaneously, another subgroup, consisting of three hundred comrades, attacked the police headquarters. Two other small forces were dispatched to occupy the Bureau of Public Works, the Electric Plant, and the Telephone Office.

"Ch'en Ch'i-mei and I left our secret headquarters in the French Concession for the Chinese City when the guns on the *Chao Ho* were roaring with fury. We thought all was going according to plan. As we hurried southward, we saw that some of our men were quickly retreating. When we arrived at the gate of the Bureau of Public Works, we found we were the only survivors left, and, what was worse, the guns of the *Chao Ho* were by then silenced. In the distance, we saw many enemy soldiers springing up as from nowhere, and more and more men appeared. Luckily it was fairly dark, and they could not distinguish who we were. Our men had failed to capture the police headquarters, and our reinforcements had been intercepted and were now unable to supply any aid.

"It was now obvious that the *Chao Ho* could provide no help to us, and we soon learned that all our forces had been defeated. A small motorboat was anchored in the river outside the Bureau of Public Works. Ch'en Ch'i-mei and I jumped into it and made our escape.

"We had hardly got back to our secret quarters and gone upstairs when suddenly police and detectives of the French Concession broke into our building and started to arrest our men. Ch'en Kuo-fu, Ch'en Ch'i-mei's nephew, purposely screamed at the top of his voice, protesting his arrest. This warned us that police were in the house. Very softly Ch'en Ch'i-mei and I climbed over the next building and from there went into hiding in my private room on Avenue Joffre.

"The only good that came from our failure was that we had inspired the province of Yunnan to declare its independence of Yuan Shih-k'ai. Other provinces soon followed, such as Kweichow, Kwangsi, Kwangtung, Hunan, Kiangsu, Chekiang, Shantung, Anhwei, Szechwan, and Shensi. They all declared their independence, one by one. Most of the heads of these provinces were formerly Yuan Shih-k'ai's supporters, and their betrayal disheartened Yuan. Telegrams arrived at his Imperial Palace denouncing him for his ambition. As a consequence, on March 22, 1916, only eighty-one days after he had ascended the imperial throne, he decided to reassume the presidency. But it was too late. He had lost his popularity with the people.

"Although we were financially straitened, our fighting spirit never wavered. Through adversity, our resistance to tyranny became stronger than ever. All means were tried to recuperate our losses. The days, however, seemed dark and bleak at this period.

"The failure of our revolutionaries was due not so much to a lack of manpower as to a lack of money—despite the fact that small remittances came in continuously from Overseas Chinese patriots. But expenses were large. Most revolutionaries were unemployed; they had to be fed and given other assistance. This alone consumed almost all the remittances received. Most revolutionaries were living from hand to mouth.

"Yuan Shih-k'ai, learning of our financial difficulties, secretly sent an emissary named Li Hai-cho to contact Ch'en Ch'i-mei in Shanghai. Li Hai-cho suggested to him a plan to raise a substantial sum of money from a Japanese financier, using a certain mine belonging to a friend as collateral. This seemed a good proposition, and Ch'en Ch'i-mei turned the matter over in his mind for several days. Suspecting treachery, I warned Ch'en Ch'i-mei to decline the offer. 'What have we to lose?' he asked me. 'Li Hai-cho is one of us; is he not a Kuomintang member!' This indeed was true, and I became speechless.

"As Ch'en Ch'i-mei's sole aim was to obtain funds to enable us to carry on the resistance, he made an appointment through Li Hai-Cho to meet this Japanese financier. The date was May 18, 1916, at an office of a mining company, purportedly to discuss the loan and close the deal. It was decided that an agreement would be signed by Ch'en Ch'i-mei before the money would be handed over. Thinking only of this marvelous offer, Ch'en Ch'i-mei threw caution to the wind.

"On the day of the appointment, Li Hai-cho appeared in the mining office with four men. One tall man was introduced to Ch'en Ch'i-mei as manager of the mining company and a friend of the Japanese financier. In fact, he was an assassin in the pay of Yuan Shih-k'ai.

"After introducing the men to Ch'en Ch'i-mei, Li Hai-cho made an excuse and said he would get the contract for signatures. As he made his exit, the tall man took out a revolver and, then and there, fatally shot Ch'en Ch'i-mei in cold blood.

"When Ch'en Ch'i-mei died, I felt that the world was lost to me. The blow altered my outlook on life and drove me to a life of debauchery. Feng Chieh-wen had become my good friend, and that is why he speaks so openly about my exploits. But I can assure you that since the day that I met you at the House of Chang, I have loved only you and no one

else. You were my lifesaver, my hope of psychological rehabilitation."
He looked at me tenderly and asked, "Do you believe me?"

In my heart I felt a great pity for him, and to make amends I said sympathetically, "Yes, I believe you."

"Thank you, my dear, dear wife, I was so afraid you would misunderstand and think ill of me."

"No, I do not misunderstand," I said in an effort to pass the matter off lightly. "You and Ch'i-mei consecrated your lives to rebuilding China, and when one arm was lost, the other was thrown out of balance. I can quite understand that. But the past is past, so don't blame yourself. In fact, I admire you more for giving up that wild part of your life."

"You do not hold it against me then?" he asked anxiously.

"Not at all. I was only a little shocked at first. Now that you have explained the situation, let us forget it."

"Do you love me?"

"Very much."

"How much?"

"As heavy as the mountain and as deep as the sea," I answered truthfully. Then I added: "I have learned so much since we have been married. Here in Soochow alone, I have learned many, many things. You are wonderful to me, and I do love you so."

Our next spot to visit was the magnificent Precious Girdle Bridge. it consists of fifty-three arches and is built entirely of granite. This and many other bridges in Soochow are well worth seeing and are famous throughout China.

Then we went on to see the famous garden called the Liu Yuan. This garden was formerly owned by a high Manchu official. The property was seized by the republican government and was open to the public. One may wander at leisure through the many walks and rock gardens. The Liu Yuan is one of the finest examples of Chinese gardening and reminded me of the willow-pattern plate. One may tramp through many shaded spots, rich in historic lore.

Soochow is also widely known as the home of the most famous women. Soochow women are noted for their beauty and the pleasing softness of their dialect. As a result, fashionable women from other parts of China imitate the Soochow accent. Although Soochow is not as large as Shanghai, it has retained its reputation as a center for the production of high-grade silks and beautiful brocades.

Because Soochow is noted for its silks and satins, Kai-shek and I made a tour of the silk filatures. In former days, most of the factories we visited had provided supplies for the empress dowager, the emperor, and the imperial household. I was surprised to see these humble surroundings; little huts with earthen floors, where glorious silks were produced with their exquisite designs and perfect workmanship. Of course, Kai-shek insisted on buying me three pieces of silk and one of satin for dresses.

Our next trip was to the western part of Soochow, where Kai-shek wanted to visit the great lake known as T'ai Hu. I was enthralled to see this most famous body of water, which had been the scene of outings by residents of Soochow for the past two thousand years. Kai-shek engaged a houseboat, and we spent three hours on the lake. We drank in the beauty of the skyline of Soochow with its many temples, pavilions, nunneries, monasteries, and pagodas.

Kai-shek said: "What is called China Proper was, roughly, the provinces north of the Yangtze River and east of the Han. All outside of that radius," he made a sweep with his arm in a wide survey of this famous place, "was barbarian land." Then he added: "Did you know that the natives of Wu allowed their hair to grow long and tattooed their bodies? That was only two thousand years ago, but they attained a fairly high degree of civilization. They were a maritime people, for the country was even more marshy and intersected with canals than it is today. They spun silk, too, and knew something of art. On the whole, however, they were a warlike tribe and resisted our Chinese encroachment most fiercely. It was the Great Emperor Ch'in who conquered them."

I thought to myself: The Chinese were not always a peaceful people, and every student knows that no nation has had a more blood-stained history than China. And no nation has records of more heroic deeds by her valiant people. But when will China be unified and become a strong nation? I looked at the ancient pines and weeping-willow trees framing the Soochow shores. No wonder its beauty was praised by famous Chinese poets so many centuries ago. Such scenic beauty desperately needs peace. I prayed that the day would come when the warlords would all be ousted and our country unified under one government. That was my devout wish.

When we got back from Soochow, I found a rash had broken out over my body. I tried one kind of skin ointment after another on the affected parts, but instead of healing, the rash became worse. Then I discovered I had a rash on both my legs. Then two blotches like ringworms appeared on my wrists above my pulse. These did not itch, but they looked so bad that it worried me. All my life I had never suffered this kind of ailment.

Kai-shek took me to see his friend, Dr. Li T'ien, who had his office on the corner of Szechwan Road and Peking Road. Dr. Li was a graduate of the Heidelberg Koch's Institute in Berlin and the Tropen Institute of Hamburg, specializing in bacteriology and venereal diseases. Dr. Li took blood samples from both Kai-shek and me for tests. After three nerve-racking days, the serologist announced that our blood was positive.

As soon as I heard this bad news, I was frantic. I jumped up from my seat, dashed out of the office, and rushed down the steps until I got to Jinkee Road, where I engaged a taxi to take me to my mother's home.

"Oh, Mother," I wailed. "I have a venereal disease. The doctor told me so. Look at my skin!"

Within half an hour, Kai-shek arrived and explained that the disease was a mild one. Treatment with 606 would give a complete cure. It was his old complaint—and he had infected me.

Mother scolded Kai-shek in no uncertain terms, and after half an hour of tongue lashing, he acknowledged his "sin."

"I will not go back to you anymore," I shouted. "You are an evil man. I will divorce you!"

"What can I do to make you believe that I am truly penitent?" he asked pleadingly. He stood there with bowed head and was so solemn and grave.

"You must immediately go with him to the doctor's for the necessary treatment. The most urgent question now is to have the disease stamped out of your bloodstream."

Late that afternoon, Kai-shek took me again to Dr. Li's for treatment. Before the injection, Dr. Li said to Kai-shek: "This is not a pleasant subject to discuss, so let me talk to your wife alone. Will you please wait in the waiting room?" When Kai-shek left, Dr. Li administered the 606 injection intravenously in my arm and said to me: "You will be cured after ten shots, that is, if you will patiently continue the treatment. I will now be very candid and tell you that the gonorrheal germ, after entering your body or, to be exact, your tubes and ovaries, may sterilize you.

Your case however, is mild, so there is no need for you to worry about it, if you will keep up the treatment.''

Having finished, I went into the waiting room while Kai-shek took his turn to enter the doctor's office. After he had his injection, Dr. Li told him: ''You should have completed your last treatment before your marriage. By not allowing yourself sufficient time to get perfectly well, you have infected your wife. From now on, you should continue the treatment in order to be completely cured. You have had epididymitis, which has left you sterile. Henceforth, it is unlikely that you will be able to produce any more children.''

To show his remorse, Kai-shek said to me, ''In repentance I swear to you I shall never again touch a drop of wine.''

I sat there glum and miserable, not uttering a word. ''I swear to that,'' he repeated. ''The day I again drink wine, or even tea or coffee, you will know that I have broken my oath. I will drink only plain boiled water and nothing else all my life. This is a self-imposed penalty. Please believe me.''

I was too miserable to argue. What could I do? What could any young wife do under these circumstances, except to forgive? So, I forgave Kai-shek. And true to his promise, he gave up liquor and all kinds of liquids except boiled water.

9

Canton and the General

On December 1, 1921, Kai-shek and I left Shanghai on the SS *President Taft* for Hong Kong, en route to Canton. Although only two-and-a-half days' journey, our whole trip was most pleasant and interesting. It was my first experience on board a large foreign ship, and everything impressed me as being very luxurious and modern. Kai-shek felt just as delighted and even agog with excitement, for he loved the great expanse of the ocean. But he was particularly excited because he would soon see the hero he worshiped, Dr. Sun Yat-sen. We spent much time strolling on deck. When tired, we sat on deck chairs and chatted.

From our long talks, I learned more and more about Kai-shek and his early days. He indeed worshiped his leader, and from this connection he drew strength.

"I am very ambitious," he confided. "I want to be something more than an ordinary leader so that you can be proud of me. With Dr. Sun's influence and connections, my path is plain sailing." Then he told me that one of his sad experiences had been with General Ch'en Chiung-ming three years before. It was on March 3, 1918, when Kai-shek had left Shanghai for Canton at Dr. Sun's request to join a newly formed army, headed by the Kwangsi clique. When he arrived at the southern city, he found conditions to be precarious for his leader because the Peking government, which was the legal government, regarded Dr. Sun as a rebel. It planned, therefore, to send an expeditionary force to subdue him. Besides, the warlord Luk of Canton had become hostile. Realizing that Canton had become untenable, Dr. Sun left to seek help from General Ch'en Chiung-ming, who was stationed at Changchow in Fukien. General Ch'en Chiung-ming was the head of an army and very sympathetic to the revolutionary cause. Subsequently, Dr. Sun introduced Kai-shek [to him] to help work out a plan to take over Canton and use it as a revolutionary base.

Everything would have passed off pleasantly had it not been for one hitch. General Ch'en Chiung-ming's idea was to have in his army only Cantonese, consistent with his slogan, Canton for the Cantonese. He thought the slogan would rally the Cantonese public spirit to oust warlord Luk, who bestrode Canton like a colossus. This warlord was a non-Cantonese, so the slogan was significant. He was a hated Kwangsi man.

Since Dr. Sun had recommended Kai-shek, it was difficult for General Ch'en Chiung-ming to refuse him a job, for that would be considered an affront to the leader. For the time being, Kai-shek was given a position as head of the Field Operations Department. Kai-shek received this appointment on March 15, 1918, despite the fact that he was not a Cantonese.

But things did not go smoothly. Kai-shek continued by telling me of his sad experiences under General Ch'en: "At the time I was appointed head of the Field Operations Department, I made extensive tours and drafted operational plans for the expedition. The first stage of operations started with our main force advancing from the left to harass the enemy and also to threaten his rear supply base. This plan failed. I drafted a revised plan of operations, hoping to concentrate our strength on the right flank for an attack.

"It happened that the town of Tai Pu was lost at this time. The enemy was approaching, and our headquarters was preparing to withdraw. Ch'en Chiung-ming found his hands tied, not knowing what to do. I advised him not to retreat and again altered the plan of operations. The main forces on the right flank were immediately shifted to the center to launch a counterattack on Tai Pu. For three days and nights I did not sleep and went to the front to give directives. Luckily the battle brought us a decisive victory. But instead of receiving praise, I was blamed for blundering. That is why I returned to Shanghai. When I reflect on General Ch'en's ingratitude, I feel a pain in my heart."

Hearing this, I realized there existed an undercurrent of conflict between the two domineering personalities. This conflict, though subdued and kept under control, was nevertheless there. Unless it was cleared up, it would lead to ill-feeling and perhaps trouble. It was obvious we had a difficult situation to face when we got to Canton. So I said: "Don't feel too badly about it. The past is past. One day Ch'en Chiung-ming will come to realize your good work and feel grateful to you."

"That will never happen," answered Kai-shek. "He dislikes me intensely, but the dislike is mutual."

The most memorable thing that happened on the ship was in the dining room. For the first time, I acted as Kai-shek's interpreter. He only knew a smattering of English, so I had to read the menu to him and order the dishes that he wanted.

After each meal, he would collect the menu, and when we sat on deck he would patiently have me, item by item, course by course, explain the pronunciation to him. Then he would try to memorize all the different words by writing them down on a sheet of paper. In this way, he could learn in two days the meanings of many words.

Before we left Shanghai, Kai-shek left most things for me to attend to. Our two male servants, Ah Shun and Sui-Chang, traveled by steerage, so they were not allowed to come to our first-class cabin without special permission. Kai-shek had no head for practical things and lacked good sense in money matters. So I had to take charge of his suitcases and money, look after his collection of maps, diaries, books, and various papers, not to mention his wardrobe. Papers alone filled two suitcases. It was a new experience for me and I enjoyed it. I realized that one of the secrets of being happy was to enjoy whatever one was doing, especially for a husband who loved his wife so ardently.

I also had my own books and wardrobe. I had bought quite a number of books so that I could study up on all phases of the revolution and the party in order not to feel that I was being "drowned" when questions on these subjects were discussed. Many times, I must confess, I had felt quite out of my depth when Kai-shek spoke of the Kuomintang and its members. Later I was glad that I had made this effort because I could then follow Kai-shek's conversations on that subject.

Upon our arrival in Hong Kong, we did not stop to visit friends because Kai-shek was anxious to get to our destination. We took the Hong Kong–Canton train and four hours later were met on arrival by politician Liao Chung-k'ai, who whisked us off to the Asia Hotel on the Canton Bund. Immediately he and Kai-shek went into conference. I looked at this middle-aged, thin, diminutive man, who seemed to be very alert and active. Kai-shek had already told me about him and his wife, who had worked with Dr. Sun from the earliest days of the revolution. When I saw him now, he seemed an old friend, I knew that he ranked third in importance among Dr. Sun's followers. Ranking first was Wang Ching-wei, and the number two was Hu Han-min.

Chung-k'ai was dapper to the point of being a dandy. He said to Kai-shek: "After General Ch'en Chiung-ming successfully captured Canton and ousted warlord Luk, he invited Dr. Sun to come here to run the government. But Dr. Sun's mind was solely on organizing a Northern Expedition against the various warlords and to unite China under one government. General Ch'en disagreed with this plan, saying that such an expedition would cost a lost of money, which he did not have. He urged, 'Why not allow me to consolidate my gains first, and then we can speak about the expedition.'

"But Dr. Sun contended that there was no time like the present because the warlords in the North were experiencing hardship and dissension. If the campaign were started immediately, half the battle would be won. They couldn't agree. Dr. Sun was adamant and finally said to General Ch'en: 'I have decided to go to Wuchow to organize the expedition. Later we will go to Kweilin, where we will begin our march. You, as commander in chief of the Cantonese Army and governor of Kwangtung and Kwangsi, will collect the taxes and allocate a part of the proceeds to me for supplies and ammunition for my soldiers. I have appointed General Teng Heng to be liaison officer for ammunition and Liao Chung-k'ai as liaison officer for finance and supplies.'"

Having briefed Kai-shek, Liao said: "I am glad you have buried the hatchet and have come to help our leader. He will be delighted to see you again. You will leave for Wuchow tomorrow morning. I have already made all the arrangements. But before you leave. I think you had better pay your respects to General Ch'en, the commander in chief."

"To tell you the truth," said Kai-shek, "I would rather not. But under the circumstances, I'll think the matter over."

When Liao Chung-k'ai left, Kai-shek turned to me and asked my opinion whether he should make the call or not. I said: "I don't want to hurt anyone, least of all you, but I do think all old grudges should be forgotten. Why don't you be magnanimous and show that you have forgiven him? After all, he is the commander in chief."

The expression on Kai-shek's face changed, and he was silent for a time. I could see he was pondering what I had said. I felt rather nervous that I may have offended him, but he said at last: "What you said is right. I'll show him that I am not narrow-minded and will call on him now."

I felt relieved to think that I had done a good deed for that day.

At noon, Kai-shek wore a long cotton gown and went by taxi to call on General Ch'en at his headquarters. At the entrance the sentinel refused him admittance. Then Kai-shek submitted his name card and the sentinel went inside to show it to the corporal. The corporal looked at it contemptuously and went into the office to telephone. Kai-shek was kept waiting at the front gate, and he began to regret that he had come. But there was no turning back without losing face. So he called upon all his patience and waited and waited.

After twenty minutes, the corporal came out with a patronizing smile and ushered Kai-shek into the commander in chief's private chamber. When they met, they chatted like old friends, but the slight, which was intentional, burned deeply in Kai-shek's heart.

General Ch'en Chiung-ming told Kai-shek: "I strongly advised our leader to postpone the Northern Expedition until I had consolidated my position here. But our leader is most obstinate. He said he had decided and would not change his mind. Then I told him: 'You have too many wild ideas, and your plans are impractical. You suggest too many things and achieve little.' But he merely answered: 'If I spend days and nights thinking out plans, it is solely for the purpose of completing our revolution. If we don't take this opportunity now to launch our expedition, when will we start? Wait, wait, wait, you say. But this continuous waiting is driving me crazy!'

"'Indeed, you are crazy,' I said to our leader in exasperation. 'I told you that we have not consolidated our gains in Kwangtung and Kwangsi, and conditions are not yet normal. We have not yet regained our equilibrium. The people are nervous. Taxes take time to collect because the people have been drained white by warlord Luk. There is turmoil on the east and on the west. The soldiers are war weary. How can you ignore these conditions and speak lightly about launching an expedition? What makes you think that you can win victory so easily?'

"But our leader merely said to me: 'You don't have to underestimate your own ability and overestimate the enemy's strength. I have decided on the Northern Expedition and will not change my mind.' He paused for a few moments and added: 'When I lead this expedition and am successful, I will then go north to Peking. Even if I fail, I will not return to

Canton, so I shall entrust Kwangtung and Kwangsi to your care. My only request now is that you approve my appointment of General Teng Heng to be liaison officer for arms and ammunition, and Liao Chung-k'ai for finances and supplies. Please, do not stop me from carrying out this long cherished plan.'

"Seeing no way out, I agreed. On October 15, 1921, therefore, our leader sailed west for Wuchow on the Cantonese gunboat *Pao Pi*, where he is now. In his retinue were twenty persons, including Hu Han-min. And now," said Ch'en Chiung-ming, looking at Kai-shek, "our leader is in Wuchow waiting for your arrival. He has appointed you his military adviser and strategist."

After this explanation, General Ch'en Chiung-ming became very friendly and insisted that Kai-shek remain for lunch in his Officers' Mess. The lunch was served at a long table around which sat a dozen Cantonese officers of the highest rank. One of them was General Ip Chu, General Ch'en Chiung-ming's right-hand man. After introductions were made, there was bantering going on throughout the meal. Suddenly Kai-shek heard General Ip refer to Dr. Sun as "Sun, the Great Cannon." This was Dr. Sun's well-known nickname. It meant "Sun, the big talker."

Kai-shek took exception to this. He rose abruptly from the table and asked General Ch'en Chiung-ming to accompany him into the conference room. "How can you allow your officer to insult our leader by calling him Sun, the Great Cannon? I noticed you didn't say a word to correct him!"

"Where is your sense of humor?" asked Ch'en Chiung-ming in exasperation. "There is no insult intended. I think you are too touchy. It's bad for your nerves! Forget it!"

"But it is a downright insult!" insisted Kai-shek.

"Every Chinese has a nickname, no matter what his name may be. It is a common custom and not meant as an insult at all!"

Kai-shek was furious and, without another word, turned on his heels and left.

❧ 10

Quarrels with Dr. Sun

On December 10, 1921, Liao Chung-k'ai, Kai-shek, and I arrived in Wuchow, where we found Dr. Sun more optimistic than ever in his Generalissimo Headquarters. He and Mme Sun welcomed us and made us feel at home. In fact, as we arrived, Dr. Sun was in the midst of drafting a telegram to General Ch'en Chiung-ming requesting him to come to Wuchow for an urgent meeting and inquiring when supplies and ammunition would be forthcoming. The following day his reply came "Cannot leave because of several important meetings stop shall come as soon as I possibly can." This telegram gave Dr. Sun a feeling of new encouragement, and he waited patiently in keen anticipation.

Kai-shek was appointed Dr. Sun's military adviser and strategist. He was kept busy with meetings every morning for many hours. Each afternoon was devoted to an outing, and Dr. Sun would invite us all to join him in climbing the famous Wuchow Mountains. One section of these hills was unique and well worth seeing. The hills were shaped like bamboo shoots, or ice cream cones turned upside down. We made no attempt to climb them. From afar, however, we could see that this part of the hills seemed barren, where boulders were strewn everywhere. The tricky light seemed to give these strange-shaped hills the appearance of emerald green. I could see why the natives called these hills Jasper Hairpins. Kai-shek said to me: "Look at Dr. Sun. See what a good walker he is. He is an expert on topography. Everywhere he goes, he makes it a habit to climb mountains to get a bird's-eye view of the place to see if there is a possibility of building a railway there."

I looked and saw what Kai-shek had said was indeed true. Dr. Sun walked with strong steady strides and appeared as cool as a cucumber. Hu Han-min, on the other hand, straggled behind, breathless from the effort. It was obvious that he had never done much walking in his studious life. But he was, indeed, a scholar par excellence and served as Dr. Sun's secretary.

As the days passed, Dr. Sun sent Ch'en Chiung-ming another telegram. And again there was no reply. Dr. Sun had not, however, lost hope. He handed a batch of files to Kai-shek and said: "These will keep you up-to-date. As you know, after you left for Shanghai, Chiung-ming fought his way back from Changchow and successfully captured Canton. He was very brave and deserves the title commander in chief of the Cantonese Army—and, indeed, all the honors I can bestow upon him." He pointed to the files and added: "There are the records. You will see that Hsu Ch'ung-chih is vice commander, and there are ten other mixed-army groups that have joined us. Each day we can recruit more and more disbanded soldiers who have no leaders. These may be trained and later incorporated into our Cantonese Army. We must have an army that is so strong that the northern warlords will have to take notice."

Kai-shek wanted to say, General Ch'en Chiung-ming is not to be trusted. He has only contempt for you as a leader! But seeing Dr. Sun's enthusiasm, he kept silent.

"The Treasury Department of Canton is run by Chiung-ming and his men," continued Dr. Sun. "The expenses and supplies, etc., for our Northern Expedition, therefore, must all come from him. It may be slow in coming, but I feel sure it will arrive in good time." In the week that followed, Dr. Sun sent General Ch'en Chiung-ming a third, fourth, and a fifth telegram. When no reply came, he decided to proceed to Kweilin to get matters started there. So far, he had at his command two regiments, consisting of 2,400 men, under Captain Ho and Captain Hsu Ching. These were to act as vanguards.

Leaving Wuchow for Kweilin was a new experience for me. Our expedition consisted of almost 100 steam launches and wooden junks of all kinds and sizes. It was thrilling to see them all assembled on the Wuchow River. When we began our journey, the long string of junks carrying our two regiments of soldiers led the way; then came the junk carrying Dr. and Mme Sun, Hu Han-min, and staff secretaries and others. Kai-shek and I, with other staff members, followed in another junk. I did not actually count them all but was told there were 100 junks in our train.

On our way, we passed many sandy beaches, and we sailed upriver against the tide. Naturally our progress was very slow.

What seemed new and exciting to me was that each of our junks had a password, [for use] especially at night. This was for the purpose of protecting ourselves from marauders or spies of the enemy.

Each junk had its own servants and cook to provide meals for us. On the whole we fared very comfortably. Our first town of call was Chu-Ping, where the magistrate of the place welcomed Dr. Sun on our arrival. The soldiers formed an honor guard, and Dr. and Mme Sun marched off to review the troops. Hu Han-min, Kai-shek, and I waited until the reviewing was over; then we joined our leader, followed by officers and other members of the staff. We were conducted on a tour of the countryside and were glad to have this exercise after being cooped up in the junk. We saw the small town and waterfront and then climbed a low hill. On the roadside, Kai-shek and I each bought a pair of cloth shoes for easy walking. And we cut branches from trees to serve as staffs. After an hour of climbing, Dr. and Mme Sun rested on boulders while tins and biscuits and other refreshments were handed around to us by the servants.

Two hours later, our junks weighed anchor to continue on our journey to Kweilin. The currents of the river from here onward became very swift, and our progress was slow, only about ten miles a day. The water was shallow but very clear. I could see the riverbed laid with oval-shaped pebbles of all sizes, which showed that the current was very strong.

For a few miles we passed more beaches and rode against the tide. The boatmen got off the junks to act as trackers to haul us upstream against the swift current. Long ropes, made of woven bamboo splints, were used. Some ropes were tied to the junk's mast and bow while the other ends were tied into loops that went over the shoulders of the trackers. Ten trackers pulled our junk. They sang ditties as they pulled.

I was intrigued by the spectacle and watched the men pulling with all their strength. Kai-shek said to me, "The Russians have trackers too, but they are called Volga Boatmen."

Just then, Dr. Sun's junk stopped. As we came nearer, we saw him and Mme Sun debark to walk along the shore. "Come and join us," shouted Dr. Sun. "Walking is faster than the junk, so we have time for a snapshot of that wall yonder." Kai-shek and I obeyed, and we, too, got off to join them. It was lots of fun walking. As we came to the outer edges of the town wall, I saw Dr. Sun snapping pictures with his camera. Fortunately I had with me my camera, too, and going up to Dr. Sun, I asked, "May I snap your picture, Dr. Sun?"

"Please do," he answered smilingly. "But do not be upset if I break your camera!" He posed especially for me, holding his camera. When I had finished, he took several pictures of Kai-shek and me standing together. Returning to the junk, we continued the journey, which took almost another twenty days to complete.

Each day Dr. Sun would ask Kai-shek to go over to his junk to spend a few hours discussing the plans for the Northern Expedition. Soon the conversation would turn to the question of the supplies promised by General Ch'en Chiung-ming. Since nothing so far had arrived, Kai-shek was irked to hear his leader incessantly praising Ch'en Chiung-ming. After one of these meetings, Kai-shek came back in a huff and told me: "I know that Ch'en Chiung-ming is treacherous and will one day betray our leader. But Dr. Sun refuses to listen to my warnings. What can I do to convince him?"

"Have you any proof?" I asked.

"There's no need of any proof," he answered abruptly. "I can feel it in my bones. A man who has no respect for his leader or his party can have no loyalty in his heart."

"If you feel so sure about it, why not write a letter to Dr. Sun stating your grounds for suspicion?" I advised. "That will perhaps be more effective than mere talk."

"You are right," he said thoughtfully. Then, taking up a sheet of paper, he wrote: "In writing this letter, my heart sinks heavily. I can hardly bear to write it, yet I cannot keep silent. I have repeatedly warned you about Ch'en Chiung-ming's treacherous nature, but you always laugh it off. I beg you to believe me, because that man is not capable of loyalty." The following day when they met, Dr. Sun said to Kai-shek: "I received your letter. Tell me what is on your mind? What do you want me to do?"

"The wisest thing to do is to curb Ch'en Chiung-ming's power by dismissing him from his post as commander in chief. Issue an order so that I can strike at him quickly, remove him from office, and take over command of his army. I can then turn back to wipe out his forces in

Kwangsi, which are now under the subcommand of Ip Chu. With this accomplished, we can carry out the Northern Expedition without hindrance," advised Kai-shek.

"But Ch'en Chiung-ming has not yet openly opposed me, so please don't create trouble," exclaimed Dr. Sun. "I have faith in him. Besides, the troops in Kwangsi are my brothers-in-arms, with whom I have fought side by side for many years. What you suggest is unthinkable! Now, listen to me," Dr. Sun patiently told Kai-shek, "to achieve peace and harmony, it is essential first to foster a spirit of trust and tolerance, and to be willing to listen to the other person's point of view: to discuss all problems in open forum instead of harboring unfounded suspicions and passing them off as established facts. You would serve me better if you would only cooperate wholeheartedly. Instead, you try to force me to fight a brother officer who has proven his loyalty these many years!"

"But I can see that Ch'en Chiung-ming will turn against you one of these days," said Kai-shek, not a little flustered.

"This kind of talk will do us more harm than good," said Dr. Sun. "It is true that Ch'en Chiung-ming's army could strike the first blow upon the slightest provocation, but I will not provoke him. You must realize that your irresponsible suggestion could easily set Canton aflame. There must be no room for doubt, suspicion, or hatred. I do not wish to listen to your repeated line of talk against Chiung-ming, and I implore you to adopt a spirit of understanding and cooperation. You are a good military strategist and should concentrate your mind on the strategy of harmony."

Seeing that Dr. Sun was adamant, and that there was no way to make him change his mind, Kai-shek turned, broke down, and wept bitterly.

The following day, Kai-shek was glum and irritable. He said to me: "Get ready, for we are going back to Shanghai as soon as we get to Kweilin. We will take the first available boat back because I want to get out of here as soon as possible."

I was naturally surprised at this sudden decision and instinctively knew that he had had a tiff with Dr. Sun. He then told me what Dr. Sun had said to him.

＊　＊　＊

Back in Shanghai, Kai-shek kept in constant correspondence with the scholarly Hu Han-min, who informed us of all the new developments. He reported that Ch'en Chiung-ming had broken his promise and refused to send supplies and funds to Dr. Sun. Although two liaison officers went back and forth between Dr. Sun and General Ch'en, no new supplies materialized. Thus the two men found their hands tied.

Under pressure from Dr. Sun, one of the liaison officers, General Teng Heng, made one last effort and spoke to his commander, Ch'en Chiung-ming: "I am your maternal cousin, so I dare to speak to you plainly. You promised to our president that you would fully support the Northern Expedition with arms and ammunition. But now you renege, putting him off, week after week. Why do you do this? Do you wish to sabotage the expedition?"

"You needn't bother yourself with this matter. Just relax," answered Ch'en Chiung-ming bluntly.

"But I am your liaison officer, appointed by you! How can I not bother? I think your attitude is very wrong. If you are against Dr. Sun, be man enough to say so! Do you realize you are making fools of us all?"

"Since you force my hand, I will tell you my reasons for withholding supplies," said Ch'en Chiung-ming agrily. "The president is not qualified to organize the Northern Expedition, and I have made up my mind not to supply him with any ammunition, funds, or supplies!"

"But why?" asked Teng Heng.

"He listens to the instigations of that Chekiang rogue, Chiang, who wants me dismissed from office."

"Impossible! I don't believe it," exclaimed Teng Heng.

"Read this report! Here are the very words he wrote to the president!" Teng Heng took the paper and read as follows:

> In the present situation in Canton, you, our leader, can only hope that Ch'en Chiung-ming will act within the limits of his authority. His growing power must be curbed; he might even be dismissed from office. If you hope for him to take your orders in a crisis, or to defend the party against its enemies, you will find he is not the man. He is not trustworthy. I venture to reveal to you my innermost thoughts and beg you to believe them.
>
> *Chiang Kai-shek*

"So, this is another report of Chiang Kai-shek's plotting! Do you think I will give guns and ammunition to be used against me?" asked Ch'en Chiung-ming.

Teng Heng was speechless. Seeing this rupture and sensing the hopelessness of the situation, he acted independently. In order not to disappoint Dr. Sun's hopes of obtaining weapons, Teng negotiated with several friends, including the politician C. C. Wu [Wu Ch'ao-shu] (son of Wu T'ing-fang). He then went to Hong Kong to sign a contract for a large quantity of arms and ammunition with the importing firm of Simpson and Company. Teng's secret mission leaked out when he wired the Canton Custom House asking for permission to bring the shipment there.

General Ch'en Chiung-ming regarded this as a plot against his life. In retaliation he ordered his men to ascertain when General Teng would return to Canton and to assassinate him at the entrance to the railway station. The assassination was carried out on March 21, 1922. When news of the assassination reached Dr. Sun, he broke down and wept, for Teng had been an upright man of whom he was very fond.

The Chinese have a saying, Prosperity seldom comes twice—adversity never travels singly. This saying now fit Dr. Sun's situation precisely. For soon after Teng's assassination, the Hunan warlord, Chao Heng-t'i, turned against him. Chao had had a secret understanding of cooperation with Dr. Sun, agreeing that he would allow Dr. Sun's Northern Expeditionary forces to pass through Hunan province. But now word arrived that Chao had changed his mind. This refusal was a serious blow to Dr. Sun's plans, and he had to hurriedly map out another route. After much discussion, he decided that the original western route would have to be changed to a central route, through Kiangsi. This being the case, it was no longer necessary for him to remain in Kweilin, and he therefore instructed his staff to get ready to return to Canton. The two regiments under Captain Ho and Captain Hsu Ching were also ordered to return to Canton to await orders.

And here is where a great misunderstanding took place. Unaware of the cancelation of arrangements by the Hunan warlord, Ch'en Chiung-ming mistook Dr. Sun's return as part of a plan to retaliate against him. He foresaw a showdown in which Sun would try to remove him from power. To quash the rumors and to show he was not grabbing power as alleged, Ch'en Chiung-ming sent Dr. Sun a letter of resignation as commander in chief of the Cantonese Army.

Dr. Sun's return from Kweilin to Wuchow took only four-and-a-half days because of favorable tides. From Wuchow to Canton took another day. On arrival, Dr. Sun found that Ch'en Chiung-ming had left Canton for his native stronghold at Kaichow. And instead of a cordial welcome, he received Ch'en's letter of resignation.

Dr. Sun knew the resignation was only a face-saving maneuver. But Dr. Sun was annoyed with Ch'en for his duplicity in withholding supplies, ammunition, and funds. He therefore quickly accepted the resignation and made no effort to retain Ch'en. He then appointed the venerable Dr. Wu T'ing-fang to be governor of Canton. This was lauded as an excellent choice because Dr. Wu had twice been China's ambassador to Washington and was a seasoned statesman.

It was just at this time that Kai-shek sent the following letter to Ch'en Chiung-ming:

In cutting off a friendship, a gentleman will not use bad language. This is my last appeal to you, and I hope you will not regard it as harsh. It is regretable that you did not go to Wuchow to see our leader. If you and Dr. Sun had held a frank discussion, some arrangements could perhaps still have been made. Now that you have left Canton, however, it appears that there is no longer any hope of mediation. I have returned to Shanghai and cannot be bothered to hear anymore of the complications of the situation. For the sake of our past friendship, I urgently advise you to retire once and for all or at least for the time being.

I now venture to speak frankly to you, concealing nothing. I think you are too proud. If you persist in your insubordination, the future will become darker and darker. No matter what may be the practical results, both parties are bound to suffer heavy damages, and the calamities will be unthinkable. If you are defeated, you will lose your good name, and all for nothing. And even if you win, your spiritual suffering will be even greater than that of those whom you have defeated.

You can ill afford not to make known your attitude nor to disregard our leader's wishes.

Neither listen to the ill words of the mean nor fall into the traps of the wicked. Obey our leader, and help him in his Northern Expedition.

Chiang Kai-shek

Kai-shek expected an immediate reply from Ch'en Chiung-ming, but days passed and none came. Ch'en's silence increased Kai-shek's hatred for the man. What was worse, Dr. Sun regarded Kai-shek's warning with cold indifference and refused to give credence to his words.

Ten days later, Ch'en heaped insult upon injury when Kai-shek's letter to C'en was returned unopened. On the back of the envelope, however, appeared these words: "Upstart—jealous—ill-tempered—stupid—egotistical mischief maker."

To a degree, the return of the two regiments of loyal troops to Canton had been intended as a means of checking Ch'en Chiung-ming's rebellion, if any. But now, because General Ch'en had resigned and left Canton, their presence in the city seemed unnecessary. Dr. Sun thought, therefore, that he could go on sublimely with his plans for the Northern Expedition and lead the troops through Kiangsi without hindrance.

General Ch'en Chiung-ming, on the other hand, now believed the rumors he had heard. Dr. Sun did, indeed, want to curb his powers and dismiss him from office. The fact that Dr. Sun had accepted his resignation without any show of regret proved that. So he bided his time.

During the next few weeks, Kai-shek sent a number of urgent telegrams and letters to Dr. Sun's loyal general, Hsu Ch'ung-chih, and other friends urging them to take preemptive action and oust Ch'en Chiung-ming. But these plans fell on deaf ears.

Because the situation in Peking was eroding rapidly, Dr. Sun's thoughts were focused solely on the Northern Expedition. A golden opportunity seemed to present itself in the North because the Manchurian Army, which had helped the Chihli clique defeat Premier Tuan Ch'i-jui and followers, now quarreled with its former comrades-in-arms. Besides, General Chang Tso-lin had brought his men from Manchuria into China Proper in order to be close to Peking in readiness to fight Ts'ao K'un, the warlord of Chihli, and his lieutenant Wu P'ei-fu. Dr. Sun, regretting that he had already lost so much time in shifting the route of his troops from Kweilin to the Kiangsi border, now became impatient.

Meanwhile, Ch'en Chiung-ming's chief of staff, Ip Chu, brought more than fifty battalions into Canton. His intentions were obvious, but no one suspected anything.

General Hsu Ch'ung-chih on May 3, 1922, sent a reply to Kai-shek's several telegrams and letters, stating:

> *Your letters and telegrams have been presented to our leader for perusal. The General Headquarters will arrive at Hsu-Chow on the sixth; I*

will personally go there earlier. Two regiments of the first and second divisions from Kweilin, in addition to various other forces, will join the Northern Expedition. The navy has been brought over to our side.

Ch'en Chiung-ming has declared that he will not resign his post as war minister. In fact, he has asked us to make arrangements to billet his troops, which are coming back from the capital of Kwangsi. If we assign them the duty of maintaining peace on the Kwangtung and Kwangsi borders, they can be kept out of mischief. Our leader and I hope you will come back soon.

To Kai-shek's despair, Ch'en Chiung-ming was stronger than ever. He was now appointed director of military affairs of Kwangtung and Kwangsi. And he retained his post as war minister. Although he had resigned his command over the army, his chief of staff, Ip Chu, still held military power in the palm of his hand.

Since Canton was now without a strong garrison, Ch'en Chiung-ming decided to demand more power. Acting under Ch'en's instructions, Ip Chu and other officers of the Cantonese Army petitioned Dr. Sun to set aside Ch'en's resignation and publicly reinstate him as commander in chief of the Cantonese Army and as military governor of Kwangtung province. This irked Kai-shek beyond words, although it made no difference to Dr. Sun. He had no mind for anything except the Northern Expedition.

By the end of May 1922, Kai-shek was so bursting with fury tht he sent a number of telegrams to various loyal supporters of Dr. Sun, urging them to attack Ch'en Chiung-ming's forces under Ip Chu. His bitterness knew no bounds.

Liao Chung-k'ai, a most trustworthy follower of Dr. Sun and an intimate friends of ours, replied as follows:

To My Brother Chiang Kai-shek:

Your telegram has been received and understood. Unless rebellion has actually broken out in Canton, there is no way to call our forces back from the front. It would not be permitted under any circumstances. None of us wish to see such a move. If the Second Army under Hsu Ch'ung-chih followed your advice and acted unilaterally to oust Ch'en Chiung-ming, the action would be opposed by all the rest. What we hope for at this time is to win our battles against the enemy outside our province

and to be calm and steady within our province. Your repeated sugges-
tions can only cause serious trouble.

You, my brother, ought to come here soon so that you can go to the
front immediately to help Hsu Ch'ung-chih. How can you bear to leave
him and the rest of us to bear all the hardships?

Liao Chung-k'ai
May 31, 1922

The following day, Liao again wrote to Kai-shek, saying:

My Brother Chiang Kai-shek:

I have returned from Hsuchow and have read your second telegram. I
reply as follows:

1. Ip Chu's troops have come to Canton. Except that he has petitioned
for the reinstatement of Ch'en Chiung-ming as the chief of the Cantonese
Army, he has taken no other action.

2. Ch'en Chiung-ming has repeatedly refused to accept any post
connected with the Northern Expedition. He cannot be blamed because
he is already fully occupied in Canton.

3. Ch'en Chiung-ming has promised to come either to Canton or
Chaoching, and to order Ip Chu's troops to return to their original
stations.

4. If Ip Chu's troops gradually leave Canton, all will be well. If they
do not, then, and only then, will what you suggested be the unavoidable
measure to be taken. Our immediate need is to have someone at the front
who can look after the whole campaign, devoting equal attention to
what goes on at the battlefield and at the home front. I hope you will set
out this very day to help us. Please delay no longer. Do not harbor old
grudges, and be magnanimous!

Liao Chung-k'ai salutes you.
June 1, 1922

Rumors travel fast and become exaggerated beyond recognition. In
all the tea houses during late May and early June, it was being said that
Dr. Sun had decided to place General Ch'en Chiung-ming under arrest,
strip him of his posts, and destroy his native stronghold at Kaichow.
Fearing that these unfounded rumors would cause mischief, Hu Han-
min wrote Kai-shek:

Please desist from urging our leader to attack General Ch'en Chiung-ming. He has repeatedly told you he would not do so, and I am sure he will not change his mind. But your many letters and telegrams to various brothers asking them to rise up and strike Ch'en Chiung-ming a fatal blow will only cause great mischief. For the sake of our leader's peace of mind, which you should respect, please desist. Much ill-feeling has already been created. Worst of all, if Ch'en Chiung-ming believes these rumors, Canton can easily become a bloody battlefield.

Hu Han-min
June 1, 1922

Despite the rumors, the situation in Canton seemed calm. To allay the fears and misgivings of the general public as well as of the army, Dr. Sun decided to return to Canton from the front for a few days and stay at the Presidential Palace. He was accompanied by only a handful of guards, which showed that he had no belligerent intentions. He arrived late in the afternoon of June 1, 1922, and sent a telegram to Kai-shek urging him to return to Canton by the first steamer to help in the Northern Expedition. Kai-shek still insisted, however, that Ch'en Chiung-ming and his forces be removed before he would compromise.

Realizing that Dr. Sun would not take any action, Kai-shek again sent an urgent letter begging General Hsu Ch'ung-chih to strike at Ch'en immediately. He said that even if Ch'en Chiung-ming and his followers retreated or compromised, Hsu Ch'ung-chih must nonetheless bring his army back home to solve the fundamental problems in Canton. Otherwise peace and safety could not be assured. His letter read:

If we fall into Ch'en Chiung-ming's trap, our party will be destroyed and our army will be lost. You must never rest easy, even if General Ch'en compromises a little. We must strike before he does, regardless of whether his forces are concentrated in the East or in Canton. If we strike first, it will not be difficult to wipe out his forces. But if we hesitate, our hands will be tied, and it will be too late to save ourselves from destruction! Whatever happens, act quickly! It will produce only a little trouble, whereas procrastination will result in great calamity. Give my suggestion the benefit of your thought, and give me an answer. My mind is greatly disturbed and I cannot rest. Even as I write this letter to you, I feel terribly agitated.

Chiang Kai-shek

Hsu Ch'ung-chih, however, was too busy to send an answer to Kai-shek. He led his army northward and on June 13, 1922, captured the city of Kan-Chow in Kiangsi. This was a feather in his cap and made Dr. Sun deliriously happy because it was the first victory in this campaign against the warlords.

During this period I often thought of the saying "We are never more discontented with others than when we are discontented with ourselves." This aptly applied to Kai-shek, for I knew in his heart he regarded himself as a dragon confined to a small pool with nowhere to soar. As a result of his own frustrations, he took umbrage at Ch'en Chiung-ming, who was his rival for Dr. Sun's favor.

Kai-shek thought himself superior because he was the only Japan-trained military expert available. He had fought for the Chinese Republic with veteran Ch'en Ch'i-mei, who, before being assassinated, had been Dr. Sun's right-hand man. Now, having pledged his life to serve Dr. Sun in the revolution, he yearned for recognition.

Ch'en Chiung-ming, on the other hand, thought himself superior to Kai-shek because, from the very earliest days, he had served the Chinese Republic. He was commander in chief of the Cantonese army and had successfully ousted the warlord Luk and restored Dr. Sun to Canton. He was, unquestionably, the most important military man in South China. His slogan, Canton for the Cantonese, was cleverly used to rally the support of the people of Canton because the warlord Luk was not from Canton. General Ch'en Chiung-ming's idea was to have only Cantonese on his staff. So, when Dr. Sun recommended Kai-shek, who was not a Cantonese, Ch'en Chiung-ming accepted him reluctantly. Kai-shek realized this, and thus an undercurrent of rivalry, jealousy, and even bitterness developed between the two men.

To protect Dr. Sun, Kai-shek repeatedly reminded Dr. Sun of Ch'en's treacherous nature. He advised Dr. Sun to issue an order curbing Ch'en's growing powers or even dismissing him from office in order to stave off a rebellion. Rumors travel fast, especially bad rumors. Ch'en Chiung-ming therefore learned of Kai-shek's advice and feared that Dr. Sun would eventually be persuaded to sign such an order. This instilled a definite unrest and fear in his mind.

Kai-shek's uncompromising spirit troubled Dr. Sun a great deal. The following correspondence, which is on record, will give insight into the matter:

To My Dear Brother Chiang Kai-shek,

When brother Ch'en Chiung-ming captured Canton, he used all his strength to serve our party and our country. We in turn used all our strength to help him. With only one aim and one view, our cooperation was no ordinary alliance. I hope brother Ch'en Chiung-ming will act as Huang Hsing did before 1912, and as Ch'en Ch'i-mei did after 1913. I esteem him exactly as I did those two patriots. All I ask of him is that he observe my principles and my policy—to respect my democratic faith for which I have worked these many years. Am I a tyrant who is pleased only when obeyed blindly? You, my brother Kai-shek, who worked with Ch'en Ch'i-mei the longest, should know how I trusted him. But you have a fiery temper, and your demands are often excessive. This often causes you to be quarrelsome and suspicious. It is often difficult, therefore, to work harmoniously with you. Because I expect you in the future to shoulder heavy responsibilities for our party, you should modify your opinions, overlook trivial differences, and try to compromise. This is merely for the sake of peace within our party, and it has nothing to do with anything personal. Would you, my brother, agree with this?

Sun Yat-sen

Dr. Sun and his other followers did not share Kai-shek's suspicions of Ch'en Chiung-ming, nor did they give ear to Kai-shek's charges. They deplored his constant nagging, but what could they do? I, for one, could see that trouble would ensue because Ch'en would surely resist being dismissed. Even if Kai-shek's suspicions were accurate, there was no proof. And Dr. Sun, anxious to compromise for the sake of peace, gave General Ch'en the benefit of the doubt, regarding Kai-shek's accusations as the result of irrational prejudice.

Although Kai-shek and I were back in Shanghai getting settled in our new home, we kept abreast of conditions in Canton through Dr. Sun's secretary, Mr. Lin Min-chi. He wrote and told us that, after our departure, rumors were becoming rampant, and that Dr. Sun was making every effort to quash them. He therefore sent for General Ch'en to come for a heart-to-heart talk, hoping to set things right. In the ten days that followed, Dr. Sun sent three similar letters to Ch'en. There was no reply. In the last of these letters, he pleaded:

Dear Brother Chiung-ming,

Do not lightly believe the rumors you hear. You must work for the common cause. Please come immediately for a meeting to map out detailed plans. I am thinking of you. I will tell you more when we meet.

Sun Wen

11

Rebellion and Reversal

*I*t was nearing midnight on June 15, 1922, when Dr. Sun, weary and worn after a heavy day's work, was getting ready for bed. Suddenly, secretary Lin Min-chi rushed in to warn him and Mme Sun to flee for their lives, General Ip Chu, Ch'en Chiung-ming's chief of staff, would stage a rebellion at midnight. Dr. Sun refused to believe this and said he would remain at his post. After repeated urgings from Mme Sun, he finally prepared to leave. As he was dressing, he heard the roar of cannons in the distance, and the noise was increasing in intensity. There was no time to lose. Dr. and Mme Sun and secretary Lin, together with the palace staff and servants, hurriedly left the palace. The latter were told to go home and await orders.

Dr. and Mme Sun, led by secretary Lin, made their way to Wai-Oi Road and then turned into side streets and byways to avoid Ch'en's soldiers, who had taken over the city and were now patrolling the streets and questioning pedestrians. Other soldiers rode by in lorries to concentrate at other vital points. The firing continued, on and on, without a stop. It was a nerve-racking ordeal to sneak the two miles from the palace to the Bund. They expected, at any moment, to be stopped or detained. Worst of all, heavy fire was continuously booming, and shrapnel was falling left and right. Several times they had to stop and flatten themselves against a wall when flashes of light momentarily brightened the night, and heavy shells ripped into nearby buildings.

Pale and shaking, the trio finally reached the East Bund Wharf. From there they engaged a sampan to take them to Navy Headquarters on the Pearl River islet. But there they were told the building could not withstand a bombardment. So secretary Lin engaged two motorboats, one to take Mme Sun to Fa Ti district. There she could temporarily stay with friends, while Dr. Sun, accompanied by a group of loyal naval officers, went by motor launch to board the gunboat *Yung Feng,* which was anchored on the Pearl River.

Once safely on board, Dr. Sun gave orders to alert the personnel of all seven gunboats docked nearby: the *Yung Chang, Chu Yi, Chu Chang, Tung On, Kwang Yu, Kin Yi,* and the *Pao Pi.* Although small, these cruisers were adequate for the purpose of protecting Dr. Sun from being captured.

By daylight, the bombardment continued, and many parts of Canton City were in flames. Dr. Sun's Presidential Palace was looted and set afire. The city was in turmoil and the riffraff, together with the troops, took advantage of the situation to loot shops and homes. There followed days of lawlessness.

Dr. Sun sent Kai-shek a telegram dated June 18, 1922, that read:

> *Ch'en Chiung-ming started his rebellion. Cannons fired on Presidential Palace. I am safe on gunboat* Yung Feng, *outside Par Chow harbor. Preparing to launch a comeback.*
>
> *Sun Wen*

"Look at this," said Kai-shek, and I was shocked at the news. "I predicted it! I predicted it!" he screamed at the top of his lungs as he paced the floor. He shook with fury. I had never seen him so emotionally upset. Then suddenly turning to me, he ordered, "Pack up! We are leaving for Canton by the first ship!"

"Not again?" I asked incredulously.

"Yes, again," he answered angrily. He then cursed Ch'en Chiung-ming in no uncertain terms.

I stood there not knowing what to do. The drapes I was trying to hang in our new flat fell to the floor and I began to fold them up. I asked myself: What kind of life have I brought upon to myself? Was I destined to lead a makeshift life? It was like child's play! Suddenly I am asked to go to Canton. When there, I am suddenly asked to go to Kweilin. Before we can land at Kweilin, I am asked to go back to Shanghai. And now, just as we are getting settled in our new home, I am asked to go back to Canton again. All this running around—up and down, back and forth we go—all due to hot tempers and dissensions. When will it all end? I asked myself.

That night Mother brought brother Bun to my new flat for dinner. When she heard we were to leave for Canton again, she said: "I think you are being unwise; you are looking for trouble. Why do you want to go to Canton again?"

"It's Kai-shek's decision, so that's that," I answered resignedly.

Then Mother turned to him and said: "You are a man, and if you wish to risk your life in fighting, I have no way to stop you. But I think it is very wrong of you to drag your wife to face this precarious situation. Bringing your wife to Canton at this time is like delivering a lamb to a tiger's mouth. Why don't you leave her behind in Shanghai? She can come home and stay with us until you return."

Kai-shek's cheeks flushed and his ears turned red. He said heatedly: "Your daughter and I will fight shoulder-to-shoulder in all our battles. Unless she objects, where I go, she goes." He turned to me and asked: "Do you object, Chieh-ju? Would you rather stay in Shanghai with your mother? Tell me the truth!"

I was in a quandary and had to make a quick decision. Of course I did not want to go, but in this case there was no choice. I looked at Kai-shek and then at Mother and tried to comfort her: "Dr. Sun is now in trouble, Mother, and he desperately needs Kai-shek; otherwise he would not send that wire. Kai-shek, in turn, needs me, and I'm not afraid to go to Canton with him. It is true that we have agreed to fight shoulder-to-shoulder in all our battles, and I don't want to let him down at this last moment. We will be quite safe, so don't worry about us."

So on June 20, 1922, Kai-shek and I set out from Shanghai for Canton via Hong Kong. On the 29th, we arrived on the Pearl River, but we did not go ashore. Through the kindness of the ship's compradore, we engaged a motor launch and sped directly toward Par Chow, at the other end of the Pearl River. There we saw seven blue-gray gunboats with smoke issuing from their funnels. We went on board the warship *Yung Feng* to meet Dr. Sun, who a few days previously had moved from the gunboat *Chu Yi.*

When Kai-shek and I boarded the *Yung Feng,* Dr. Sun looked at us with tears welling in his eyes. For a moment he was unable to speak.

When at last he found his voice, he had so much to tell us that he talked on and on, without a pause.

It was soon reported that all the remaining loyal troops on shore had either been wiped out or overpowered by Ch'en Chiung-ming's forces. Following this, the men on duty at the forts also had to surrender.

Kai-shek immediately took command of the small fleet of seven gunboats. He thought it prudent to move farther upriver for safety. After we had left the danger zone of the two main forts, there was yet a third fort called Che Wai, which we had to pass on our way. As a precaution, Kai-shek insisted that Dr. Sun and I take cover on the lower deck, while he stayed on the bridge with the ship's captain to give directions. Our gunboat zigzagged its way along the Pearl River, firing at the fort furiously. Meanwhile, the fort's guns were not idle. They answered in kind, shot for shot, concentrating their aim chiefly on the *Yung Feng*, where we were. It was very humid that afternoon. I watched Dr. Sun sitting at a table writing out a speech, and I noticed that beads of perspiration appeared like pearls on his wide forehead and then rolled down to his eyebrows. I took up a damp face towel and handed it to him to wipe his face. I then stood behind him with a palm-leaf fan, moving it left and right, in an effort to cool him.

It was precisely then that a shell struck the bow of our gunboat, which shook so severely that I was thrown to the floor. Dr. Sun held onto the table, but his chair fell on top of me. When I rose, I felt my drawers sticking to my legs, and I knew I had unconsciously urinated from shock. It was a harrowing experience, especially when six other blasts followed. But thanks to the Great Buddha, we suffered no serious damage, although it took us more than half an hour to pass through the danger zone.

As the days passed, Dr. Sun's only hope was the army under General Hsu Ch'ung-chih. It remained loyal and was stationed at the Northern Expeditionary base in Kan-Chow. Before Ch'en Chiung-ming rebelled, Dr. Sun had been determined not to call it back from the front, but now he had no choice. It was the only weapon that could save him. But alas, this army could not be moved on short notice because one of its divisions had defected to Ch'en Chiung-ming's side. This lowered the army's morale, and when it was attacked, it quickly beat a retreat. By August 1, 1922, all the army's avenues of retreat were cut off. Its base was taken over by Ch'en Chiung-ming's men, and its newly conquered stronghold at Kan-Chow, the conquest of which had once made Dr. Sun so happy, was now recaptured by its former northern warlord. Thus, Dr. Sun's army, which had seemed so promising only a month earlier, had to withdraw toward the Fukien border. Kai-shek now realized the truth of the saying "Help that is long on the road is no help at all," and he began to see the futility of further resistance.

Thus, by August 7, 1922, Dr. Sun's feverish hope that the army would come to rescue him was blasted to smithereens. Kai-shek, as military adviser, reviewed the situation coolly. He said: "(1) Shiukwan, our original military base, is now in the hands of the rebels; (2) Kan-Chow has been recaptured by the northern enemy; (3) a division of our men has defected to Ch'en Chiung-ming; (4) there is no hope that loyal elements in the army will come to our rescue. So it is clear that our continued presence here can serve no useful purpose. Everything seems against us, and it is senseless and dangerous to stay here any longer. It is advisable to get away before it is too late."

On August 9, 1922, by arrangement with the British consul general, the HMS *Moorben* escorted Dr. Sun and us to Hong Kong, where Mme Sun joined us. The next day we all boarded the SS *Empress of Russia* and set sail for Shanghai, where we arrived on the 14th, two months after the debacle began.

General Ch'en Chiung-ming disclaimed all responsibility for the outbreak. He declared that he knew nothing of the doings of his former subordinates, for he had retired from active service. Had not Dr. Sun accepted his resignation as commander in chief? His chief of staff, General Ip Chu, after bombarding the Presidential Palace, looted it and wired all the newspapers in the whole country the startling news: "Expose of Dr. Sun Yat-sen's Alliance with Soviet Russia." The news release said:

> The newspaper reports of Canton military coup have been characterized by a great deal of notoriety not in accord with the truth. The Canton authorities wish to repeat assurances that all foreigners in Canton are in no danger and there is no need to evacuate. Political mudslingers have accused General Ch'en Chiung-ming of treachery, but the general public is asked to be the judge. Dr. Sun Yat-sen's policy is pro-Russian and Bolshevik. He is planning to introduce Bolshevism to China. Important papers found in his locked iron safe at his Presidential Palace reveal documentary proof of a far-reaching plan to communize China as a first step to usurping the legal Peking government. The Canton government therefore demands the immediate resignation of Dr. Sun Yat-sen.

Seeing that he had successfully defeated all those who opposed him, Ch'en Chiung-ming reassumed the title of commander in chief of the Cantonese Army and head of the two provinces, Kwangtung and Kwangsi.

So, Dr. Sun was once more an exile, living in seclusion in his home on Rue Moliere, Shanghai. He issued an open letter:

> *I have been leading my comrades in the struggle for the establishment of a republic for nearly thirty years. During this time, we have risked death on numerous occasions. But never have I been as disastrously defeated as this time. All my previous failures had one thing in common: I was defeated by an enemy. Now, after overcoming my enemies, I was opposed by Ch'en Chiung-ming, a man whom I had taken under my wings for over a decade. But now his treachery exceeds that of even my bitterest foe. This is not only a calamity to the nation but a black stain on humanity and morality.*
>
> > Sun Wen
> > August 15, 1922

Back in Shanghai, the cool days brought little peace of mind to Kai-shek. In all his life, he had never felt so utterly crushed as now. The mere thought of Ch'en Chiung-ming basking in his great victory in far-off Canton was like a knife in his bleeding heart. In his black despair, he found consolation in writing letters to various Kuomintang members denouncing Ch'en Chiung-ming for his treachery. This was an outlet to appease his pent-up anger. He also wrote to Hu Han-min and Wang Ching-wei, giving them an ultimatum: They should launch a comeback to unseat his enemy in Canton within ten days, or else he would never speak to them again.

Each day he was irritable and grouchy, and for the first time in our married life he made no effort to control his temper. Something had to be done for his own sake to alleviate this intense hatred; otherwise he would become a mental case. I knew that hatred does not cease by hatred at any time. Hatred ceases only by love, so I began to make him relax his tension and tried to humor him to the best of my ability. But at best, it was terribly difficult.

Then one day, he suddenly received the following letter from Dr. Sun. It read:

My Dear Brother Kai-shek,

I have just seen your letter to Hu Han-min and Wang Ching-wei in which you said, "If there is no progress in recapturing Canton within ten days, then there is no hope, etc." Pooh! What rubbish you talk! How could you so lightly think of giving up like that?

Things do not succeed as we wish eight or nine times out of ten. Success depends upon fortitude and persistence. You must disregard jealousy, hatred, and prejudice. If you wish to give up when there is no progress within ten days, then you will never succeed in doing anything.

Even though we have made no progress, the enemy is losing ground every day. For instance, his officers and men are beginning to see the light; his unity is fast disintegrating; the people in Kwangtung are hating him more and more and thinking of us daily. These things are to our advantage, though we cannot see them. Therefore, if we can only hold firm, that means progress. So I do hope you will not give up hope. We must achieve our aim to vanquish Ch'en Chiung-ming.

Sun Wen

Onc thing that made Kai-shek lose hope was the waning of Dr. Sun's popularity. Public opinion was against him as a result of his Bolshevik connections. People, on the whole, hated Bolsheviks. Their bloody purges and atrocities in the Soviet Union during the revolution of 1917 were still fresh in the people's minds and they looked upon anything Rusian with abhorrence. So to enlist any sympathy for Dr. Sun at this time seemed out of the question.

Seeing Kai-shek's heavy burden of hatred, I knew I had to do something to remove it, for it should not be allowed to sink his heart and weigh it down like a rock. I made it my duty to get him interested in something to fill the vacuum. But what? He was a military man, through and through, so it was not so easy to find an opening outside his line to suit his personality. I therefore sought the advice of my good friend Yi-min and told her: "Kai-shek's mind is brooding too much on Canton, and he needs some diversion to make him forget. Is there something you can suggest that he can do to occupy his thoughts? I've been thinking for days but cannot think of anything suitable. My mind is a blank."

"Let him join Father in his speculation business," said Yi-min. "He is forming a stock-and-shares company and Kai-shek can join him."

"Will it need a lot of money?" I asked.

"No, not so very much," she replied. "Let us go in to see Father, and he will tell you all about it."

Old Mr. Chang Ching-chiang was, as usual, extremely kind and told me: "Our proposed company is named Sheng Tai, and we buy and sell stocks and shares. Our profit is brokerage, and it can be quite handsome at times. We have sixteen members at present, but if Kai-shek joins, he will be the seventeenth member. Our capital will be 50,000 Shanghai dollars. Each member must take at least one share at 1,000 dollars per share. Our company will be entitled to four seats on the Shanghai Exchange. I am only the adviser of our company. Mr. Chang Ping-san is our big shareholder and manager, but I will ask him to include Kai-shek in our group. I am sure, he will agree."

Thus, through old Mr. Chang Ching-chiang's influence, Kai-shek took four shares in the company under the name of Chiang Wei. He read up on financial literature and how to make decisions on stocks-and-shares investments. It was a novelty to him, and the excitement of the fluctuation of rates of the many types of stocks and shares soon occupied his mind, especially on his potential gains. Which were the high-grade stocks and which were the bad? In this way, he gradually forgot the bitter hatred that was in his heart.

Being one of the privileged few who could occupy a space in the big hall of Shanghai's Stock Exchange, Kai-shek worked hard and with enthusiasm. The Stock Exchange transactions were an integral part of Shanghai's financial world. Thousands of speculators, who depended upon it to eke out a living, packed the premises to capacity every day. Kai-shek watched the market tendencies like a hawk, and he bought and sold like a veteran, making a profit. The most popular shares were those on textiles, grain, land, and public utilities. But all was not peace and quiet. During times when buying and selling fluctuated, the situation became frenzied and often violent, for people battled to buy or sell to cover their positions.

Five days a week, Monday to Friday between 10 A.M. and 4 P.M., the exchange building swarmed with anxious investors. From September 1922 to February 1923 Kai-shek spent his days in this line of business.

In the meantime, during the month of December 1922, Dr. Sun successfully persuaded a Kwangsi Army chief named General Liu Chen-huan to oust Ch'en Chiung-ming from Canton. To be doubly assured of an overwhelming victory, General Liu secured the help of the Yunnanese Army chief, General Yang Hsi-min, to work in conjunction with him. With these two well-trained armies, success was a foregone conclusion.

On January 5, 1923, these two armies launched a fierce attack on Canton. Ch'en Chiung-ming, taken by surprise, was forced to flee the city and take refuge in his stronghold at Waichow on the East River, eighty miles away. But General Liu pressed on in hot pursuit and annihilated a large part of Ch'en's troops. General Yang, too, did very well, and these two forces easily conquered the city of Canton and environs and welcomed the return of Dr. Sun and General Hsu Ch'ung-chih to take their rightful places in Canton. General Hsu not only recruited leaderless, scattered Cantonese troops but also reorganized his ill-fated Northern Expeditionary army, which had taken refuge in Fukien province the year before.

On March 21, 1923, Dr. Sun resumed his authority as generalissimo over Canton, and his headquarters was again established. Kai-shek was appointed military adviser and strategist in absentia and was urged to return to Canton to assume his duties. But Kai-shek was tied up with the Stock Exchange and could not leave immediately.

Now in possession of Canton once more, Dr. Sun found his government in greater need of money than ever before. On his flight, General Ch'en Chiung-ming had emptied the coffers, and Dr. Sun faced a dilemma. He had not only his own government to finance but also several large armies that had fought valiantly to restore him to power. He was in urgent need of funds, and more funds.

In desperation, he thought of the Canton Customs Service, which was associated with foreigners. It should be explained that because of China's observance of treaties made by the Manchu regime with the foreign powers, all the customs were controlled by China's foreign creditors. Under the peace treaties signed after the Boxer War in 1900, China promised to pay £900 million sterling as an indemnity. This debt, according to treaty, was to be paid chiefly from China's customs revenue. China's customs were controlled by foreigners, and any surplus from the fixed rate was to be handed over to the legal Chinese government.

Thus the surplus from the Canton Customs House was being sent to Peking. It was now an ironical situation that the Peking government should be using the money from Canton to pay the soldiers who were trying to oust Dr. Sun's government. Meanwhile, Dr. Sun himself was in urgent need of money to pay the armies that were loyally serving him and his government. Dr. Sun naturally thought it fair to request that the foreign diplomatic bodies turn over the surplus revenues from the Canton customs to his southern government—rather than to his Peking enemies. This request was made in the spring of 1923. Because this was an international question, Dr. Sun was flatly refused. In December, however, he publicly declared that he would, nonetheless, seize and keep the Canton surplus by force.

This threat was answered on December 7, 1923, when the Great Powers, headed by Great Britain, gathered an international naval force of seventeen gray warships along the shores of Canton to intimidate Dr. Sun. The commander in chief, Admiral Leveson of the British Fleet, China Station, superintended the demonstration personally. The occasion was truly international, for the flags of many countries flew on these ships: British, American, French, Japanese, and even a Portuguese flag were seen.

During this demonstration, Dr. Sun ordered his foreign minister, Eugene Chen (Ch'en Yu-jen), to bring to him representatives of Reuters and other members of the press. He declared to them that because his repeated requests to Britain and America for sympathy had failed, as shown by this flagrant display of gunboat diplomacy, he would now accept Soviet Russia's proffered hand of friendship. Actually that was just a threat. He was still hoping that he could get help from the democracies.

In January 1924, when the First National Congress of the Kuomintang was in session, the Labour Party in England was victorious in the general election. Dr. Sun, on behalf of his party, sent his friendly congratulations to Ramsay MacDonald. If he had not wished to promote good relations with Britain, he would not have risked being snubbed. But according to government records, his congratulatory telegram was not even acknowledged by a secretary of the new prime minister of Great Britain.

On the very next day, news came that Lenin had died. The Canton congress sent a telegram of condolence. The meeting then adjourned for five minutes of silence to indicate its respect for the deceased revolutionary leader, and its sympathy with the Russian people. M. Chicherin, the Russian foreign commissar, sent a telegram in response.

It expressed how much the Russian people appreciated this gesture. These two small incidents helped Dr. Sun and his followers decide which direction to turn.

Since the Kuomintang had now decided to go left and approach Soviet Russia for help, Dr. Sun enlisted the services of a large number of new people with leftist tendencies. This marked the beginning of the policy of accepting Communists as members of the Kuomintang.

As mentioned before, Kai-shek could not leave for Canton to join Dr. Sun so easily. His transactions in the Shanghai shares market showed a large deficit, to the amount of 20, 000 dollars, as a result of his misjudgments. He had overbought textile shares, and prices had dropped. Like the sweet angel he was, old Mr. Chang Ching-chiang came to Kai-shek's rescue. He paid off the debt and then packed Kai-shek and me off to Canton to join Dr. Sun's new government.

We arrived at the southern capital on April 20, 1923, and Kai-shek immediately assumed his position as military adviser. Although the position was called by that name, in actual fact, Kai-shek was under General Hsu Ch'ung-chih, the commander in chief of the Cantonese Army. Thus he was a subordinate officer, on a par with General Hsu's secretary. He had to take orders from his big boss Hsu and not directly from Dr. Sun.

But Kai-shek and his boss got on well together. They understood one another perfectly and had a mutual respect for each other's strong qualities. On the one hand, Kai-shek had a good military record with Ch'en Ch'i-mei and was also known for his loyalty to Dr. Sun. General Hsu Ch'ung-chih considered himself lucky to have such a man on his staff.

On the other hand, Kai-shek looked upon his superior with a respect that seemed to be fired with devotion. General Hsu was a man of glamor. His grandfather was a man of vast wealth and position, having been governor of Fukien under the empress dowager. His father was an early modern who advocated reforms. And he, of the third generation, had gone to Japan in his youth to become a revolutionary under Dr. Sun. For his loyalty over the years, Dr. Sun regarded General Hsu Ch'ung-chih with an affection comparable to that for a son.

Besides, this was Kai-shek's first steady job in eight years, and he wanted everything to go off well. He was ready to devote all his energy to the revolution. But he noted a little unhappily that among all the officials, he himself was a mere junior and had hardly any standing at all. Fortunately, he had ambition. He knew that if given a chance, he would soon win recognition from the Kuomintang government.

Having learned a lesson in the past, and not wishing to repeat the mistake, Dr. Sun discussed with Kai-shek the ways and means to start a military school, which would train its own soldiers to be loyal and true to the Kuomintang. Dr. Sun contended that, in China, he who headed the army had the power to rule a province or the whole country—whether he was a scholar, thief, or bandit—as exemplified by the warlords. To prevent any cadet from defecting to the enemy, the newly trained soldier should be instilled with the will to fight for a cause, to be patriotic, and to study the Three Principles of the People. With this idea in mind, it became Kai-shek's chief aim to establish such a school as quickly as possible.

12

"Living Angel Liu"

*T*hrough General Hsu Ch'ung-chih's favor, Kai-shek and I were invited to Mr. and Mrs. Wang Ching-wei's dinner party given in honor of the "Hero of the Day." This hero was General Liu Chen-huan, who was chiefly responsible for the victory that ousted Ch'en Chiung-ming from Canton and thus restored Dr. Sun to office. Dr. Sun, in his deep gratitude, had nicknamed General Liu, "Living Angel Liu."

We arrived punctually at six o'clock at the Wang Ching-wei villa at Tungshan, a newly developed residential district of Canton. There, we were greeted warmly at the door by our host and hostess.

I was especially glad to meet my hostess. I had known her by reputation for years. She was an Overseas Chinese born in Penang, so she had the advantage of a Sino-British education. She was about five feet four inches tall, with luxuriant black hair, large eyes, well-shaped mouth, and a strong chin that gave an immediate sense of determination. I was almost as quickly aware of her very feminine flair for sizing up people. I could see that she looked at me critically and took in every detail of my attire. But I smiled at my wealthy hostess, who was commonly known to her friends as Becky, short for her maiden name, Chen Beck-Chun. Both she and her handsome husband were early revolutionaries who had lived in Japan before the Chinese Republic. Our host, especially, was regarded as Dr. Sun's right-hand man and heir to the revolutionary throne. Both host and hostess were charming.

The drawing room was spacious, with tall French windows opening onto a large terrace. The whole color scheme was in yellow and black.

The fawn-colored walls were decorated with scrolls of landscapes and calligraphy by famous modern scholars. The most eye-catching decorations, however, were the two silk flags that covered the whole space over the fireplace. The flags were crossed; one, that of Nationalist China, was red with a white sun on a blue square, while the other was simply the white sun on a blue square without the red. This was the party banner of the Kuomintang. There were a large number of people standing or sitting about. They looked modern, intelligent, and smart, dressed either in Chinese clothes, Chungshan suits, or soldiers' uniforms. The ladies wore Chinese-silk long gowns of all hues of the rainbow. Becky introduced Kai-shek and me to "Living Angel Liu," who wore a gold-braided uniform. He was standing at the fireplace talking to Dr. Sun and surrounded by a group of men. I looked at Dr. Sun and could see that his pallid face had many more lines than the year before. Plainly, he was not at all well. Becky said in a sonorous voice: "Allow me to introduce Mr. and Mrs. Chiang Kai-shek. Our leader, Dr. Sun, and General Liu Chen-huan."

While we shook hands, Dr. Sun exclaimed: "You young people must remember, without our 'Living Angel Liu,' I would not be here today! He suffered two bullet wounds on my account. I am forever grateful for his bravery."

"To hear such a fine compliment from our leader is indeed a great honor," said Kai-shek in a jovial voice to General Liu. They shook hands cordially and went on talking. I looked at this "lion of the hour." He seemed only about thirty-five years of age, small of stature and build, with squarish face and determined jaws. He wore thick glasses over his alert eyes. His unassuming manner, close-cropped hair, and lingering smile gave him the appearance of a young man instead of a brave soldier of such indomitable energy and will. Kai-shek had spoken to me of this man before, especially during the recent events at Waichow, when this hero's troops were heavily shelled by Ch'en Chiung-ming's forces in the retreat toward Poklo. General Liu had pursued the enemy doggedly, and as a result he received two bullets that pierced his shoulder and stomach. Little wonder that Dr. Sun had given him such a complimentary nickname.

Looking at Kai-shek and me, Dr. Sun continued: "Great credit is due to the stern military discipline in Japan, where General Liu received his military training. He knows the art of war. Better yet, he is always on the firing line with his army. He is patriotic and ever conscious that he is fighting for a cause—our cause! He is not easily tossed about by the winds of chance or fortune. To him the word *surrender* has no meaning. And though his ranks may dwindle, there still breathes the soul of one who knows no fear. No praise is sufficient to describe his undying loyalty to me and to our constitutional government. Through thick and thin, he never hesitated to render his service for righteousness. He is a great credit to China!"

Kai-shek was much impressed with General Liu, especially after Dr. Sun's lavish praise. He did not want to leave this great personality, so I left him there talking while Becky graciously steered me round the room until I had met practically all the forty-odd guests—the great and the near-great—including General Liu's wife, Mme Sun, Mr. and Mrs. Hu Han-min, Mr. and Mrs. Liao Chung-k'ai, and General and Mrs. Hsu Ch'ung-chih. All were Dr. Sun's intimates; many I knew by reputation or had met previously.

Promptly at seven o'clock we went into the large adjoining dining room to sit down to an elaborate Chinese banquet. There were four round tables, each accommodating twelve people. Although we considered ourselves modern, the women kept to themselves and refused to mix with the men. I had no choice but to give in to their wishes.

When the sizzling-hot food was served, the lady guests of my table just sat there and stared at the food. They refused to eat, although I felt sure that in their hearts they longed to devour the tempting delicacies. But "face" had to be maintained. So I, too, had to follow suit. But when the first and second platters of food were taken away by the waiter practically untouched, and the third dish appeared, I screwed up my courage and told the guests in very much the same way as if they were children: "Our host and hostess have prepared a very lovely dinner for us, and it is ungracious of us not to appreciate it. So far, you all are too courteous and have not eaten anything. Let me help you." I then rose, took up a spoon, and dished the food out, serving each guest a portion on her plate. Then I sat down, lifted my chopsticks, and urged them to eat.

To my surprise, the ice was broken, and the guests began to eat heartily. Seeing this happy sign, I continued: "Not eating at a formal dinner such as this is an aspect of Chinese ancient custom that I feel should definitely be revolutionized. We are revolutionaries, and it is not only unfair to the host and hostess but a kind of hypocrisy handed down from the old days that regarded eating as 'ugly' and eating heartily as bad form. But today is different, so let us eat and not stand on ceremony!"

Just then Becky and her husband came to our table to urge us to make ourselves at home. They had seen me helping the guests and Becky said: "How sweet of you, Mme Chiang, to help me. Keep up the good work, but don't forget to help yourself."

The chief topic of conversation at the table was the recent friendship of China with Soviet Russia. The Russians had proffered their friendship on a silver platter to China and Dr. Sun had accepted it. And with Soviet help, the goal of the unification of China did not seem so remote. Other guests talked of how to defeat the warlords from the northern provinces, and how to establish a central government. Then some ladies turned to tell me exactly why all the previous revolutionary attempts had failed and what "iron-heeled" tyrants the warlords were— as if I did not know about it. I listened politely, however, and did not want to show that I was bored by their half-baked views.

Dr. and Mme Sun left soon after dinner, and we all adjourned to the drawing room. Kai-shek spoke to "Living Angel Liu" long and enthusiastically. Before we left he said: "I would like to invite you and your wife to take a trip to Hong Kong for two days. Would you like to go?"

"Very much, indeed," answered General Liu. "I have been wanting to go for some time but have been kept too busy to leave. Do you know many people in Hong Kong?"

"Yes, I do. My best friends are the Lees of Robinson Road.* They are our leader's friends. The father, the late Lee Po, and another merchant, named Mei Quong-tart, were the two most prominent merchants of Sydney at the turn of the century. They were exceptionally public spirited men and very patriotic. Both possessed the confidence and esteem of the entire Chinese community. When our leader was in difficulty, these two men were always ready to help financially to keep our revolution going. Mr. Lee Po has died, but his widow and several sons and two daughters have their home in Hong Kong. They are Westernized Chinese, and you will enjoy meeting them."

So, two days later, Kai-shek and I, together with our honored guests, General and Mrs. Liu Chen-huan, sailed on the eight o'clock morning steamer for Hong Kong. Kai-shek had wired his friend Mr. James (Shih-

---

*The Lee family discussed in this section is the family of James (Shih-min) and Yinson (Yin-sheng) Lee, who assisted Jennie Ch'en in writing and trying to publish this memoir. See "Introduction: The Elusive Manuscript of Chiang Kai-shek's Second Wife, Ch'en Chieh-ju." —L.E.E.

min) Lee in Hong Kong to meet our steamer and arrange hotel accommodations. Kai-shek had made the trip many times before, but never had I seen him in such a jolly mood. He was extremely grateful to General Liu, even more so than Dr. Sun, because General Liu had ousted his bitterest enemy, Ch'en Chiung-ming, from power. Furthermore, Kai-shek was anxious to get to know General Liu better and to create a good impression. That was the reason for this trip: to show General Liu that he had influential friends in Hong Kong.

Of course, General Liu was anxious to know more about Kai-shek's friends in Hong Kong, too. Westernized Chinese seemed to create a certain air of sophistication and even glamor, so they chatted away while Mrs. Liu and I sat there, simply being "good listeners."

"Lee Po," Kai-shek explained, "helped Dr. Sun substantially with finances for the revolution several times. He admired Dr. Sun and hated the powerful Protect-the-Emperor clique under K'ang Yu-wei. But Mr. Lee passed away ten years before and is survived by his widow, several sons, and two daughters. They are Overseas Chinese and all received a good English and Chinese education. The eldest son is Yinson Lee, a businessman of Shanghai, very active in welfare work and at the Baby's Clinic. The second son is Li Chor Chi (George Lee), chief secretary at the Ho Hong Bank and a leading Hong Kong singer. The third son is James Lee, who is in charge of the Cable Department of the same bank. One sister is Rose Lee, married to Y. K. Chow, the son of Sir Shouson and Lady Chow. The second sister is Alice Lee, who is engaged to C. L. Chow of Penang, Malaya. They are British subjects and prominent in Hong Kong society."

Entering the harbor of Hong Kong any time of the day is a pleasant experience. Its quiet, lakelike beauty never failed to impress me. It is most thrilling to see Victoria Peak, with its many palatial buildings built on the various upper levels. Then there are the ranges of high mountains opposite Hong Kong, in the area called Kowloon, which connect to the mainland at Shumchun. The seawater of the harbor is placid, and steamers from all parts of the world come and go incessantly. They bring all kinds of foreign products and export rattan, tea, silk, and chinaware. The city streets rise, one above the other, like terraces, and many of the homes are of palatial dimensions.

When our steamer docked at the waterfront wharf, we were met by Kai-shek's friend James Lee, who insisted that we be his house guests. He said he had two guest rooms awaiting us and would not take no for an answer. We therefore drove by car to his home on Robinson Road. There we were shown two comfortable rooms for the four of us, where we were to stay during our two-day sojourn. After we freshened up, we went into the drawing room, and in accord with custom, we paid our respects to our hostess, Mrs. Lee Po, who received us graciously and bade us welcome. She was a short, stoutish lady with a charming smile, grayish hair, and small bound feet. Kai-shek, especially, was very attentive and full of politeness to this grand old lady. He stood at her side and refused to sit down until she was comfortably seated. He asked most concernedly after her health and displayed an unusually respectful mien such as I thought belonged only to the twenty-four heroes of filial piety.

Turning to General Liu, he explained: "Mrs. Lee Po's husband is the Mr. Lee that Dr. Sun constantly praises. When he was a merchant in Sydney, he helped Dr. Sun with financial aid to carry on our revolution." Then turning to Mrs. Lee Po, he continued: "I've heard Dr. Sun praise your honorable husband many times. He called your husband a real patriot!"

After refreshments, Mr. James Lee took us for a car drive to the upper levels and then on to the peak, where we saw Hong Kong sprawled out before our very feet. It was a fascinating vista. After an hour of sightseeing, we drove on to the Repulse Bay Hotel, where we had tea on the spacious verandah. Kai-shek was greatly impressed. I was thinking of how well constructed the building was, its commanding view of the sea, the beautiful furnishings and attractive appointments, when Kai-shek suddenly exclaimed: "What I like best about this hotel is its proximity to the sea. I love to hear the sound of the waves. It charms my ears!"

"Yes," said General Liu, "this is an ideal spot. Let us stay here for a few days when we come to Hong Kong the next time."

"That's a promise," said Kai-shek happily.

After driving to Stanley Beach and other places, we returned to Robinson Road through Wanchai and then on to Queen's Road Central, which is the shopping center of Hong Kong. This busy street never failed to interest me. There were such varied crowds of people in the street: Elegant ladies and well-dressed men, soldiers of all nationalities in uniforms, students in Chinese or European clothes, and, of course, the hordes of merchants and the poorer class of men and women. It all made a colorful spectacle.

When we got back to the House of Lee, it was time for dinner. In the drawing room Kai-shek continued his filial politeness to Mrs. Lee Po. He refused to sit down until she was seated, and when she arose to give orders to the servants or crossed the room to get something, Kai-shek also stood up and was full of solicitude to help her in every way. When the sumptuous dinner was served, we sat at a round table. There were our hostess Mrs. Lee Po and her two daughters, Rose and Alice, Kai-shek and I, General and Mrs. Liu, and James Lee. The two other guests invited were Sir Shouson and Lady Chow. Sir Shouson was a grand old man who told us many jokes about Shanghai, Peking, and Tientsin. Kai-shek and General Liu were delighted with him.

After dinner, Mr. Lee played his newly acquired Victor gramophone, the very latest model, which was said to be the only one of its kind in Hong Kong. A number of records were played, but what seemed to appeal to Kai-shek most were the two records Gounod's "Ave Maria" and Schubert's "Ave Maria." These were played twice for Kai-shek's benefit. When they ended, he asked for their names and made a notation in his small calendar notebook. I myself enjoyed Rose and Alice Lee. They were charming and well read. After a while we were calling one another sisters.

The following day, Sir Shouson and Lady Chow invited us all to luncheon at their house at Excelsior Terrace, 91 Robinson Road. It was an elaborate meal. What struck Kai-shek most, however, was the terrace's name, Excelsior Terrace, which in Chinese was called "Miao Ko Terrace." He told me happily: "I shall borrow that name when I build my own house in Hsi-K'ou. Do you remember the spot I pointed out to you on the left of our village home? "Miao Ko" sounds splendid, and it aptly describes the landscape that can be viewed from Wen-Chang Kuo, my favorite spot in the whole of Chekiang."

That night after dinner, James Lee phoned his English friend, Inspector Joseph Brennan of the Central Police Station, asking him to come to the Hong Kong–Canton Steamship Company's wharf to meet us so that he could get the officer on duty to exempt all our luggage from police inspection. The red tape of searching by revenue officers was usually long and tedious. Then at 9 P.M., we said good-bye to Mrs. Lee Po and family after a very enjoyable visit. Mr. James Lee took us by car to the wharf, where he introduced us to Inspector Joseph Brennan. The inspector was very friendly and graciously accompanied us on board, giving us a royal send-off. Kai-shek was fascinated by the inverness cloak, a full-length sleeveless cape that Inspector Brennan wore. He asked me about it twice. Knowing that he liked it, I asked Mr. Lee if he would have his tailor make a replica for Kai-shek. What was needed was only the height, so I gave him Kai-shek's measurements. At 9:55 P.M. the ship's gong sounded for visitors to leave. We all thanked Mr. Lee for his kind hospitality. Kai-shek and General Liu invited him to visit us in Canton as soon as convenient.

13

Soviet Friendship

*T*o encourage China's friendship, Soviet Russia offered to restore to China the control of the Chinese Eastern Railway in Manchuria. She also promised to waive Russia's share of the Boxer indemnity, to give up all extraterritoriality rights of Russians in China, and to surrender all other special privileges that were contrary to the principle of the equality of nations.

That seemed a friendly act because after a century of incessant greedy exploitation of China by the Western Powers, including Japan, many Chinese began to overlook Bolshevik atrocities and regard Soviet Russia as the only friend despite European disgust and horror. Ever-conscious of Western aggression and exploitation, the younger Chinese generation, especially the college students, started to read as much as possible about Russia. Thus, values changed considerably. Only two years before, when Lenin sent his envoy to Peking, Bolshevik officials had seemed offensive to Chinese eyes. But now, with the change to a favorable feeling, Russia sent another Communist representative to China, by the name of Adolph Joffe, who was a very shrewd diplomat. Previously, he had come to Peking in August 1922 to represent Lenin in negotiating a fair and just treaty between Russia and China. The basis for this treaty was the manifesto issued by Leo Karakhan in 1919. Chinese officials in Peking had rather disliked the looks of this uncouth, unkempt person. The Corps Diplomatique in Peking felt disgusted at the brazen arrival of Joffe and warned Chinese authorities to be careful of involving themselves with communism.

The Western Powers had good reasons to fear the Communists. If they befriended Soviet Russia, they had nothing to gain and everything to lose. Besides, the late czar was a cousin of most of the monarchs in Europe, and he and his family had been murdered in cold blood by the Reds. But what about China? In accepting the friendship of Soviet Russia, China had nothing to lose and everything to gain.

Adolph Joffe's stay in China was welcomed cordially by the college students and the radicals. The chancellor of Peking University thanked him in public for the generous offer from Soviet Russia, which was to help the Chinese expel imperialism from China. This chancellor was a veteran member of the Kuomintang. It was obvious to Adolph Joffe where he should go to make connections.

Dr. Sun negotiated with this special Russian representative and told him about affairs in general in the Far East and the solution to these problems. All these matters were thoroughly discussed. Due to unfavorable public opinion, however, they had to conduct all their talks *in camera*.

During this period Dr. Sun, Kai-shek, and Liao Chung-k'ai exercised the greatest discretion in negotiating with Mr. Joffe. The trio successfully kept the matter to themselves until the Sun-Joffe Manifesto was publicly issued. In order to give the lie to those who said that Dr. Sun had sold his party to the Communists, the most important part of the document read as follows:

> Dr. Sun Yat-sen holds that the communistic order, or even the Soviet system, cannot actually be introduced into China because there do not exist the conditions for the successful establishment of either communism or Sovietism. This view is entirely shared by Mr. Joffe, who is further of the opinion that China's paramount and most pressing problem is to achieve national unification and to attain full national independence; and regarding this great task he assured Dr. Sun Yat-sen that China has the warmest sympathy of the Russian people and can count on the support of Russia.

The other points in this manifesto were Mr. Joffe's confirmation of Russia's offer: to relinquish all the rights and privileges obtained by czarist Russia through the unequal treaties; proposals for a conference about the return of the Chinese Eastern Railway; and the promise by Russia not to encourage secession of Outer Mongolia from China. On the other hand, Dr. Sun agreed that the Soviet army could remain in

Outer Mongolia to prevent White Russians from attacking Soviet Russia. The reason was the Peking government was unable to prevent such an attack from Chinese soil.

This arrangement was, in fact, the nucleus of the first fair and equal treaty that China had ever been offered by a foreign power. The final agreement stated that the Soviet system should be studied before it would be introduced to China as an experiment. This was designed to appease the public who feared communism.

*   *   *

I was happy when our hotel boy delivered to our suite a parcel posted from Hong Kong containing the inverness cape that Mr. James Lee had made for Kai-shek. It was of black woolen material with dark-gray silk lining and a velour collar. When Kai-shek returned from office, he was delighted to get it. He put it on over his uniform and found it to be a perfect fit. He swaggered about like a magician. I had never before seen him so enthusiastic about a piece of clothing. As a rule, he was quite indifferent to the fabric or cut of his wardrobe. But this cape was different. It appealed to him intensely. When he looked at himself in the mirror, I could see his cheeks flushed for a moment with indescribable pleasure and there was a gleaming joy in his eyes: "We must refund Shih-min for what he has spent," were his first words.

"This card says it is a gift," I told him as I showed him the card that came in the parcel.

"Then I will write him a letter to thank him for it. I shall reciprocate his kindness later."

"You do like the cloak, don't you?" I asked.

"Yes, this is something I really like, and you had it secretly ordered for me. Whenever I wear it, you will know my thoughts are of you." Kai-shek's words stirred me and were engraved on my heart. I hoped that he would always be as happy as he was that day. "Don't you like it?" he asked, noting my silence and not understanding what I was thinking.

"Certainly I like it," I said, feeling too happy for words.

*   *   *

Kai-shek and I had been in Canton for several months; we were now on the move again. Our trip was to fulfill the last phase of Dr. Sun's agreement with Russia, namely, an inspection tour. It was called Dr.

Sun Yat-sen's Mission to Soviet Russia. Its aim was said to be to pay a goodwill visit and study the political conditions and party organizations of Soviet Russia and "to regard Russia as our teacher." Kai-shek was appointed to represent Dr. Sun. We had to return to Shanghai, where an appointment was arranged for Kai-shek to meet the Russian representative, Mr. Maring, on August 5, 1923. At this meeting, they would discuss and finalize plans regarding the mission to Russia.

So we left Canton on July 28 and reached Shanghai on August 2, 1923. Mr. Maring quickly settled the matter. Kai-shek was to head a four-man mission. The other three delegates chosen were Messrs. Sheng Teng-yi, Wang Teng-yun, and Chang T'ai-lei.

Kai-shek urged me to accompany him, but I declined because I had never had any desire to go to Russia. It was just my natural feeling without any prejudice. So on August 14, 1923, the party left for the North, crossed the frontier into Siberia at the station of Manchouli. From there Kai-shek wrote me:

August 25, 1923
My Darling Wife,

 I arrived at Manchouli this noon and must say that I miss you very, very much. I am glad to see this town. There are only a thousand families inhabiting the place, roughly half of them Chinese and half Russian. Conditions are primitive. Every train is inspected thoroughly on arrival, and we will have to change trains because the coaches cannot pass through. Our group was courteously shown the actual frontier on a conducted tour. I was much surprised to find that it was only a long and narrow strip of road with no guards on duty to guard it. One could cross or recross the frontier with entire freedom. I shall write again as soon as I reach Moscow. Please do not worry about me. I am very happy and looking forward to learning much. I think of you morning, noon and night.

           Kai-shek

Kai-shek's second letter:

September 2, 1923
My Darling Wife,

 I have safely arrived in Moscow. The customs are very strict here. Our luggage was given a thorough inspection. The most surprising thing to me is the European atmosphere. Everything looks so different from Asia. Shall make a visit to Petrograd and then return here. I will visit various organizations to study them and call on a number of people who are connected with China. My great regret is that Lenin is very ill. In fact, he is in a coma and visitors are not allowed. How I wish you were here to enjoy the trip with me. Here are two snapshots. Please note I am wearing the cloak you gave me, which means I am thinking of you!

With much love,
Kai-shek

Kai-shek's third letter read:

September 12, 1923
My Dear Wife,

Enclosed are some pictures taken in Moscow. You will be glad to see me wearing the cloak, which means I love you. So far, the first important man I met in Russia is Mr. Chicherin, the people's commissar of foreign affairs. We discussed matters concerning the Kuomintang and the Communist Party. I tried very hard to impress upon him that the Chinese people were much concerned about Russian activities in Outer Mongolia. I also met and talked with Kalinin, Zinoviev, Trotsky, and other prominent leaders. Kalinin is chairman of the Soviet and seems to be an honest and sincere peasant who, when asked about important affairs outside Russia, said he did not know how to answer. What a parliamentarian for a country ruled by peasants!

I enjoyed Mr. Trotsky, whose essential qualifications for being a revolutionary are patience and activity; the lack of either will never do. Mr. Trotsky is an important man in Russia. I mentioned to him the importance of restoring Outer Mongolia to China, but he had no comment on the subject.

Here are my notes on the three reasons for the success of the Russian revolution:

1. *The workers know the necessity of the revolution.*
2. *The peasants want to have a share in the land.*
3. *The 150 different races in Russia are given the right of self-government and of joining the Soviet Union.*

Here the three drawbacks:

1. After the confiscation of factories, there are no more managers.
2. When all small factories are taken over by the state, the effect of the monopoly is too severe.
3. The distribution of profit is difficult.

Latest conditions for reconstruction:

1. Extensive compulsory education for children.
2. Military training for all workers.
3. Small factories on lease to private persons.

> More in my next letter—with love,
> Kai-shek

Kai-shek's fourth letter reads:

September 20, 1923
My Dear Wife,

Today I went to see the director-general of military training. From him I learned much about the formation of the Red Army. The political side of it is run by representatives from the Party. For a practical demonstration, I went to study the working of the Party men in the army. I found that in the 144th Regiment of Infantry of the Red Army, the commanding officer is in charge only of military matters. Political and spiritual training, and lectures on general knowledge, etc., are done entirely by the Party representatives. The duties and the authority of the officer and of the Party representative are clearly differentiated. The system works very well. I took the following notes at my meeting with the people's commissar of education:

The Tendencies of Russian Education:

1. Uniformity of educational system.
2. Increase of technical schools.
3. Getting near to real life.
4. Paying special attention to workers' schools.
5. Abolition of religion.
6. Coeducation.
7. Students administer schools.

Besides studying the Red Army, Navy, and Air Force, I also visited other places in order to gain some knowledge of social services, activities, and organizations of the Communist Party. I also participated in mass meetings, one of which had no less than 220,000 people taking part. I also attended a number of small committee meetings and discussion groups as well as official receptions and banquets followed by theatrical performances. I also examined industrial and agricultural organizations and visited several new model villages outside Moscow.

For my reading I have bought Karl Marx's Das Kapital. *I find the first half of this work very heavy-going, but the second half is both profound and entrancing.*

More news in my next letter, with much love,

Kai-shek

While Kai-shek was away in Moscow, Soviet Russia sent a new representative to Canton. Though he was not called an official envoy from Russia, his work was at least equally important, if not more so, than that of Karakhan. This man was Michael Borodin, whose original name was Grusenberg, or Berg, as he was known in the United States where he lived for a number of years. Before coming to China, he had been sent by the Third International first to Mexico, then to Scotland to promote revolutions, and last to Turkey, where he acted as adviser to Mustapha Kemal Pasha. Dr. Sun appointed him his adviser in December 1923.

Dr. Sun was now anxious to redouble his efforts to consolidate his foundations in Canton in order to expand northward. People began to realize that the so-called legal republican government in Peking was going from bad to worse. China's hope rested with Dr. Sun and his party. There was, therefore, an urgent demand to rejuvenate this party and to rebuild a strong China. It was decided to use Russia as the model. So Kai-shek's visit to Moscow was especially timely, and Russian advice and help were heartily welcomed. The policy of allowing Communists to become members of the Kuomintang was now adopted. At this time, too, Dr. Sun began delivering a series of lectures on his Three Principles of the People. Lincoln's words, "government of the people, for the people, and by the people," were borrowed and rendered into Chinese. These lectures were subsequently published in book form and used as a political program for the Kuomintang.

Kai-shek's fifth letter read:

November 20, 1923
My Dear Wife,

Today I had a very plesant surprise and two most unplesant shocks in Russia. I saw at the Ministry of Foreign Affairs three letters written by our leader, Dr. Sun, one to Lenin, one to Trotsky, and one to Chicherin. In each of them, our leader mentioned and spoke very highly of me. As for shocks, the first was on the day following my speech on the history of our Chinese Revolutionary Party on October 10, our National Day. Some Chinese students in the audience rudely criticized my speech and said I spoke of our leader as if he were a god, and my speech made it seem that I was a hero-worshipper. When I heard this, I felt very annoyed at these insolent young men who do not know the importance of respecting their own national leader. The irony is that they despise their leader although calling themselves Chinese. I got the next shock when I read the resolution about the Kuomintang's being criticized by the Third International. After I read it, I exclaimed angrily: Pooh! Look at what it says! To be so ignorant of a friendly party! With such a narrow outlook, how can it hope to be the center of world revolution?

I intend to leave Moscow on November 29 and probably reach Shanghai on or about December 15. I am counting the days until I will be with you again. I am well, so don't worry about me.

With love,
Kai-shek

Kai-shek left Moscow on November 29, 1923, and reached Shanghai on December 15. Although he greeted me most affectionately and seemed very happy, I could see that there was something that troubled him. "We leave for Hsi-k'ou tomorrow morning," he said firmly.

I was very much surprised and asked, "Don't you have to go to see Dr. Sun to give your report?"

"No, my dear, our leader can wait," he said abruptly.

I knew when to keep quiet, so there the matter rested.

That night he told me what was troubling him. He said: "Our leader has caused me to lose face. How could he accept Borodin, who was newly sent by Moscow as an adviser, while I was away in Russia? At least he should have cabled me for my advice or waited for my return to consult me. It is not ethical! Now, I'll let him wait for my report. I'll let him wait, wait, and wait."

What could I say? Kai-shek was very much upset, so I thought it prudent to keep silent. After a while I could not keep quiet, so I quoted to him an old saying: "Let us not throw away any of our days in useless resentment nor contend who shall hold out longest in stubborn malignity." This, I was glad to see, set him thinking, and it gave him food for thought. "Do you think the Russians are sincere in their professed wish to help China?" I asked.

"You cannot trust a Communist," replied Kai-shek. "But as long as we keep them under control, they will not be able to do us any harm. You see, Russia fears Japan. To counterbalance Japanese power, Russia wants to see a strong China to help her. That is one of her motives. But why should we worry as long as we utilize Russian help and turn it to our own advantage? With caution, we can accept Moscow's help!"

Each day, little by little, he drafted the report of his Russian trip but couldn't write easily because he was in a bad mood. Several days later, it was finally completed. It ran to forty pages—too long to reproduce here. I shall merely quote the most important passages:

> Regarding the question of our attitude toward the Russian Party, we must separate the practical from the theoretical. We cannot disregard the practical side simply because we want to believe it theoretically. From my observations, the Russian Party lacks sincerity. Only 30 percent of what they say can be believed. You are so enthusiastic in your belief in the Russians that I have not the heart to disappoint you by saying otherwise.
>
> Soviet Russia is willing to cooperate in the task of building a strong China by supplying, on a friendly basis, fifty military advisers, certain financial aid, and ammunitions. As a first step, a military school should be established to train a modern army. The Soviets' wish is that China will enter into a Sino-Russian alliance of mutual cooperation so that the total destruction of imperialism, colonialism, and capitalism will become a reality within the shortest possible time.
>
> Those who respect you personally are members of the Russian Communist International and are not officers of the Russian government. As for our Chinese nationals who are in Russia, they have nothing except slander and suspicion for you.
>
> The sole aim of the Russian Party is to make the Chinese Communist Party its legitimate heir. In truth, they do not believe that our

Kuomintang can cooperate with them permanently in achieving success. As regards their policy in China, I feel that they wish to make Manchuria, Mongolia, Sinkiang, and Tibet a part of their own Soviet Union. As to China Proper, they wish ultimately to Sovietize it, too.

After the report was dispatched to Dr. Sun, there was no acknowledgment at all. The reason was that communism was not at all popular in Canton. The word *Bolsheviki* inspired instant horror in China, just as it did elsewhere. Dr. Sun had to explain his view repeatedly that communism was unsuitable for China and that his own Three Principles of the People would prevail. But he needed Soviet financial aid and ammunition.

After an interminable period of nervous waiting in Hsi-k'ou, Kai-shek wrote again to Dr. Sun complaining:

> *I have spent half a year of my time, and more than 10,000 dollars, on this Russian mission. It cannot be said that I have regarded the matter lightly. But as to my report of this trip and as to what I saw and heard, you have not given it even the slightest attention. Apparently you feel that I have completely failed on the mission. Or perhaps you no longer have faith in me. In either case, I feel an intense slight and that my reputation has plunged to the ground!*
>
> *I feel, however, that my conduct in Russia was impeccable. I did nothing injurious to our party. Once, when they tried to force me to join the Communist Party, I refused by saying that I had to obtain Dr. Sun's permission first. For this I was jeered and ridiculed as being too loyal to an individual and not loyal to the State; that I was fostering an idolatrous cult by revering an individual!*

Three days later, a telegram came from Dr. Sun asking Kai-shek to go to Canton. It read as follows:

> *To My Brother Kai-shek,*
>
> *On your shoulders you have an extremely heavy responsibility from your trip. Please come immediately to Canton to make a report personally on all matters and to prepare detailed plans for cooperation with the Soviets. I wish to know what your proposals are. Whatever you suggest*

will be respected. Please persuade Brothers Chang Ching-chiang and Tai Chi-t'ao to come with you. There is important business to be discussed.

Sun Yat-Sen
December 24, 1923

✓   ✓   ✓

Because of his bad health, Joffe, the Communist envoy, had returned to Moscow the year before. Leo Karakhan was therefore sent to Peking as the representative in chief of Soviet Russia in the Far East. And Michael Borodin had been sent to serve as adviser to Dr. Sun and his government in Canton. The Kremlin wanted to get the Peking government to accept Karakhan as the Soviet envoy accredited to China. Through deft diplomacy by Wellington Koo, who was foreign minister in the Peking government at that time, Karakhan was accepted as the first Soviet ambassador to China. Arrangements were subsequently completed for returning to Chinese sovereignty the Chinese Eastern Railway, as well as terminating Soviet Russian special privileges (extraterritorial rights) in China.

The First Congress of the Kuomintang was held in January 1924, a few days after Kai-shek and I arrived in Canton. We were only onlookers and had no voice. This, I noticed, made Kai-shek feel small and unimportant. In fact, Kai-shek squirmed in his seat. The congress was attended by 165 delegates from various branches of the party all over the country, including Overseas Chinese. The meeting was called to announce, ratify, and carry out the reform of the Kuomintang. In reality it was to reactivate the party by making it a public political party rather than a secret and exclusive organization. It was also to be as democratic as possible, and members of the Chinese Communist Party would be allowed to join. It was only after this congress that the principles of the Kuomintang were made public and accessible to all who were interested. It was also on this important occasion that the resolution was adopted to organize a Kuomintang army and to establish a military academy.

But where, in the whole of Canton, could a suitable building for the academy be found? Finally, two large buildings belonging to the old Kwangtung Provincial Military School and the Kwangtung Naval School were found. The buildings, located outside of Canton on an island called Whampoa, were still in fair condition. As soon as these buildings were renovated, it would be possible to start the academy.

On January 24, 1924, Kai-shek was appointed chairman of the Preparation Committee of this academy, and the government gave him a two-room office on the East Bund. We ourselves stayed at the Asia Hotel on the West Bund.

On February 3, 1924, Kai-shek was appointed a member of the Military Council of the Headquarters of the Kuomintang.

Jennie at Ling Yin Temple in Hangzhou

Jennie with her daughter, Yiu-kwong, at the Whampoa Military Academy in 1926

CHIANG REPUDIATES WOMAN AS HIS WIFE

Does Not Know Lady Now Here From China.

SHANGHAI, Sept. 19 (A. P.).—Gen. Chiang Kai-shek, former Nationalist commander in chief, is quoted as declaring in an interview at Fenghwa on September 10 that the woman who arrived at San Francisco aboard the liner President Jackson from China early this month is not his wife.

He branded the report as "the work of political enemies" seeking to embarrass him in any way possible, adding that he does not know the "Mme. Chiang Kai-shek" mentioned in dispatches.

Chiang is quoted as stating that he divorced his legal wife in 1921, later taking two concubines, whom he "freed" this year, believing continuance of the practice of concubinage undesirable.

He asserted that at present he is entirely without a wife, but he made no mention of the report published in the United States that he intended to wed Miss Meling Soong, Wellesley College graduate and sister of Mme. Sun Yatsen, widow of the founder of the Nationalist movement.

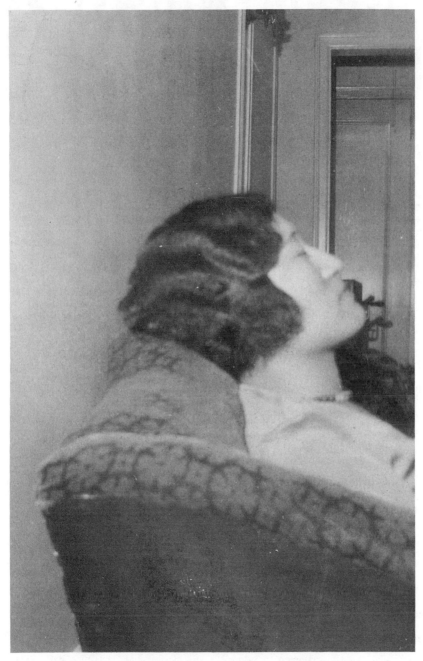

Jennie in her New York apartment, circa 1930

WHO HAS THE LOVE LETTERS CHIANG WROTE TO HER?

WHO has the love letters of the divorced second wife of Generalissimo Chiang Kai-shek?

Also, where is the dead woman's photo album — which undoubtedly contains pictures of the Generalissimo with his then wife?

These are two of the most intriguing questions being asked in Hongkong following the long-delayed funeral service yesterday of Madame Chen Lo — also known as Madame Chen Chien-ju.

Married to and divorced from Chiang Kai-shek in China in the 20s, Madame Chen died at 65 a fortnight ago — and not one of her neighbours or the friends she made in Hongkong knew her past.

Madame Chen is known to have brought treasured photographs and documents with her when she came to Hongkong from Shanghai in 1962.

Her past was well known to the Communists — and Premier Chou En-lai personally farewelled her.

It was originally believed the Communists wanted her to do United Front work in Hongkong, but it seems certain once she got to freedom in Hongkong Madame Chen did not indulge in politics and kept to herself.

Delay

Before Madame Chen left Shanghai there was some delay over the papers she wanted to take out with her.

The Communists examined them closely — but they were given back to her after being described as "trivia," and she was allowed to take them out.

The STAR's own sources report

Madame Chen got into contact with her former husband after coming to Hongkong — but by 1965 was complaining that Chiang's son by another marriage, Chiang Ching-kuo, was preventing her letters from reaching Chiang Kai-shek, and she was not getting any support from him.

It is known that in Hongkong Madame Chen gave her letters and photographs to a well-known Australian-Chinese writer who published several books.

Memoirs

He wrote her memoirs hoping to publish them in the United States — but for some reason or other they never appeared in print.

Meanwhile, the author died and the whereabouts of the memoirs he wrote is unknown.

Pictured on these pages are photographs at the cremation service held at the Cape Collinson Crematorium.

The chief mourners were Madame Chen's nephew, who lived with her before going to the US in 1965, and the dead woman's daughter and sister-in-law from Shanghai.

Both women were allowed by the Communists to come here for the funeral. They travelled via Macau and reached Hongkong at the weekend.

They are expected to return soon to Shanghai — and to take with them the ashes of Madame Chen, who wanted her remains to be returned to Shanghai.

Jennie in the late 1950s

Jennie at the Heaven Temple in Beijing in December 1961

14

The Whampoa Military Academy

On May 3, 1924, when the military academy was established, Kai-shek was appointed president. This appointment marked Kai-shek's first step in his rise to power.

The original name of the academy was the Military Cadets School. Later, however, the name was changed to the Whampoa Military Academy. Whampoa was situated at the port of Whampoa, outside Canton. It was once famous because it was here that the British and American clipper ships in the mid-nineteenth century had dropped anchor before starting their race with the first tea of the season to the American and European markets. From Canton City, Whampoa could be easily reached in forty-five minutes by motor launch. Also on the island was the Chang-Chow Fort, of which Kai-shek was now also named commander.

On may 15, 1924, Kai-shek and I moved to our home on the first floor of the military academy. It was our first permanent home since we had been married. Being an old building, newly renovated, it had only two stories, but extensive wings for lecture rooms and offices. The barracks were situated at the back.

Our own quarters were on the first floor of the main building, overlooking the courtyard leading to the main entrance. This whole flat was divided into two parts. One part, on the right side, was the large conference room. It was walled off with doors leading to our private quarters, which consisted of a living room, bedroom, and dining room. It was nicely furnished in teakwood and, on the whole, very comfortable. But for the first few days, life for me was dull and monotonous. Every morning the trumpet sounded at daylight. And I arose with Kai-shek to get him ready to go to work.

The academy itself was a citadel, and one did not want to go in and out often. This was because each time one emerged or returned through the front entrance, the guards on duty would present arms in a most formal manner. That made me feel nervous.

The conference room was large, airy, and seldom used. So I made use of it. The only furniture was a long table and twenty-four high-backed chairs. One side of the wall space was filled with the two crossed flags of the Chinese Nationalist government and the Kuomintang. On the opposite wall was hung a large map of China. Tiny green, red, and blue flags dotted its surface in a crooked vertical line, marking the course of the Northern Expedition. Some flags represented the cities, some the armies; some represented strategic positions; and some represented pitfalls and danger spots.

Kai-shek was given a free hand in running the academy, and I was in sole charge of decorating our own apartment. At first he intended to admit only about 320 students. When the examination took place, however, there were far more candidates than expected. For instance, originally it was planned to accept only 100 Cantonese students, but more than 1,200 applied. Most of them were rejected. All in all, only 500 students were accepted for the first enrollment. Because most of the candidates were educated, young, and strong, the competitive entrance examination was made rather difficult. The subjects included political science, military strategy, mathematics, general knowledge, geography, and the like.

Finances at the provincial treasury were quite low, but about 200,000 Chinese silver dollars were allocated as a start. Several organizations were called upon to contribute. For the first few months, the academy received the equivalent of about 30,000 dollars monthly, which was far from sufficient. Fifty Soviet military instructors, military equipment, guns, and ammunition were all supplied by Moscow.

Most of the academy's planning was done by Kai-shek, based on the model of Moscow's Red Army School. He made a draft of the curriculum, decided on the length of the course, set salaries for teachers and officers as well as the pay and rations for the cadets, and selected a board

Chiang Kai-shek and Jennie, probably about the time he became commandant of the Whampoa Military Academy near Canton.

of examiners. He knew exactly what he wanted and was very thorough in his planning, telling me time and again: "Once I have decided on my plans, I don't want anything changed. People are always offering suggestions and they cause confusion."

"What if some things are found unsuitable and should be changed?" I asked. "That is possible sometimes. Don't you think? "

"I am willing to make slight alterations, if things are unsuitable. But I emphasize having a fixed, basic plan. Once decided upon, it must not be altered at random. There may be some small points that require change, and those can be adjusted later. For instance, the length of time allowed for graduation is a vital point and is psychologically very important to the student. Once it is fixed at six months, it would upset our curriculum if our plans and our budget were changed to one year."

So he went ahead to assign the various members of the committee to their specific duties and said to them: "I hope you all will attend to your duties more diligently and make suggestions less. We do not want to hamper progress. While I am in Canton, I can give consideration to any of your suggestions. During my absences, you may propose and discuss changes, but they cannot be adopted unless authorized by me. Have I made myself clear?"

In consultation with the fifty military advisers from Moscow, headed by General Blücher,* the curriculum was more than full. Besides military drills, the students had to study a number of subjects such as military science and political science, in addition to lectures on the history of the Kuomintang and the Three Principles of the People. The latter were delivered by veteran members of the party. These lectures were needed because the aim of the academy was not only to train good soldiers but also to cultivate staunch supporters of the Kuomintang.

Thus the military academy brought a new image to the lives of the Cantonese. The word *cadet* sounded better than *soldier,* and many young men of well-to-do families flocked to join. The academy was an instant success.

On May 5, 1924, the first set of 500 students entered the school, and on June 24 the formal opening ceremony took place. Five hundred

---

*General Vassili Blücher, also known as General Galen, was, together with Borodin, a leader of the Russian advisers in China. —L.E.E.

guests were invited to the opening ceremony. On this important occasion, Dr. Sun addressed the cadets:

> The foundation of our Chinese Republic scarcely exists. The reason is simple: Our revolution has been carried on by the struggles of a revolutionary party, but not by a revolutionary army. Because of the lack of a revolutionary army, the republic has been mismanaged by warlords and bureaucrats. Our revolution will never succeed if this state of affairs continues. With the establishment of this school, a new hope is born. A new era for our revolution has begun. This school serves as the basis of our revolutionary army, and you students form the nucleus.

That, indeed, marked the turning point for Kai-shek and the Kuomintang. For the first time in his life, Kai-shek figured prominently in the party and in Canton political life. I felt so happy and proud of him. In his speech following Dr. Sun's, he said:

> With this new military academy we are now on the threshold of building an army to unite China. What are your duties as a soldier? You must memorize, step by step, your duties so that there is no way for you to forget them. First is discipline. Your leader's orders must be obeyed unconditionally. An army without discipline will surely fail. Secondly, whatever your individual task, you must do your utmost to complete it to the best of your ability. Do not shirk your work. Thirdly, you must regard death as glorious. It is an honor to give one's life for one's country. So, do not be afraid to die. Only cowards are afraid of death. The ancients had a saying, "One must regard death as going home." China's past history has many glorious instances of bravery on the battlefield for us to emulate. The most notable case is that of General Yüeh Fei of the Sung Dynasty. He was most brave and never feared death. That is why he is revered as China's bravest warrior. A good soldier never plans a future for himself. His future is with his army. He rises or falls with his army. So if you soldiers will all work hard and do your duty, you will be demonstrating your undying loyalty and devotion to your country.

The academy's first group of 500 cadets was the foundation stone in building a mighty army power. Because only six months were required to complete training, the academy, in a relatively short time, turned out numerous cadets ready for active service. A powerful Kuomintang army was thus assured.

To show the Communists that they were welcome, they were, beginning in January 1924, allowed to become members of the Kuomintang. But many veteran Kuomintang members strongly objected to this and began to protest. Knowing the bloody history of the Bolsheviks, they spread scathing remarks not only against the Communists but also against Kai-shek. Conditions became so bad that by July 1924, the Central Executive Committee of the Kuomintang received the first petition requesting that the behavior of certain Communist and non-Communist members be censured. The petition was signed by a few prominent veterans who were on the Executive Committee of the Canton Branch of the party. It took eighteen days for the three members of the Central Supervisory Committee, the highest supervisory body of the party, to adopt a vote of censure.

Eleven days after the vote of censure, Kai-shek made a public speech at the military academy. He praised the Russian Communist Party and its members with these words:

> Members of the Russian Communist Party are willing to work under any kind of hardship, but not so members of our Kuomintang. Russian Communists are willing to work hard for the welfare of their country and the common people, and not solely for their own private interests. We have seen how they let others have power and advantage, while they themselves do their duty, unsung and unpraised. Those who were formerly opposed to Communists joining our party now no longer do so. Not only do they support the Communist Party; now they want to join it.

He allowed those of his cadets who were Communists to form an Association of Military Youth, and those who were non-Communists to form the Sun Yat-sen Society. The primary purpose of these organizations was to discuss and exchange the revolutionary ideas of the two parties. It was also hoped that they would promote mutual understanding and goodwill.*

Because Kai-shek was a strong supporter of Dr. Sun's policy regarding the Communists, he was looked upon as Dr. Sun's most reliable

---

*In fact, these two organizations became the nuclei of destructive factionalism among the cadets. —L.E.E.

person to deal with all the anti-Communist forces in Canton. At this time, the merchants of Canton threatened to call a general strike if the financially straitened government levied any more new taxes on them. They considered themselves already overburdened with taxes. They said they had to pay taxes to the Yunnanese and Kwangsi Garrison and a dozen other departments. Besides, the businessmen and intellectuals hated communism like poison. And Dr. Sun and Kai-shek were the patrons of the Communists in China. The merchants wanted no part of it.

So, during August and September 1924, the Canton Merchants' Volunteer Corps under the leadership of the compradore of the Hong Kong Shanghai Bank, Ch'en Lien-po, planned to arm their men with 9,000 rifles, which they had ordered from abroad, purportedly to protect themselves. When Dr. Sun learned of this, he regarded it as a plot against him because the license permitting a Norwegian vessel to ship the arms into Canton had already been obtained under the name of the "Hong Kong and Shanghai Banking Corporation Compradore Department, Mr. Ch'en Lien-po." Dr. Sun asked Kai-shek to take immediate action. He did this with pleasure, for he did not like any mercenary forces, and he did not approve of any anti-Communist measures. Kai-shek therefore took quick action, ordering the seizure of the Norwegian vessel. He had the dangerous cargo unloaded and stored in the military academy.

The Merchants' Volunteer Corps protested, calling it an outrage because a license had been granted for the import of the arms. The Yunnanese commander in chief was invited to intercede, and he tried his best to negotiate for its release, but without success. Strong measures and soft means then followed alternately, but Kai-shek was unmoved. The Merchants' Volunteer Corps declared a general strike. The government responded by declaring martial law in order to ensure public safety.

While this trouble was going on in Canton, the northern government in Peking had its share of trouble. The military governor in Chekiang had started to fight against forces sent by Peking. General Chang Tso-lin, the warlord in Manchuria, was marching his army to attack the Peking government. Dr. Sun thought this a heaven-sent opportunity to join in the general uprising by starting his long-awaited Northern Expedition. So it was arranged, through the mediation of the Yunnanese commander in chief, that the Canton government would release the arms to the Merchants' Volunteer Corps on the condition that they pay a fine of a million dollars to help the government start the Northern Expedition. As the days passed, bargaining went on to and fro. The million dollars was reduced to half a million and, still later, further reduced to the amount of 300,000 Canton dollars.

But Kai-shek stood firm and would not trust the Merchants' Volunteer Corps. Then Dr. Sun received a letter from the British Consulate General in Shameen, saying that if the Chinese army fired on the Merchants' Volunteer Corps, the British navy would bombard the Chinese army. On September 9, 1924, Dr. Sun wrote an open letter that read:

> *Kwangtung is now a place of death, the causes of which are three. First is pressure of the British. If this situation continues, disorder will surely arise and the target of the British warships will be my headquarters, our gunboat, the* Yung Feng, *and the Whampoa Military Academy. Within a few score of minutes, these could easily be in ashes. We have no power whatever to resist. If we luckily avoid it this time, it may occur again any time. This is the first point. The second is a possible counteroffensive by our enemy Ch'en Chiung-ming, who is still lying low at his stronghold in the East River. If this develops, we don't know what will be the result. The third is the waywardness of so-called friendly armies in Canton from Yunnan and Kwangsi. Although they were loyal and kind in ousting Ch'en Chiung-ming for me, they will not observe discipline and are running things very much their own way.*
>
> *With these three worries, we cannot stay here a moment longer. We must discard everything to start a new way of life. Now, the best outlet is the Northern Expedition. Besides, the friendly armies of Manchuria are marching south of the Great Wall. The armies in Chekiang can maintain their own ground, and the people want to overthrow the puppet Peking government. In Wuchang and Hankow there are armies that will support us. For these reasons, we must resolve to fight forward on our long trail. We will use battlefields as the training school for the cadets; this will yield wonderful results. Comrades of our party, you must not hesitate, but heed my call!*
>
> Sun Wen
> September 9, 1924

15

Dr. Sun's
Last Journey

Dr. Sun moved his headquarters from Canton to Shiuchow, taking with him his own guards, a small air force, the Cantonese Army under Hsu Ch'ung-chih, and the army belonging to the friendly Hunanese commander, General T'an Yen-k'ai.

Hu Han-min, the conservative follower, was appointed acting generalissimo, to administer the government during Dr. Sun's absence. He constantly discussed with Kai-shek ways and means to solve the Merchants' Volunteer Corps problem.

Because Dr. Sun had taken the army and air force with him to the Shiuchow front, Kai-shek felt vulnerable on several sides. He feared that the Merchants' Volunteer Corps might retaliate by staging a raid on the military academy in order to recapture their arms, which had been seized and stored there. This was one possible threat. There were also the two armies in Canton from Yunnan and Kwangsi. They had ousted Ch'en Chiung-ming and restored Dr. Sun to Canton. They had been stationed within the city for two years. Although they were loyal to Dr. Sun, and to Dr. Sun only, they took orders from no one else. If things got out of hand, the military academy—which was a storeroom for the large quantity of Russian ammunition and for the guns seized from the Merchant Volunteers—could easily be captured, blown up, or destroyed. Thus Kai-shek was worried by thoughts of attack from these three armed groups.

Actually, Kai-shek's fears were unfounded. Nonetheless, he wrote two rather frantic letters to Dr. Sun asking him to send reinforcements to Canton, for he expected an outbreak by the Merchants' Volunteer Corps momentarily. But Dr. Sun answered Kai-shek's urgent calls with a telegram in secret code:

Dear Kai-shek,

I have received both your letters. According to my calculation, the situation is not so critical as you say. Being now in Shiuchow I have decided to break my kettle and sink my boat, concentrating on the Northern Expedition only. Since you feel there is danger in Canton, I hope you will leave Whampoa and come at once to Shiuchow with all the arms and ammunition. Also, bring the cadets. We will gamble everything on the Northern Expedition. Act immediately, as soon as this telegram reaches you. You must not be reluctant to leave. I will never go back to relieve Canton. So do decide instantly and hesitate no more.

Sun Wen
September 20, 1924

But Kai-shek refused to leave. He became bad tempered and morose. Like a caged animal, he paced the floor and cursed to high heaven.

I could stand his behavior no longer and exclaimed: "All this noise won't help. Be calm and collected. If you don't want to go to Shiuchow, don't go. It will, however, mean that you are disobeying our leader, Dr. Sun."

"I'll never give up the academy," he said with finality. In agitation he sat at his desk and began to write the following:

Your instructions received. The treacherous Merchants' Volunteer Corps is behaving more outrageously than ever. I expect danger to descend upon our academy if they start a raid. I am determined to defend this isolated island till death, so I still await your early return with your army to relieve us. We will never give up our base, without which our party will lose its foundation forever. If we hold out and show no fear, the rebels will not dare attack us. If you return, our army can launch a counteroffensive, which will proceed smoothly. With the Russian arms we now possess, we will have a good brigade of cadets within three months. With this force, we can wipe out all opposition and make Canton a safe and solid base for our revolution. I will not go even a step from here, and

I earnestly entreat you to return soon. Today is the key to our success or failure.

Chiang Kai-shek
October 1, 1924

Much to Kai-shek's relief, the belligerent attitude of the Merchants' Volunteer Corps had changed. Its head, Ch'en Lien-po, made a public statement saying he would seek peaceful means to solve their arms problem. He sent a written request asking for the cooperation of the Cantonese authorities to settle the matter at the earliest possible opportunity. In this, Kai-shek saw the corps' weakness and bided his time.

In the meantime, Dr. Sun found it necessary to change his plans regarding his Northern Expedition. Instead of "breaking his kettle" and "sinking his boat," he now found it necessary to return to Canton to discuss with his party members the latest offer from Peking, which he had just received. To understand the situation, it may be explained that the most powerful northern warlords at this time were Wu P'ei-fu, Feng Yü-hsiang, and Chang Tso-lin. The latter two were somewhat friendly to Dr. Sun. They, together with other leaders, had telegraphed him to go to Peking to attend a conference to discuss the future of China and to probe the possibility of forming a real democratic government by peaceful means. This was a golden opportunity. On October 30, 1924, therefore, Dr. Sun returned to Canton, where he held a conference with his followers in the Kuomintang.

Dr. Sun was jubilant, thinking that the unification of the nation could be attained, not with the use of force, but through peaceful discussion. The Peking agenda was to call a meeting of the Chinese National Assembly and to rally all groups—including education departments, chambers of commerce, students from the universities, and all worker groups—to protect and oppose the warlords, who were ruining the country. A demand would be made that they throw in their lot with the central government so that China might be unified in the near future.

Dr. Sun decided to leave immediately for Peking. Before his departure, he issued orders that all military affairs, including a potential Northern Expedition, be under the sole command of General T'an Yen-k'ai, while the officer administering the government would be Hu Han-min.

On November 12, 1924, a thousand of our academy cadets and officers, headed by Kai-shek, joined by me and a number of others, stood on the deck of the gunboat *Yung Feng,* which was docked at the Canton Bund, to wish bon voyage to Dr. and Mme Sun.

It was a mammoth occasion and a rather formal one. The people participating included practically all the dignitaries of Canton. These included Wang Ching-wei and his wife, Hu Han-min, General T'an Yen-k'ai, Mr. and Mrs. Liao Chung-k'ai, General Liu Chen-huan, and thousands of others. In fact all the heads of the Canton government and their retinues, accompanied by their wives, were present. And then there were groups representing the Kuomintang, the farmers, industrial workers, merchants, and students.

"How many people do you think are here?" Kai-shek asked me as we surveyed the crowd.

"A hundred thousand, I should say," I answered, at a rough guess.

"I think you have guessed rightly," Kai-shek replied. "There are at least that many and maybe more. What a day! This will go down in history," he said gloatingly.

What made the scene so colorful was the fact that all the student and worker groups held small flags of all colors and shapes. The white ones had written on them various slogans: "Down with Imperialism," "Down with Warlords," "Unite China by Peaceful Means," and "Best Wishes to our Generalissimo!"

Kai-shek and I, along with General Liu Chen-huan, Mr. and Mrs. Wang Ching-wei, Hu Han-min, and General Hsu Ch'ung-chih, stood in line with Dr. and Mme Sun. I was immensely gratified that I had this chance to participate in such a historical occasion. Then the gunboat *Yung Feng* slowly moved away from the wharf to sail down river. It was indeed thrilling to see the waving crowd and hear the shouting voices that drowned the brass band's music. We all smiled and waved back.

The gunboat headed for Whampoa and docked at the bank of the academy's parade ground. Dr. and Mme Sun and their retinue came ashore to spend the afternoon and night with us at the academy.

After a short rest and freshening up in our bedroom, Dr. and Mme Sun, Kai-shek and I made a tour of the academy. After that, I kept Mme Sun company while Kai-shek led Dr. Sun in a review of the cadets. Then a short trip was arranged for our honored guest to watch the soldiers building the defense works across the Pearl River, at the Yutsu Forts. Michael Borodin, General Liu Chen-huan, and ten others joined the group. On the way back to the academy, Dr. Sun said to Kai-shek: "I am going to Peking and am not sure when I will return. I am hoping, however, that the unification of our country will now become a reality. I am pleased to see the fine spirit of the academy. I know it will carry on my revolutionary task. Even if I should die, my spirit will be at rest."

Michael Borodin said to Dr. Sun: "I have just received a telegram from Moscow, Sir. Our government is pleased to invite you to visit Russia after your trip to Peking."

"I am unsure how long I will stay in Peking," answered Dr. Sun. "Will you please extend my thanks to your government and say that we shall discuss this matter again after I have arrived in Peking?"

Back at the academy, Dr. Sun convened a meeting in our conference room. There, the most important business fell on the shoulders of "Living Angel Liu." Dr. Sun told him: "I will remind you once again. You will leave for Yunnan tomorrow as instructed and request Governor T'ang Chi-yao to send me a wire swearing his allegiance to me and to Canton. This telegram is of the utmost importance because it will give me the prestige I need when I go to Peking. With T'ang Chi-yao's telegram in hand, I will be able to prove to the northern warlords that I have the firm backing of three provinces—Yunnan as well as Kwangtung and Kwangsi. This will greatly enhance my bargaining power at the National Assembly."

"I will carry out your wish, my leader," answered General Liu Chen-huan respectfully. "Governor T'ang owes me a debt of gratitude since I once saved his life, so I feel very sure he will not refuse this request when I ask him."

"Good," smiled Dr. Sun. "I'll not forget your loyalty. You risked your life to oust Ch'en Chiung-ming from Canton and now you are helping me to build up my prestige." He extended his hand in deep gratitude and both men shook hands cordially.

Hu Han-min and Michael Borodin listened intently, but a dark cloud passed over their faces. It seemed that they were displeased over General Liu's "thunder" because his mission to Yunnan served as a feather in his cap.

On the following morning, Dr. and Mme Sun departed for Hong Kong and arrived that afternoon. There they boarded the Japanese SS *Chun Yang Maru*, bound for Shanghai. Accompanying them were Wang Ching-wei and others. Kai-shek and I remained in Canton.

The SS *Chun Yang Maru* left that evening, and the trip was smooth and pleasant. That evening Dr. and Mme Sun appeared in the dining room for dinner. The next day, however, the sea became choppy and a strong wind made the ship roll. Dr. Sun became very seasick and stayed in bed. On the morning of the seventeenth the ship arrived at Woosung, near Shanghai, where Dr. Sun was met on arrival by the Christian general, Feng Yü-hsiang, and many others. The strain of the trip, however, had exhausted him.

Arriving at his home on Rue Moliere, in the French Concession in Shanghai, Dr. Sun felt ill. The seasickness had aggravated his old liver ailment. On the eighteenth he called a meeting of members of the Shanghai Kuomintang to discuss the latest offer from Peking.

From Shanghai, Dr. and Mrs. Sun sailed on the SS *Shanghai Maru* for Tientsin via Japan. He arrived in Tientsin at daybreak on December 4 and immediately went on to Peking. On his arrival in the ancient capital, the weather was extremely cold. And because he made many speeches on the themes of "Down with Imperialism," "Unite China," and "Oust the Warlords," he now felt quite sick. On December 6, he could hardly talk, and the following day he was confined to bed and advised to rest.

16

Chiang
Moves Ahead

*I*n the meantime in Canton, Hu Han-min, acting on behalf of Dr. Sun, negotiated a compromise with the Merchants' Volunteer Corps. Because 200,000 dollars had been given as a loan, Hu Han-min issued an order to Kai-shek for the release of the impounded arms. Reluctantly, Kai-shek obeyed. But when the arms were handed over, a quarrel between the government soldiers and the volunteers broke out. A free-for-all ensued in which several soldiers were shot and killed. The next day, Kai-shek formed a Revolutionary Committee. And on December 13, 1924, Kai-shek, in his capacity as head of the Training Department in the Headquarters of the Cantonese Army, launched an attack on the Merchants' Volunteer Corps. After two days of street fighting, the corps capitulated and was subsequently disarmed and disbanded. This marked Kai-shek's first decisive victory over enemy forces, as well as over internal opposition.

Overwork and worry are not usually associated with leaders. And so it was most surprising when Kai-shek suddenly became stricken with a severe nosebleed. The blood flowed profusely and I was terrified. Nothing I did could stop the bleeding. I made him lie flat on his back and applied a number of ice-cold, damp towels, but without effect. What made it especially difficult was that he refused to keep still. I called the academy's physician who came rushing upstairs to administer first aid. But he too, was powerless to staunch the oozing blood.

My first thought was to get Kai-shek to a hospital as soon as possible. I called an ambulance despite Kai-shek's repeated protests—protests that were sharp and cutting—but I ignored him. "I won't go to a hospital," he yelled. "I've got too much work to do!"

In many ways, I am soft and yielding, but in this case I refused to listen and was determined to have my way. In the hospital, the doctor said I had done the right thing because the case was very serious. He called it epitasis, which was caused by a small growth. After an hour of medication, the bleeding had stopped somewhat but not entirely. Kai-shek was very weak from the loss of so much blood, and his face was drawn and horribly pale. It frightened me greatly.

The doctor gave strict orders for the patient to remain motionless and quiet. After a short rest, however, seeing that the bleeding had stopped, Kai-shek wanted to go home. He was a very naughty patient and refused to listen to orders. He talked incessantly and moved about, and the blood began to flow again. But the nurse, following the doctor's instructions, was able to check the flow.

In the late afternoon, when the doctor came again, he advised me to talk more to Kai-shek in order to prevent him from talking. But this was easier said than done. I talked to him, telephoned various people on his behalf, wrote letters for him and did a hundred and one things that would help, but at best it was difficult. I was soon exhausted from trying to get him to stay quiet.

In the evening, seeing that Kai-shek was feeling better and that the bleeding had entirely stopped, I got ready to leave for home, intending to return early the next morning. But Kai-shek would not hear of it. "You must stay here to keep me company," he insisted. The nurse said she would arrange permission for me to remain there, so later she brought in a canvas bed for me to sleep on.

Early the next monring, the doctor came and gave Kai-shek more medication. But he was restless and refused to lie still. He was only allowed to drink fresh orange juice, and at each meal he insisted that I feed him personally with a straw. He behaved just like a cantankerous baby. The nurses felt insulted when Kai-shek refused to let them help him. He insisted that I should do everything. He would only drink the orange juice when he felt in the mood to do so. And my job was made doubly hard by having to humor him and cater to his every whim.

He remained in the hospital three days, until the small incision inside his nose had somewhat healed. I was glad to get home to attend to my many household duties. And of course, Kai-shek, too, was relieved to get back to the academy so that he could catch up on a large pile of accumulated work.

′ ′ ′

Kai-shek had, in fact, a triple job. First, he was still military adviser and strategist for General Hsu Ch'ung-chih's army; he was also the head of the Training Department of the Cantonese Army; and, of course, his main job was at the Whampoa Military Academy, where he was paid to train more and more cadets.

Two of Kai-shek's favorites among the students were Teng Yen-ta and Hsu Ch'ien, who were very serious, studious, and energetic young men. It was Kai-shek's secret wish to train these young men to becme his protégés. He therefore entrusted them daily with many errands, and they became frequent callers at our flat. They proved to be the handymen around the place, and both Kai-shek and I regarded them as close friends.

Although Kai-shek had many subordinate officers to assist him, his duties took a heavy toll of his time and energy. When I advised him to slow down, he told me time and again: "If I control the army, I will have the power to control the country. It is my road to leadership. Please, please, please, don't ask me to stop working."

At this point I may say something about Kai-shek's character. As a military leader, he was a very exacting commander. For instance, many a time when he and I were passing by the parade grounds to the jetty to take our motor launch to go into Canton City, he would suddenly stop to call a soldier and question why his tunic was unbuttoned at the neck or why his boots were unlaced. When the reply was unsatisfactory, he would shout for a corporal and, in a verbal blast, order the culprit to be reprimanded or even placed in the brig. Often he would shout, "Stand at attention when talking to your superior officer!" I remember another instance when a cadet stood at the rostrum of a memorial meeting to give a patriotic reading before an audience of 3,000 people. He had memorized the speech, but in the middle of it forgot a line. So, taking a soiled sheet of paper from his trousers pocket, he unfolded it and began to read.

"Stop!" shouted Kai-shek who sat on the rostrum. "You should know better than to put a folded paper in your trouser pocket where it would get crumbled! It should be placed in your shirt pocket! Remem-

ber that, you blockhead!" The audience sat agog and exchanged glances
with one another. Meanwhile the orator turned red for having been so
publicly ridiculed.

Perhaps the greatest of all Kai-shek's idiosyncrasies was his ego. He
was sensitive to criticism and quick to anger. He seldom praised anyone, and he regarded his military colleagues, even the well-known "ge-
niuses," as being very ordinary. In his intense desire to be first in everything, he inclined to be pompous. And he only cultivated those
friendships that might be useful to him in furthering his aims. Once
that usefulness was outlived, however, most of the friendships, regardless of how close they had been, died a natural death as a result of Kai-
shek's aloofness.

Owing to this attitude, he made enemies overnight. The number of
our intimate friends could easily be counted on one hand. With the exception of Dr. Sun, he had four best friends: old Chang Ching-chiang,
who was his mentor and financier; General Hsu Ch'ung-chih, who was
his boss; Liao Chung-k'ai, who was the finance minister; and, finally,
the scholar Tai Chi-t'ao. I had a difficult time keeping up with which
friend he still favored and which he did not. For instance, he suddenly
regarded "Living Angel Liu" as an enemy, for no apparent reason.

✓   ✓   ✓

During this period, Kai-shek was steadily becoming more prominent. But to carry out any project or make any changes, he had to obtain
the approval of his seniors in the party, who acted something like a
privy council. At this time, there were three ministers. The commander in chief of the Cantonese Army, Hsu Ch'ung-chih, also served
as minister of war. The minister of finance was Liao Chung-k'ai. The
minister of foreign affairs was C. C. Wu, son of veteran diplomat Wu
T'ing-fang.

But there were many departments and bureaus where Communists
served as heads. T'an P'ing-shan, who represented the Communists on
the Revolutionary Council, was also head of the Organization Department. The Propaganda Department was headed by Mao Tse-tung. Four
other departments, Labor, Peasants, Youth, and Women, were also
headed by Communists. On the whole, Communist power within the
Kuomintang at this time was said to be at a ratio of six Kuomintang
members to one Communist.

To familiarize himself with all the department heads, and ever anxious to effect reforms in the government, Kai-shek made it a habit to go to see these people at least three times a week. The members of the council listened to him patiently and usually gave their approval to most of his requests. On the other hand, toward his subordinates, he regularly encouraged the cadets and personally pinned stripes on many of them and gave them pep talks. In addition, he made many public appearances and told his officers, "We are a large family and must follow the Three Principles of the People."

It goes without saying that the academy exerted a powerful influence over the political life of South China. At the beginning, however, Kai-shek tried to be unobtrusive and was willing to take a back seat. Constitutionally, he had the power to advise his seniors, but most of the leaders were jealous of one another. I often thought that the situation was similar to the period of Julius Caesar. Next to Caesar there were Octavius Caesar, Marcus Antonius, Lepidus, Brutus, Cassius, and others. Now, next to Dr. Sun, there were, by seniority:

1. Wang Ching-wei
2. Hu Han-min
3. Hsu Ch'ung-chih
4. Liao Chung-k'ai
5. Liu Chen-huan
6. Wu Chih-hui
7. Chiang Kai-shek

All these men were distinguished but differed greatly from one another. In supporting Dr. Sun in the revolutionary movement, each of them was known for his ardent revolutionary spirit and contributions to the revolutionary cause. These, it may be said, were Dr. Sun's true revolutionary heirs. They were heirs by dint of their seniority and importance in the party. They had been willing to take government office only at the times when Dr. Sun was in power. As a result of their merits, background, and experience, they were given the title of party leaders. Kai-shek, in his capacity as head of the military academy, ranked number seven among the party leaders. He stood at the bottom of the ladder.

Kai-shek conceived it to be his duty to be well informed on all Kuomintang affairs. This soon imbued him with the authority of an expert whenever he intervened, as he often did, in matters of policy. This, of course, provoked much jealousy among the other party leaders, who considered him merely a newcomer and a junior member of the party leadership. Kai-shek fully comprehended this. Nonetheless, he regarded himself as Dr. Sun's true and only heir, standing above faction, party, or class.

By nature, Kai-shek was aggressive, stubborn, sensitive, headstrong, and quick tempered. The least frustration angered him, and he did not care who saw it. I often advised him to overcome this weakness. Knowing it to be a part of his nature, however, I realized he could not help it.

Because he had his entire head shaved, he was given the sobriquet "Chiang the Bald." This hair style was common among northern Chinese soldiers, but not in the Cantonese Army.

While Dr. Sun was in the North, the Communists' influence began to spread all over Canton, not just within the military academy, but also in trade unions, student groups, workers' guilds, and farmers' associations. Lenin's photo was enshrined everywhere. Thus entrenched, the Communists stepped up their efforts to create dissension within the Kuomintang and among cadets in the academy. The purpose was to enlarge their powers and eventually seize control of these organizations.

In watching Kai-shek deal with his military affairs, I was impressed most by his persistence. Although fully occupied with the work of the academy and his other political activities, he took time out to think of ways and means to annihilate General Ch'en Chiung-ming. The mere thought that his old enemy basked in comfort in his stronghold in Waichow, less than ninety miles away, made Kai-shek's blood boil. He was anxious to wipe Ch'en off the face of the earth, come what may. His bitterness seemed to have no bounds, and I often watched him, sitting in deep thought, trying to figure out the best way to achieve this end.

One day he gave me a fright when he suddenly jumped up from his chair and exclaimed at the top of his voice: "I've got it! My slogan will be 'To unite China, first unite Kwangtung!' I'll pulverize that traitor!" And from that time on, the military academy propagandized this slogan. Soon everyone spoke of Ch'en Chiung-ming as a treacherous man.

In fighting his enemy, Kai-shek was shrewd enough to realize he faced a formidable foe. Ch'en had 30,000 well-equipped soldiers. In fact, when he had fled Canton, he took with him the bulk of his army, which was still almost intact. That is why Waichow became known as an arsenal. But in attacking Ch'en, Kai-shek planned his strategy carefully.

Being a promoter of good relations with the Soviets, and an ardent supporter of Dr. Sun's policy of cooperation with the Soviet Union, Kai-shek actually wore a red tie daily. He knew the Communists' ammunition he had in the academy would help him exterminate Ch'en Chiungming. He therefore regarded help from communism as the only salvation for China—on the condition, of course, that he be the leader, second only to Dr. Sun.

More Chinese Communists were consequently allowed to join the Kuomintang. Actually, at this time, there were only a very few Communist members. One Communist whom Kai-shek recommended was Chou En-lai, who was appointed a military judge in Kai-shek's army. This was because Chou En-lai was able to write a good petition, and such work was well rewarded. In the modern sense of the word, there was no authorized class of lawyers in China, just as there were no trained physicians. All authorized ones were Westernized. Chou En-lai was very progressive and had a quick wit and a measure of scholarship.

In spite of repeated opposition by various influential people in the party and the government, the fifty Russian Communist advisers took over the vital work of serving as instructors in the academy. This was because the Whampoa Military Academy was modeled after the Red Army School. These fifty Russian officers did their best to Sovietize the Chinese cadets.

In the government, however, there was a group of die-hard conservatives—intellectuals who, from the very first, had hated the Communists worse than poison. They knew, however, that an uprising might result in the overthrow of the Canton regime. Those who merely wanted to get rid of the Communists, therefore, thought it advisable to keep quiet for the present. They hoped that the government would eventually realize its errant policy.

Kai-shek played an important part in handling this difficult situation. Since he was a supporter of the policy of collaboration with the Communists, he regarded those who were anti-Communists as his chief enemies. They were eyesores. In a way, however, the anti-Communist sentiment suited his purposes well because the most enterprising and energetic elements in the party at this time were the academy graduates and the Communists and pro-Communists. They had all flocked together under him, and he had the pick of the best of them.

The cadets started as a Training Corps. Besides ordinary officers, such as corporals, lieutenants, captains, and majors, there was in each unit a party representative. In larger units, there were Political Departments, each with a head and a small staff. These party officials looked after the welfare of the soldiers and imparted to them political knowledge. They were also trained how to use their wits and how to act in the event that the commanding officer was killed in battle. In other words, they were taught initiative.

In the beginning, quite a few posts in Kai-shek's army were filled by Kuomintang members who were also Communists. The reason was, simply, that their political knowledge was, on the average, greater than most others. And it was necessary for them to know a little about international affairs. The system seemed to work very smoothly this way. Chou En-lai, who was now serving as a military judge, was recommended by Kai-shek to be head of the Political Department attached to the First Army, which was Kai-shek's original revolutionary army. Chou and Kai-shek became good friends.

When the first 2,000 cadets graduated from the academy, Kai-shek decided it was a good time to have a showdown with Ch'en Chiungming. Until this time, he had commanded no troops of his own. But now that he had his own troops, he thought it best to strike as early as possible with his 2,000 cadets.

As a military expert, Kai-shek fully knew that Waichow was a tough nut to crack. He planned and organized and burned the midnight oil, trying to solve the immense difficulties. He quickly whipped his newly trained cadets into shape and made elaborate preparations for the attack. Flying Swallow Hill, at Waichow, was something like a miniature Gibraltar. Experts had declared that any aggressor that presumed to attack Waichow would only meet with death and defeat. Kai-shek set about to solve the problem of attacking this fortress.

On February 1, 1925, as Dr. Sun lay ill in the Peking hospital, Kai-shek led two regiments, consisting of about 3,000 men, to storm his enemy's stronghold. His slogan was to unite China, first unite Kwantung!

General Hsu Ch'ung-chih, commander of the Cantonese Army, was named commander of the campaign. But because this was Kai-shek's own battle, only a part of General Hsu's army joined the expedition. Two thousand cadets had to bear the brunt of the fighting.

On February 15, 1925, a decisive battle was fought in the strategic town of Tamshui, about twenty miles south of Waichow. This was

Ch'en Chiung-ming's first line of defense. The battle lasted for a day and a night until Kai-shek's two regiments of cadets stormed and occupied the city. The next day Kai-shek, who was directing the campaign, gave a pep talk to his officers and men: "The defeat of the enemy at Tamshui was due to your brave attack. With but 2,000 revolutionary cadets we have defeated 6,000 soldiers of the enemy. We have taken prisoner more than 2,000 officers and men. We have captured more than 1,000 rifles. I have telegraphed this report to our leader Dr. Sun in Peking, who will certainly be cheered by the news.

"With loyalty and courage, you officers and men have shown discipline and bravery. You have astonished everyone. Because you have received only a short period of training, this achievement proves again that our party's doctrine is inspiring and great. Now that the enemy's strength has been reduced by half, it will be but a matter of days until the East River will be cleared of them. I congratulate you on your bravery!"

By mid-March 1925, the stronghold of Waichow was attacked. A fierce battle was fought in which over 1,000 cadets and 2,000 infantry routed more than 10,000 of the enemy. But the price of this victory was heavy.

Waichow was General Ch'en Chiung-ming's nearly impregnable bastion. He had protected the outer city walls with four different types of barricades. First, there were rows of barbed-wire loops; then a wide floor of thick wooden boards that were densely covered with three-inch protruding nails; then there were wooden-block "horses," with more coils of barbed wire; and, finally, the wall itself was defended by an electrically charged steel netting, fifteen feet high.

When a unit of soldiers attempted to dismantle the barbed-wire loops, a fusillade of shots rained down from the top of the city wall, mowing down the attacking cadets. Unit after unit followed, and finally a part of the loops collapsed. Then the order was given to cross the wooden floor of sharp nails, which was thirty feet across. The cadets charged forward. This ordeal of nail walking took a heavy toll because the infantry wore only cheap, thin leather boots. As the soldiers pushed forward, their soles got stuck on the nails. And unable to extricate themselves, they became easy targets. As the soldiers fell, other cadets and soldiers advanced over the pile of dead bodies to reach the third barrier. Then another wave of cadets came with loads of dried straw to set fire to the electrically charged wire netting. As the fire burned fiercely, more and more soldiers advanced with straw, while bullets and bombs showered down upon them from above. With the netting finally down, many places in the city wall were blasted with dynamite. As Waichow was thus tottering to its fall, Ch'en Chiung-ming and his generals took flight on their gunboats, which had been anchored in Waichow Bay.

The victory at Waichow cost the lives of 3,000 young men. Kai-shek thought it worthwhile, however, for his bitterest foe had been defeated. He occupied the city, did the necessary mopping up, and reorganized the army that had surrendered. After a month, seeing that his work was completed, he was anxious to get back to Whampoa and other business. He handed over the administration of the newly captured city to his boss and mentor, General Hsu Ch'ung-chih. Before departing, Kai-shek delivered a victory speech saying, in part: "In this battle, more than 3,000 men fell in battle, or were totally disabled. Of the cadets of the first unit that came with me, and of those cadets who followed later, more than half are now dead. When I think of this, my heart aches. But victory today is ours."

∕　∕　∕

Waichow, even at its best, was but a small, old town, untouched by modernity or the excitement of nightlife. Despite the fact that General Hsu Ch'ung-chih had the prestige of being the town head, lived in the most aristocratic house, which was adorned with red-lacquered columns and a green-tiled curved roof, and was served by numerous servants, he soon became bored with this country life. He longed for the lights of the city, where life was glittering and amusing. He thought of the tinkling music of the singsong girls, the speed of motor cars, the merry night spots, and his witty friends. No, Waichow was not for him. So, after a month of this Spartan life, he decided to return to Canton. He named his friend, Lieutenant General Hoong Lok, to represent him, handing over to him the seal of office of the Waichow territory.

General Hsu did this without consulting anyone. For, in fact, General Hoong Lok, the new town leader, had a link with Ch'en Chiung-ming—being a cousin of Ch'en Chiung-ming's right-hand man, General Hoong Chew-lun. As a result, within forty-eight hours after General Hsu left for Canton, Hoong Lok threw open the city gates of Waichow to Ch'en Chiung-ming and his hordes. Thus Waichow had, once more, come under Ch'en Chiung-ming's control. And the town's defenses were soon repaired and refortified.

When news of this reached Kai-shek in Canton, he became almost hysterical. He shook with fury. His face was white as he paced the floor, clenching his hands and swinging them upward, cursing to high heaven, using a string of swear words that I had never thought possible. What could I do? What could anyone do? Even as a wife, it was not tactful to say anything. So I sat in silence and let him unburden his mind to his heart's content. But it was painful to see him so unhappy. When night came, he sat at his desk with his head bowed between his hands, as though in deep meditation. The whole night he sat thus and refused to go to sleep.

Because General Hsu was Kai-shek's good friend and boss, he was in a dilemma regarding how to punish the offender. Kai-shek felt strongly that Hsu must be punished for a crime that had resulted in the loss of more than 3,000 lives. Yet these young lives had been thrown away for merely a whim. If a court-martial took place, Hsu would have to be shot. But after much thought, Kai-shek decided that he must make the best of a bad bargain.

Naturally, an unpleasant tension existed between the two men when they again met. But Kai-shek was calm when he spoke: "What happened is unfortunate. It means that a large number of my cadets and soldiers have died in vain. However, I will lead another expedition to recapture the city. For me to accomplish this, however, you must furnish me with some of your troops."

"Certainly! I'll be glad to arrange that," Hsu replied, now most eager to please Kai-shek.

"But the discipline of your whole Cantonese Army, from top to bottom, is deplorable," said Kai-shek haughtily.

"What do you suggest be done?"

"Let me reorganize your army for you. Will you grant me permission to do that?"

"I will agree to whatever you suggest," said the contrite Hsu.

"To make a success of it, however, I must have a period of one year and a free hand to do a thorough job."

"What do you mean?" ask Hsu Ch'ung-chih in perplexity.

"I cannot reorganize your army while you are here in Canton. That you can well understand. It will take me a year to do a good job, and you during that period must go to Shanghai for a holiday. When your army is fully reorganized, I will invite you to come back and resume command."

"Marvellous," exclaimed General Hsu, who thought of the good times ahead of him. He would splurge and for a whole year paint Shanghai red!

The change of command being agreed upon, then, a meeting was held the following week for the transfer. All the commanders and lesser officers of the Cantonese Army were present when its commander in chief, General Hsu, announced: "Beginning today, General Chiang Kai-shek of the Whampoa Military Academy will serve as commander in chief of our Cantonese Army for one year in order to reorganize the army. I empower him to be your new boss. Henceforth, you are to take orders directly from him." So saying, he handed to Kai-shek the jade seal of office of the commander of the Cantonese Army, an army that numbered ten regiments, or 100,000 men.

Everything ran smoothly the first day. But two officers, Lieutenant General Liang Hung-k'ai and Major General Yang Kam-lung, refused to take orders from their new commander in chief. In fact, they ignored Kai-shek. Lieutenant General Liang Hung-k'ai accused Kai-shek of sanctimoniousness, cajolery, and cunning, while Major General Yang Kam-lung told his former commander, Hsu Ch'ung-chih: "You have fallen into a trap! You may as well say good bye to the army, for it will not be returned to you even after thirty years! Remember Kingchow? That territory was borrowed but never returned."

Kai-shek, who is a stickler for discipline, regarded these two men as "mutineers," but he allowed the incident to pass. Then, two days later, in the name of the Whampoa Military Academy, these two generals, Liang and Yang, were invited to a banquet at a private dining room in the Tai San Yuen Restaurant on the busy Canton Bund. Thinking that a compromise was in the offing, the two generals readily accepted the invitation. Being one of the better restaurants in the city, the place was crowded that night. As wine flowed, glasses clinked, and toasts were drunk, in marched a batch of soldiers led by an officer holding a warrant for the arrest of the two recalcitrant generals. They were driven to the Eastern Parade Grounds and shot without benefit of a court-martial.

Now as the commander in chief of the Cantonese Army, Kai-shek's powers were greatly enhanced, and I could clearly discern a sudden change in his temperament. His important post gave him a new psychological outlook, and he basked in his infallibility as a budding leader. Dissatisfied with existing conditions, he issued imperious commands for new changes, even far beyond his own domain. He became a kind of self-appointed dictator.

As mentioned before, there were in Canton, besides the Cantonese Army, the Yunnanese Army, under General Yang Hsi-min, and the Kwangsi Army, under General "Living Angel Liu" Chen-huan, who had originally restored Dr. Sun to Canton. In order to carry out an expedition to recapture Waichow and be assured of a quick victory, Kai-shek thought he could make use of these two friendly armies, which were garrisoned in Canton. The heads of these armies were invited to participate in the campaign to oust Ch'en Chiung-ming from Waichow. But the two generals said nothing. Silence meant, Nothing doing. Seeing this, Kai-shek suddenly felt that these men were thorns in his side. He issued an open report to his Cantonese Army with these words:

> It is now almost two years since Canton was restored to us. We have in Canton today no fewer than 100,000 friendly soldiers under Generals Liu and Yang. But the traitor Ch'en Chiung-ming remains in Waichow, basking in comfort. The people of Kwangtung are suffering more and more. Is this because our friendly forces in the city are too tired or too weak that we cannot wipe out a small army of 30,000 rebels with our 100,000 men? No! It is really because suspicion and jealousy are rife among ourselves, and there is no coordination among us. When a force is not united even in spirit, not only can it never defeat an enemy, but there is even a possibility of its being defeated by the enemy!"

Kai-shek's message went unheeded. The refusal of the two commanders to cooperate engendered in Kai-shek's breast a profound hatred for them. He regarded them as his new enemies who were eating off the fat of the land. If they were removed, once and for all, Canton would come under his sole control and direction. It therefore became Kai-shek's obsession to plan their downfall. But he bided his time.

17

Life at
the Academy

At the academy, Kai-shek's daily routine began at 5 A.M. , when he rose from bed. At 6 A.M. he watched his men at drill. At 7 A.M. he came home to eat with me a plain breakfast of rice, vegetables, and fish. Meat was served only in small quantities. At 8 A.M. he went downstairs to his office on the ground floor, where military officers or important Canton officials came to discuss business. Interviews were strictly scheduled to last only twenty to thirty minutes. Intimate friends came to our private rooms on the first floor. Since he was now much occupied, I took charge of Kai-shek's mail and from it made a memorandum with details about the purpose of visitors before each interview or what replies were to be given to questions asked. Each morning I gave the list to our boy Ah Shun to place on Kai-shek's desk. From 11 A.M. to 1 P.M. he gave lectures or made announcements to the cadets.

Hu Han-min and Liao Chung-k'ai came to the academy at least once each week. Kai-shek had a high regard for these two important officials, although he complained to me privately that they never once let their hair down when they were with him. They always kept him at arm's length and were always most ceremonious on all occasions. Try as he might, he could not get close to them.

Despite his position as head of the Whampoa Military Academy, Kai-shek's salary was only $1,500 per month, which was hardly enough for expenses. Only $50 monthly went to Mao Fu-mei, and it was through my efforts that monthly remittances were kept up and sent to her to augment her income for subsistence.

Being the head of the academy, Kai-shek could always get credit from most shops. Although there was always a shortage of cash, we did not, therefore, experience many difficulties in our houschold. In fact, through thrift over a period of months, I could save a little cash for a rainy day.

Under pressure of work, Kai-shek would now and again revert to his old type of bad temper. A common Chinese proverb says, Kingdoms may change, but tempers remain, which is very true to life. I now found married life rather difficult. When things did not go smoothly in his dealings with the military, Kai-shek would return home sullen and grouchy. At times, he would fly off the handle. This was especially diffi-cult for me because if I knew what was going on in his mind, I could look out for it and be on guard. Irritating things would be allowed to pass without a single word of complaint, but then, all of a sudden, a molehill would suddenly be made into a mountain. Life became a series of tantrums and shoutings. To give in repeatedly was eternal submis-sion. For the sake of peace in the family, however, I meekly endured his outbursts as best I could.

Kai-shek finished work at 6 P.M. We spent most evenings quietly. I continued my studies of the Chinese classics or browsed through story-books or current magazines, while Kai-shek practiced calligraphy on old newspapers. He would fill ten sheets of old newspapers with charac-ters before he would put his brush down. He did this as consistently as he could, and I could plainly see the great improvement he had made in the past months. One evening while watching him practice, I pointed to his paper and remarked, "That written character has strength, but that one is too weak; you must put more of the 'iron stroke and silver hook' into it."

My words tickled his fancy, and he burst out laughing. Then he asked, "Do you think my calligraphy is good enough for the academy's slogan?"

"Write and let me see it," I answered, and he unrolled some sheets of white paper and wrote the four characters that I had seen him practice for the last few weeks. They read: "School slogan: Affection with Sin-cerity!" and then he signed his name at the side.

I told him truthfully that I did not like it, and he agreed that it was not to his satisfaction either, so he wrote another and yet another until the seventh one pleased us both. This was later mounted on silk, framed, and hung on the academy's office wall.

Although the humidity was oppressive with the heat of summer, I kept all the windows of my rooms wide open. I preferred to work each day in the conference room, which was not often used. From there, a large part of the cement driveway directly below could be clearly seen. The sentries on duty as usual presented arms to all the officers who passed in and out of the main gate. I often wondered why they had to do it. It seemed so unnecessary, but it was regulation, so the shouting and salutes went on and on.

The long table in the conference room was usually piled high with papers, and each day I helped Kai-shek put them in order before filing. Since he had many positions besides that at the academy, he shifted the major part of his paperwork onto my shoulders. I was glad to be of some help because it increased my knowledge of Canton affairs. In other words, I had become Kai-shek's filing clerk and private secretary.

Acting as Kai-shek's private secretary, I had to be very careful about one thing, for he considered a part of his correspondence *secret*. He kept it unknown to the general staff and even the officers. To such proportions did the correspondence reach that I found it difficult to cope with, for there were also my normal chores to carry out, and these had increased very considerably.

For instance, amid a pile of letters for Kai-shek were several marked "Secret" in bold letters on the left-hand corner of the envelope. Most envelopes were very large, this being a characteristic of officialdom. One secret letter would read: "It is reported that General Wu P'ei-fu of Hupei has recently remitted a sum of 10,000 dollars to Yunnan General Yang Hsi-min as tea money through the Central Bank. This may be regarded as an attempt by the remitter to buy General Yang's support. Please treat this as secret."

Another letter read: "Wang Ching-wei and Hu Han-min held a meeting yesterday afternoon to discuss ways and means to restrain you from your aggressive interference in Kuomintang affairs. They claim that you are not even one of the twenty-five founding members and have no right to make drastic demands."

Yet another letter read: "Your rapid rise is being watched with enmity, especially by some members of the Cantonese Naval Headquarters." These messages startled me, and I had to inform Kai-shek at once to come upstairs to our flat to read them.

"Because these letters are marked secret," said Kai-shek, "you will have to make a record of them in a special book that I will give you. A number should be given each letter before placing them in a file marked 'Secret.' This is kept upstairs under lock and key."

These letters caused Kai-shek deep thought. He sat there for a time without saying anything. After many minutes, he took up his pen and wrote a letter to Shanghai to invite Ch'en Kuo-fu to come to the academy to assume a position as secretary. He showed me the letter and said: "I will get my old friend Ch'en Kuo-fu to help me organize an intelligence department so that I can keep my fingers on the pulse of Canton political intrigues. It is very necessary." He realized that his growing powers had caused much jealousy. In my heart I was glad to be relieved of this type of "Secret" responsibility.

Pending the arrival of Ch'en Kuo-fu, who was the nephew of Kai-shek's former boss Ch'en Ch'i-mei, I continued to look after all my husband's correspondence. I was in the midst of doing some filing work when the servant Ah Shun came in with a boy who approached me timidly.

"Mother!" he said most politely with a deep bow. I was certainly surprised to Kai-shek's son, Ching-kuo. He wore a long white-linen gown and leather European shoes and looked quite the little gentleman. His unexpected appearance had taken me aback, but looking at him and hearing him call me mother awoke within me a maternal instinct, and I suddenly felt a deep affection for him.

"Please sit down and make yourself at home, my good son. When did you arrive and where are you staying?" I asked.

"I arrived yesterday and am staying with some friends in the city. I have already finished my studies at the Wan-chu Middle School at South Gate, Shanghai." He glanced at me to see my reaction. When he saw the smile on my face, he said courageously: "I have a scholarship from the World Scholarship Society given to me by Master Li Shih-ching. It is for me to study in Moscow. I plan to leave in ten days' time."

"How wonderful! But you are so young to go alone to such a faraway country," I observed.

"You need not be worried," he answered. "General Feng Yü-hsiang's son is going with me, and he will be my constant companion. In fact, we will all look after one another." Then he laughed, showing a row of crooked teeth.

"That is wonderful," I exclaimed. "Are you very happy about your trip?"

"Oh, yes, I am."

"Did you go back to Hsi-k'ou to tell your mother about it?"

"Yes, I did."

"I am so glad to hear that. Your mother loves you and you must never, never, forget her. What do you need? Have you enough clothing? Moscow is very cold in winter, and you must take along some woolen underwear."

"Uncle Ch'en Kuo-fu has already supplied me with many things. I have enough clothing, thank you."

"But what can I do to help? I must get you a silk-floss padded coat and some extra woolen underwear to keep you warm," I said.

As I was thinking of what else a young man needed on a trip, he said uneasily: "There is one thing you can help me with, Mother. I hope you will tell my father about it and ask for his consent."

I looked at his squarish face, his large mouth, and closely cropped hair and advised kindly: "You must tell him yourself, Ching-kuo. You are a big boy now, and if you plan to go to another country, you must learn to do things yourself." He suddenly became agitated and shook with nervousness. I said to him in a sympathetic voice: "He is your father, Ching-kuo. I know he loves you very much. You are his son and I know that you, too, love and respect him. This being the case, you must get used to talking with one another and have mutual confidence. I am only your stepmother, and it is not good for me to be a go-between for father and son. It is not right at all. Do you understand what I mean?"

He nodded and blinked and I could see he was trembling. After a few minutes, he pleaded: "Only this once! Please, please help me, Mother."

I could see how terrified he had become and felt so sorry for him. In order to put the boy at ease, I said chidingly: "Only this once then, for your sake, Ching-kuo. But you must learn to ask your father directly in whatever you want to do. Do you understand?"

"Yes, Mother, I understand, thank you, thank you," he replied profusely.

"You must learn to live in harmony with your father and not be frightened of him. I have already spoken many times to him about you, and he promised me that he would not scold you anymore or be abrupt with you. So please, do as I say and do not be frightened of him anymore. Will you promise me that?"

He nodded his square little head and blinked his heavy-lidded eyes again. I thought he resembled more and more his mother, Fu-mei, than his father, and although he had no aristocratic features to speak of, still I felt a warm spot for him. He reminded me of an uncut diamond.

"I promised your mother I would help you all I can," I told him. "And my wish is that you will grow up and a become a man of great importance. So you must study hard and learn as much as you can." After this chat Ching-kuo left to meet his friends. We made an appointment to meet on the morrow.

That night I told Kai-shek of Ching-kuo's arrival and request for permission to go to Moscow. Without waiting for me to finish he snapped: "That block of wood is useless!"

"Don't say that," I pleaded. "He is your only son and is very sensitive. His mind is most receptive in his formative years and whatever you say to him now will always be remembered. So do be gentle and kind to him." Hai-shek kept silent and did not answer me. Then I urged: "Will you speak to him nicely and stop being so harsh and abrupt? He is going away soon, and I do want him to remember how good you are to him."

"Then you approve of him going?" he asked me.

"Yes, I do."

"What's the use of his going away so far?" he shouted. "I can't afford his expenses. Tell him not to go."

"Don't speak like that," I argued. "The lad has his mind all set on the trip and will be very disappointed if you object. He has specially come to ask your consent, so do say yes. Besides, he has a scholarship, and it will hardly cost you anything. Only a very little. Besides, the son of Chu Chi-san and the nephew of so-and-so are going too. The three of them will look after one another. Will you give your permission?"

"You are always spoiling the young," he said in a scolding voice. "Since you seem to be so pleased about it, I will give my permission."

"How wonderful you are," I complimented him. "I am sure you will be proud of Ching-kuo when he graduates. He is a very good and sensible lad, and I feel sure he will make good."

"You see to it that he does," he grumbled, but I knew that behind his rough words lay a kind heart.

"Tomorrow," I said, "we will take Ching-kuo and his friends out to lunch and have a photograph taken as a souvenir. It will be nice for him to have copies to take to Moscow. It will remind him of us always."

"If he needs a photograph to remind him of his parents, then he can't be any good," remarked Kai-shek glumly.

"But it will be a nice souvenir anyway," I argued. "Why do you always misconstrue things? Why do you behave like that?"

The following afternoon, as planned, Kai-shek and I took Ching-kuo and his young friends to the Nan Yuan Restaurant near the East Canton Bund to have lunch. There were eight of us, and we all enjoyed a very pleasant meal. Kai-shek impressed upon the young people the importance of discipline, decency, and decorum. Then he reminded them of filial piety and finally about their duty in serving their country. I was glad to see that Ching-kuo was now relaxed and did not feel so nervous in his father's presence. Hitherto, he was all tension and dared not utter a word. Now we were having a pleasant time. After lunch we went to the nearby photo shop to have our pictures taken. Kai-shek was in a good mood, and he allowed me to make all arrangements and objected to nothing.

He and I posed for the first photograph. I sat on a seat on the left, while Kai-shek stood at my right in a formal pose. This done, we had a family group picture taken. In this picture, Kai-shek and I sat on chairs while Ching-kuo stood between us. Two of Ching-kuo's older friends stood on the right and left of us. Before the photographer could say "ready," I looked at our positions and found that Ching-kuo was terribly stiff and self-conscious. He stood like a log of wood, so I said: "Ching-kuo! Sit with your father and try to appear more natural!" The photographer objected and said it would be too crowded in that position. Of course, he did not know my purpose, so I insisted and said, "Sit there, next to your father, Ching-kuo!"

Kai-shek edged over from his seat to make room for his son, so the two sat close together on one seat, which was what I wanted. I hoped that this act would bring father and son closer together as it should be. In the past, there had existed an invisible wall between them.

The third picture taken was of Ching-kuo and his three little friends. Two of them were the son and daughter of Wang Ching-wei; the other was little Miss Chu, daughter of Chu Chi-san, a well-known revolutionary. They all posed naturally and charmingly.

After all our pictures had been taken, we said good-bye to the photographer and went for a drive to see Canton City. Although Kai-shek and I had been in Canton many times, we had never had the chance or the inclination to see any of the highlights of the place. So I thought it a good idea to kill two birds with one stone and see the famous scenery with Ching-kuo. I told him what I knew about the place, for I had made a study of Canton only recently by reading a book called *Eighteen Vistas of Canton.*

"Canton," I told him, "in comparison with our northern cities, is practically new in Chinese history. The Cantonese were called *Man* at the time of Confucius, meaning 'wild tribe.' According to local tradition, at the beginning five holy men arrived from the North riding sheep, each bearing a stalk of grain and a message bidding the aborigines of Canton to live in peace and prosperity. The legend says the holy men disappeared, while the sheep turned to stone. These five stones can still be seen by the skeptical in the Temple of the Five Genii. From this story, Canton is known as the City of Rams.

Kai-shek then told what he knew. He said: "The reason for Canton's progressiveness is that the early Chinese living near the coast went abroad to Europe, America, Java, Siam, Malaya, and Japan. After years of amassing fortunes, they returned home to advance ideas of good government. Having lived abroad, they had acquired a broader view of the world than those secluded at home. There is a common saying, Everything new originates in Canton, and this is especially true of things political. It was in Canton that the plots that resulted in the overthrow of the Manchu Dynasty were hatched. And during the revolution, Cantonese led by Dr. Sun provided the leadership."

Our car traveled along the Bund, and we could see the well-paved streets, 80 to 150 feet wide. For miles along the bank of Pearl River, we saw thousands of sampans, on which 100,000 people were said to live and eke out a living, just as their families had done for centuries. Their boats were also called water taxis. Then we came to the end of the Bund and saw the island of Shameen. This place was originally near a spot called Sup-Sam-Hong, where Europeans did business. A hundred years ago this small island was a mud flat, granted to foreigners as a place of residence and to transact their business after Sup-Sam-Hong was destroyed. One-third of this island was administered by the French and two-thirds by the British.

Other spots that we visited were the Flower Pagoda, still in a good state of preservation despite its venerable age of 1,000 years. It was built during the Sung Dynasty. Then we visited the Five-story Pagoda, Big Buddha Monastery, and then on to "Yellow Flower Hill."

Getting out of our car, we left the road to enter an expanse that looked like a well-kept park. There on the ground in even rows of bare, gray stone was a maze of low graves of the seventy-two revolutionary martyrs, all marked with their names. At the farthest end stood the main wall of gray granite. Atop the wall stood a miniature Statue of Liberty. The wall itself, serving as an altar, had four huge Chinese characters engraved upon it, written by Dr. Sun, meaning Great deeds live forever. This sacred spot seemed to hold special meaning for us and impressed us all alike. It was in March 1909 that the seventy-two revolutionaries had attempted to capture Canton City from the Manchu viceroy in a rebellion. When their plot was discovered, they were arrested, tortured, and finally decapitated. This was their burial place, which had become a Mecca for us revolutionaries.

Kai-shek said to us, "Come, let us stand here and pay our respects." We obeyed and stood in a straight line. Then he continued: "We are here in proud and solemn company among these heroic martyrs who gave their lives to overthrow the Manchu oppressors. These seventy-two heroes were our comrades, our brothers, and our uncles. They rest here at this shrine; their glorious courage and sacrifice are to be kept in lasting memory down through the ages. Let us show our deep respect by bowing to them three times."

We all bowed our heads three times. This done, I said, "May these heroes rest forever in honored and hallowed peace."

We then walked around the grounds, and Kai-shek stood long and meditatively looking at the four large, gilded characters written by Dr. Sun, meaning Great deeds live forever. Kai-shek placed his fingers on the wall lovingly to trace the lines of Dr. Sun's writing and said to me: "Now you know why I am anxious to improve my calligraphy. I expect to be writing a lot of such large characters one of these days."

"Your constancy of practice will surely reward you," I assured him. "You have greatly improved in the last three months."

"Do you really think so?" he smiled with deep satisfaction.

Our drive home was very pleasant. Ching-kuo was full of boyish glee and smiled and chatted with his young friends, which showed his happiness. In due course we dropped him and his little friends at their friend's home at Tai-ping Gate; Kai-shek and I took our motor launch to return to the academy.

Altogether Ching-kuo stayed in Canton for ten days, and each day we would meet for a visit or have a meal together. As a stepmother I wanted to shower my affection on the boy, not because I had promised his own mother, Fu-mei, to look after him, but because I wanted him not to feel slighted in a strange city. On the tenth day, he came upstairs to my flat and said: "I have come to say good-bye to you first, Mother, and then I will go downstairs to say good-bye to Father. He is now busy in the office. Thank you for making Father like me."

"I'm sorry you cannot stay a few days longer, Ching-kuo," I said emotionally. "Must you really go?"

He looked at me full in the face and said, "I'm sorry to leave you, too, but our plans are all set and cannot be changed."

I gave him two packages of woolen clothing, socks, handkerchiefs, some edibles, and 100 Cantonese dollars to buy something he liked.

He thanked me profusely and I looked at him forlornly, as if I was losing a part of myself. For a moment I could not speak and tears welled in my eyes. Somehow, I stuttered the words: "Look after yourself, Ching-kuo. I hope to see you after five years. Be sure to study hard and write me whenever you can."

He looked lovingly into my eyes for a minute, unable to say anything. Then he bowed to me respectfully and quickly went downstairs to say good-bye to his father.

The Chung shan Boat Incident

18

*E*arly in March 1925, Kai-shek, with self-confidence verging on fanaticism, led his cadets and soldiers to capture Waichow for the second time. He was deeply conscious of what he had experienced in the last hideous battle. He was also conscious of the responsibility and gravity of this decision to rush regiments of young men to their deaths. But in planning the campaign, he could only see that such sacrifices were justified on the grounds that his bitter enemy, Ch'en Chiung-ming, had to be exterminated at any cost.

So by sheer force of personality, high morale, political skill, a numerically superior force, and ample ammunition, the Whampoa cadets, under Kai-shek's direction, stormed Waichow. They engaged in spectacular assaults and displayed unbelievable bravery. As a consequence, the defense of the pivotal fort collapsed, and the great fortress of Waichow fell like a house of cards. This new victory earned for him the title "Chiang Kai-shek the Indestructible."

Having captured Mei-hsien on the East River a week earlier, Kai-shek sent for me, and we stayed in this antiquated town for a few days. Since Waichow had now fallen and mopping-up operations were taking place, we were planning to officially enter the city. But just then the sad news of Dr. Sun's death came from Peking. We were all deeply grieved, and immediately I got Ah Shun to buy some black cloth to cut into strips to make arm bands for Kai-shek and the officers to wear. The

176

House of Shen, where we were staying, flew our Kuomintang flag at half-mast.

Kai-shek was busy mapping out plans for the administration of Waichow, and he did not grieve as much as I thought he would. He was miserable when the news came, but then he braced himself for the situation before him. He had much work to do for the country. He took it for granted that he was the genuine heir to Dr. Sun's revolutionary work. Everyone understood that all followers of Dr. Sun would now move up a step in the invisible rankings within the Kuomintang. Wang Ching-wei and Hu Han-min were by seniority the logical ones to take the leader's place. Hu Han-min was acting generalissimo, administering the government. But the fever of leadership entered Kai-shek's veins, so he forged ahead to achieve his ambition in an astonishing way.

I accompanied him to enter the fallen city of Waichow when he officially took over the city. After a few days, when conditions became normal, he as commander in chief of the Cantonese Army called meeting after meeting. He outlined his plans to fight back to Canton in order to oust the two formidable forces bestriding the city, namely "Living Angel Liu" (Liu Chen-huan) and Yang Hsi-min. He told me: "I can feel our leader's charge, which says, Go ahead and unify Canton first and then start immediately on the Northern Expedition!" He spoke the words seriously enough, but he could see my cynical look. He hastened to assure me: "I would not have you think that there is anything superstitious about this, but it is true. Those are the exact thoughts that were on Dr. Sun's mind when he died."

"How do you know that?" I asked.

"I can feel it in my bones," was his reply.

"But Dr. Sun would not approve of you fighting 'Living Angel Liu.' After all, he regarded Liu as a living angel!"

"The past is past," he answered abruptly. "Liu Chen-huan has outlived his usefulness. He must be eliminated along with the others."

"But he risked his life to restore Canton to you and Dr. Sun. Does that no longer count for anything?" I argued.

"Not any more," Kai-shek said with finality. "He has collected taxes from the Canton citizens for over a year and has been amply repaid for whatever services he rendered."

"But to be fair, all the taxes collected went to the upkeep of the armies that were garrisoned in Canton. I remember Dr. Sun had earmarked those taxes solely for that purpose; is that not so?"

"To tell you the truth," he confided, "I am planning to take control of all the armies in Canton. This is impossible so long as the Kwangsi and Yunnanese leaders are in my way. The only way is to use this opportunity to oust them, once and for all. So, please see it my way, will you?"

I kept silent, but it gave me much food for thought. This was Canton politics. One may risk one's life for the party or the government, and yet, within a year, one's sacrifice and loyalty will be forgotten. But I could see why the Kwangsi and Yunnanese had to go. They cramped Kai-shek's style and prevented him from realizing supreme command of the armies in Canton.

The following week we received from Tai Chi-t'ao in Peking a report of Dr. Sun's hospitalization. It read:

> In Peking, Dr. Sun's condition steadily became worse. His liver not only had calcified, but there was a tumor that the doctor said required an immediate operation. On January 26, 1925, Dr. Sun was transferred to the Peking Union Medical College Hospital. There he underwent an operation under the supervision of four doctors of four nationalities, namely German, Russian, Chinese, and American.

After the operation it was announced that Dr. Sun was suffering from cancer of the liver and was not expected to live. Besides his wife and son, Dr. Sun had with him at his bedside eight of his disciples: Wang Ching-wei, Eugene Ch'en, Ku Ying-fen, Wu Chih-hui, and others.

Since the Westernized doctors had given up hope for Dr. Sun's recovery, it was decided to try Chinese herbal treatments, which could do no harm and might do the patient good. Since it was unethical to do this in a Westernized hospital, Dr. Sun was removed to the home of Wellington Koo. Herbal treatment was administered and for the first time in weeks Dr. Sun could sleep, long and soundly, for eight hours. The swelling of his feet too, subsided.

Despite these good signs, Dr. Sun's condition gradually worsened. He passed away on March 25, 1925.

᛭   ᛭   ᛭

To celebrate the victory of Waichow, Kai-shek told his men: "Our leader struggled forty years for the liberty of all the Chinese people, and all he got was a toehold at Canton. He wanted to use this as a base to liberate the oppressed people of the whole country. Now, if we lose this

base, Dr. Sun's work will all have been in vain. No matter how powerful the Kwangsi and Yunnanese armies bestriding Canton are, we shall
kick them out of our base. I will then adopt a new policy: Unify the control of finances under our government, reorganize our armies into one,
and put our revolutionary doctrine into practice. This I cannot do without your help. So I ask you, one and all, to show your loyalty to our government."

Michael Borodin had once suggested that Kai-shek use a psychological weapon in order to throw fear into the enemy. So now, on June 10,
1925, before Kai-shek marched his troops back to Canton, all workers
on the railways and public transport in and near Canton, by prearrange-
ment, went on strike in sympathy with the returning army. This threw
a scare into the hearts of the Yunnanese and Kwangsi commanders,
who were wholly taken by surprise. Unable to move their forces
quickly to meet the emergency, they were utterly at a loss to know
what to do. Indeed, Borodin's psychological Communist weapon was
most effective.

On June 12, 1925, Kai-shek entered Canton victoriously with his
men, having met little opposition, for the enemy had fled. He assumed
the position as commander of security of Canton, and this new title
gave him added importance.

A large part of the defeated armies had surrendered, while a smaller
part had escaped. Some of these escapees had scattered at the outskirts
of the capital, and the new commander of security was kept busy
mopping them up.

Now, with the successful conclusion of this homecoming campaign,
the General Headquarters was headed by four men: Wang Ching-wei,
Hu Han-min, Liao Chung-k'ai, and Kai-shek himself. Thus from the
seventh rung in the Kuomintang hierarchy, Kai-shek had now jumped
up to number four!

Kai-shek had his own ideas regarding what should be done for Canton. He took it upon himself to reorganize the government according to
his own ideas. This could only happen, however, if he quickly staged a
coup d'état to seize all the power in Canton for himself. This was how
he did it. June 20, 1925, was the date for the meeting of the Central Executive Committee. On that day he asked to be elected a member of the
committee and was made commander of the armies. As a result of his
recent victory, no one dared to refuse him. While the meeting was still
in progress, he peremptorily declared martial law. He then established

in his headquarters a virtual replica of the Kuomintang's system of administrative offices, arrogating to himself the right to veto all acts by civil and military officials. He then submitted to the Central Executive Committee a set of resolutions that were, of course, passed with nervous alacrity. The Central Executive Committee was made the highest body in the government. And the Generalissimo's headquarters, which used to be the revolutionary government, was now reorganized into a formal Nationalist government. The various armies under different names were reorganized, to be called the Nationalist Revolutionary Army. He automatically became the army's commander.

It goes without saying that many members of the Kuomintang, especially the veterans, were indignant and expressed their opposition to Kai-shek's dictatorial powers. They started a smear campaign against him. The slogans they created were: A new warlord is born; A Ningpo Napoleon has risen; If you wish to be arrested stay in Canton; and Canton is a police state.

When wholesale arrests took place under Kai-shek's orders, many Kuomintang members, fearing incarceration for their outspoken dissatisfaction, left Canton for Peking. There they held a meeting at the Purple Monastery in the Western Hills, where Dr. Sun's coffin was resting pending burial.

These discontented Kuomintang members bowed before Dr. Sun's casket and wailed out their long list of grievances. They accused Kai-shek of betraying the party, usurping power, and persecuting them. They wanted their dead leader to know their grief. Later, these men constituted the opposition, the so-called Western Hills Faction. For a time, there were grave schisms in the party that almost threatened another rebellion. The Communists, too, countered with more intensive efforts to create dissension in the party by spreading suspicions and causing provocations. They branded Hu Han-min and all anti-Communists as rightists and declared that Wang Ching-wei, Liao Chung-k'ai and all pro-Communists were leftists. This friction between the left and right wings soon became very serious. Liao Chung-k'ai, an extreme leftist, was a die-hard Communist and, therefore, was hated intensely by all conservatives. Communist influence in China was attributed to him. Because he used his growing position and power to support communism, his enemies plotted to assassinate him. This they did on August 20, 1925, when he was shot in the street on his way to attend a Central Executive Committee meeting. He died the same day.

The suspected assassin was believed to be none other than the brother of Hu Han-min, the rightist. In view of the gravity of the matter, a combined meeting of the various government branches was held to meet the emergency. The two leaders, Wang Ching-wei and Kai-shek, were given unlimited powers to deal with this political case. In his capacity as commander of security around Canton, Kai-shek sent out part of the Fourth and Fifth Regiments of the Training Corps to arrest the assassin or assassins.

As Liao Chung-k'ai had been the party representative in both the Whampoa Military Academy and the revolutionary army, a memorial service was held in the academy. At this service, Kai-shek said: "The death of our party representative Liao was entirely due to a plot hatched jointly by the imperialists and the reactionaries. We must realize that those who struck at our party representative Liao did not aim at him alone. They actually aim to annihilate us, our party, and our army as a whole. They plan to destroy you and they plan to destroy me!"

On September 1, 1925, the Special Committee met for the eighth time within twelve days. At the meeting it was resolved that Hu Han-min, because of his brother's crime, be requested to go abroad on an "inspection" tour. His brother and the others involved were imprisoned. So with the death of Liao Chung-k'ai, the absence of Hsu Ch'ung-chih, the departure of Hu Han-min, and the ousting of "Living Angel Liu," Kai-shek was automatically promoted to the number-two place in the Kuomintang hierarchy. He was now second in leadership only to Wang Ching-wei.

On the recommendation of Mrs. Liao Chung-k'ai (Miss Ho Hsiang-ning), Kai-shek now rented a small, modernized house next to hers at Tungshan, where many of the prominent officials lived. This was quite convenient for us because Kai-shek held several positions in Canton that necessitated his presence there.

The house was self-contained, consisting of two bedrooms, a dining room, and a parlor. In the bedroom there was a big double bed, low, according to the new fashion, with an embroidered bedspread. There were two bedside tables and a chest of drawers of teakwood. On the chest of drawers stood a few ornaments consisting of some porcelain vases, a clock, and two small flower pots. A door led to the bathroom, all white, with nickel-plated taps and fittings. Everything was new, clean, and orderly. The parlor was spacious with dark-green curtains and green up-holstered chairs and a sofa. Best of all was the telephone, which Kai-shek could use to keep in touch with the academy.

It was on March 18, 1926, that our telephone rang shrilly. It was Becky (Mrs. Wang Ching-wei), who inquired, "Is Kai-shek in?"

"No," I said. "He has gone to a meeting."

"Do you know when he will leave for Whampoa tonight? We want to see him on urgent business."

"I cannot say," I answered. "But I know he has a meeting at the academy this evening and most probably will leave Canton before six o'clock."

"By which jetty will he leave?" she inquired.

"Why do you ask?"

"Because Ching-Wei has an appointment with your husband and wants to go with him to Whampoa. There are two landings, so I want to know which one Kai-shek will take."

"As Kai-shek is not here, I cannot give you the information. Can I phone you as soon as he comes back?"

"Please do," said Becky and she hung up.

Within two hours, Becky phoned again and again, five times in all, asking me urgently the same questions without variety.

That is strange, I told myself. Why is she so anxious? What kind of a plot is she hatching? It was well known that haughty Becky never did anything without a purpose, so the more I thought of it, the more suspicious I became.

When Kai-shek returned that afternoon, I asked, "Did Wang Ching-wei make an appointment to go with you to Whampoa this evening?"

"No, he didn't," he said casually.

"But Becky Wang said he did."

"Not to my knowledge," answered Kai-shek.

"In that case I smell a rat," I said. "You had better stay here tonight. Don't go to Whampoa until tomorrow. I have a hunch that something funny is going on."

"But I have an important meeting at 7 P.M.," he exclaimed.

"Then postpone it," I insisted and took up the telephone to phone the academy.

When I made the connection, Kai-shek spoke and was surprised to be told by the academy dean that the gunboat *Chung shan* had been sent down river from Canton to Whampoa for fueling.

"Who issued the order for it to leave?" Kai-shek asked in an excited tone.

"Wang Ching-wei issued the order."

"Then he will be held responsible," hollered Kai-shek indignantly. "He had no authority to issue an order without informing me."

The next day, Kai-shek made extensive inquiries. He learned that a plot was afoot to kidnap him and ship him to Moscow. That such an abduction could be conceived seemed outrageous. Here are the facts that Kai-shek gathered: On March 18, 1926, Li Chih-lung, the Communist acting director of the Naval Forces Bureau, received a mysterious order to sail the gunboat *Chung shan* from Canton to Whampoa. He informed the dean of the military academy that he had the commandant's (Kai-shek's) orders to send the ship there for the purpose of loading enough coal for a long voyage. This done, the ship returned to Canton. Being in Canton, Kai-shek knew nothing of this matter. Throughout the night the *Chung shan*'s engine was kept running and its lights were left on. Precautions of the most rigorous kind were enforced on board. At the time, however, it was suspected that plotters intended to stage a revolt. No one had any idea of the extent of the Communists' plans. Only after it was all over was it revealed that the plan was to seize Kai-shek when he boarded the boat to return to the military academy that evening. The scheme was to send him as a prisoner to Russia, via Vladivostok. This would remove the Communists' major obstacle to their scheme of using Canton and the Nationalist revolution as a means of setting up a "dictatorship of the proletariat."

That night, Kai-shek made a decision, which he carried out the next morning. In his capacity as Canton's defense commander, he declared martial law and had Wang Ching-wei arrested and detained at the Goddess of Mercy Hill. Li Chih-lung and the other Communists involved were imprisoned. All members of the Communist-dominated Canton–Hong Kong Strike Committee were disarmed and all strikes called off. Simultaneously, Kai-shek sent troops onto the gunboat to regain control. This was a startling move.

On March 22, 1926, a representative from the Soviet consulate in Canton came to see us at Tungshan and later spoke to Kai-shek about this incident. He asked: "Was this raid directed against Wang Ching-wei or directed against Soviet Russia?" Kai-shek told him that it was against Wang Ching-wei.

"But we disapprove of your dictatorial methods," he countered. "In the first place, Borodin was entirely ignored. He is the Soviets' representative in the government and should have been consulted. In the second place, Wang Ching-wei is your superior, so how can you take it upon yourself to place him under arrest without the party's approval? I demand that you call a Central Political Committee meeting at once."

Kai-shek called the meeting that same day, and Wang Ching-wei was brought before the meeting. In front of eighty Kuomintang members, he denied that he had issued any orders for the removal of the gunboat *Chung shan*. Looking at Kai-shek, he thundered: "Who do you think you are? You are only an upstart! Your name is neither among the twenty-five Kuomintang founders nor are you one of the five supervisors! You are only a newcomer and a junior member, but you browbeat your betters with your brazen warlord tactics. If you wish to grab my position, go ahead and do so. Let our dear leader watch you from the great beyond! Let the whole nation see you do it; let history record it! But don't frame me with false charges!"

He then turned to the party chairman and asked to be allowed to move to a hospital for medical treatment. He also requested old Mr. Chang Ching-chiang, my godfather, who was on the Central Supervisory Committee, to serve as his guarantor. On the strength of this, Wang Ching-wei was sent to the hospital to rest. He stayed there all through the month of April, and on May 11, 1926, without a word, he secretly left Kwangtung for France, ostensibly for reasons of health. With Wang Ching-wei's departure, Kai-shek took Wang's place and became the most important leader in Canton. He was now on the top rung of the ladder of Canton politics.

Through the months that followed, the situation in North China waxed and waned. Internecine warfare flared up in one province, was quickly settled, then another started, like the changes of the moon in its constancy. But whatever fighting went on in the North, Kwangtung and Kwangsi were solidly united under the new leadership of Kai-shek. His doctrine for the salvation of China was Dr. Sun's Three Principles of the People. This slogan served as a beacon signaling Chinese nationalism from a high tower that flashed across the length and breadth of China, giving hope of a new day to a war-weary, oppressed people. At last, they told themselves, they were on the threshold of a new, strong, and honest government headed by a new leader. That leader was Chiang Kai-shek! This gave his name an aura of glamor, and his popularity spread far and wide. He was dubbed the most important Chinese leader. But on the other hand, a news extract sent me by my Mother from Shanghai read:

One of the favorite sports in Canton at present seems to be driving important government members from office—almost all of whom are Cantonese. For instance, General Hsu Ch'ung-chih, Liu Chen-huan, and Hu Han-min. Now the latest is Wang Ching-wei. It is the general belief that these men were forced to leave Canton because they stood in the way of the ambitious schemes of General Chiang Kai-shek, the new leader, who wishes to gain supreme control of the political administration as well as of the army. Like it or not, he is the most prominent leader of the Kuomintang today! (*Shen Pao* [the Shanghai daily]: May 20, 1926)

19

The Dinner Party

*I*t was a Saturday evening in our new house, where we spent our weekends. Out of the blue, Kai-shek said to me when he returned home after work: "We have an invitation to dine with Mme Kung tomorrow night. She tells me she is going to make a very special pigeon dinner just for you and me. She wants us to be there at three o'clock, but you may go first from here because I will not be able to get away from the academy until after work at 5 P.M." He spoke as he walked up and down the room in great excitement. His throat seemed contracted with tenseness. "An invitation!" he repeated to himself. "I never, never expected it. And now, at last, after all this time, you and I have a chance to dine with this great personage. It is really too wonderful to be true." He strutted the floor like a peacock and refused to sit down. He seldom behaved in this agitated manner.

"Why so excited?" I asked airily. "It's only a dinner. The weather is so hot that I really hate to go anywhere. Why don't you go alone and enjoy yourself? You can make excuses for me."

I poured him a glass of boiled water from the thermos and offered it to him. He placed it on the table without drinking it. "You still don't understand," he chided me quickly. "You must be sensible and realize how very important it is to me to get closer to the Soong family. You know that I wasn't able to get as close to our leader all those years as I had wished, so this is a chance to get closer to his relatives. Don't you understand that?"

Of course, I couldn't deny the truth of that statement.

"You know, just as well as I do," he continued patiently, "Canton is full of military experts, but by a stroke of pure luck I was made head of the academy. I have position, but I lack prestige. So my strategy is to cultivate the friendship of his nearest relatives. I want the names of Sun, Soong, and Chiang to be linked tightly together."

I looked at him and knew what he meant by luck because at the very beginning, Dr. Sun's choice as head of the academy had been General T'an Yen-k'ai of Hunan. But being bitterly anti-Communist, General T'an had declined the position.

Kai-shek reached out for my hand and held it firmly and lovingly and in a coaxing voice advised: "We are on the threshold of great achievement. You must stand shoulder-to-shoulder with me to win success, both in our revolution and in cultivating friendships. You know how much this means to me. You must not refuse to go to the dinner."

"I promise," I assured him. "I'll do everything to help make your wishes come true. I'll go wherever you want me to go. Are you now satisfied?"

Kai-shek laughed happily and crushed me to his body. "You are wonderful," he said happily. "I know you can see everything eye-to-eye with me, and that is precisely why I love you so very dearly. But do you love me?" Without waiting for an answer he continued: "I want you to love me every minute of the day. Don't ever stop loving me. Will you promise me that?"

"I promise," I said affectionately.

On the following afternoon, I wore my best white crepe de chine silk dress and white kid shoes, carried a white-beaded handbag and a sandalwood fan, and tried to look fresh and smart so that Kai-shek would feel proud of me. Since he could not go until five o'clock, I went alone at 3 P.M. to the Standard Oil manager's home, where Mme Kung was staying. This was at No. 309 East Section of the Canton Bund, near the South Garden, called Nan Yuan.

I knew this section well. Mme Kung's house was a low, detached, two-story white house shaded with many cedar trees. The Cantonese called this type of house *yang-lou,* meaning foreign building. It nestled in a green garden. The walk that led up to it was flagstone, all embedded in blue-green, well-trimmed grass. Potted flowers were placed everywhere to add color, and the whole scene was entrancing.

When I arrived at the house, I found other guests were already there. Mme Kung, with her heady French perfume, welcomed me heartily and exclaimed worriedly: "But where is Kai-shek? He promised me faithfully he would come!"

"He will be along later," I assured her.

Then she led me into the drawing-room. I knew those present. Her sister Mei-ling Soong, the well-known diplomat and scholar Eugene Chen [Ch'en Yu-jen], and Mrs. Liao Chung-k'ai were there. I shook hands all around and we chatted pleasantly.

The living room and dining room were made into one, blocked off only by a large, beautiful embroidered screen of heavy blackwood. The whole setting was as quaint as the house itself, filled with lovely furniture, Persian rugs, old porcelains, and heavy lace half curtains.

My hostess and her sister were dressed in bright-colored Chinese-silk gowns of the latest Shanghai fashion. Their smooth black hair was dressed in chignon style with the bun at the nape of their necks, which was considered very chic and aristocratic. Indeed, they looked as if they had stepped out of a Shanghai fashion book.

"How good of you to come in all this heat, Mme Chiang," cried Mme Kung. "It's terribly hot again today, and the heat is unbearable. But you look as cool as a cucumber. How do you manage it?" She patted the perspiration from her forehead with her lace handkerchief. She and her sister looked at me as if they were prima donnas. They stood in front of the three eighteen-inch electric fans placed on side tables, which oscillated, at full blast. Mei-ling Soong kept fanning herself with a large, carved-ivory, silk fan. It was obvious she was posing.

"What do you expect in Canton in August?" asked Eugene Ch'en, broadly grinning in his white linen suit. "Shanghai is just as hot, if not worse. Every summer is the same. We'll be lucky if it doesn't get worse."

"This summer is comparatively milder than last year," remarked Mrs. Liao Chung-k'ai.

"But Shanghai is not so sticky and utterly miserable as here," chimed in Mei-ling Soong.

"It's the humidity," I said airily. "I agree that conditions are far too stifling for any comfort." Soon two maids brought in trays of ice-cold drinks in tall glasses and plates of hors d'oeuvres and passed them around. The drinks helped to keep us cool.

"Forget the heat, Ai-ling," advised Mei-ling Soong, trying to humor her sister. "We'll go back to Shanghai on the *Empress of Japan* next week."

"Fine! I like that ship. It's the best on the line. Don't you think so?" Mme Kung asked me.

"I usually travel on the Dollar Line but shall make it a point to try the *Empress of Japan* one of these days."

"It's a must," she assured me. "The cabins are large, food and service good, and you'll never regret it."

Eugene Ch'en started to talk about politics, oblivious of my presence. But I was a good listener. The conversation soon drifted to rates of gold dollars, stocks and shares, speculation, latest bank buying and selling, margins, real estate, and dividends in thousands and tens of thousands of dollars. What they were saying went completely over my head, for I knew nothing about the money market and cared less. They must have thought it pitiful to see that I was not at all interested in money speculation.

"Show Mme Chiang the house," said Mme Kung to Eugene Ch'en. He got up politely and we left the room. I looked at Eugene Ch'en in admiration and told him how much I admired his speeches. He was known as a seasoned diplomat, although a little radical. There was much talk of a possible match between him and Mei-ling Soong, but judging by their behavior toward one another in the drawing room, the rumor probably was unfounded. One reason, in my opinion, was excessive pride on both sides. I must confess, however, I liked Eugene Ch'en for his keen mind and patriotism, while I thought Mei-ling Soong a snob, which showed so plainly through her polished veneer.

"This house belongs to the manager of the Standard Oil Company, who is now in New York on furlough," Eugene Ch'en told me as we looked the house over. From the three bedrooms we went into the little kitchen and saw the nicely arranged rows of shining aluminum pots and the glistening crockery and glassware on shelves.

"Of course this house is built for utility and is not as spacious and grand as our Chinese houses," he explained.

"I never saw anything so compact as this," I declared, as I looked around and admired the place. "My little house in Tungshan is not so well appointed. Now I have some ideas as to how to arrange it just like this."

"Do you like staying in Tungshan?" he asked.

"Yes, it is very nice and quiet."

"Do you entertain much?"

"I have very few friends here in Canton," I said, "and we are kept too busy to do any entertaining. Besides, I ply between Tungshan and Whampoa. The academy is really home to me, since I stay there most of the time."

"Whampoa is such a long drag to town. It wastes so much time traveling back and forth."

"That is true," I fully agreed with him. "But Kai-shek and I are used to it by now. It was only through the persuasion of Mrs. Liao that Kai-shek rented our Tungshan house from her. She has been quite lonely since her husband's death. The rent is low and the district select. We now usually spend our weekends in town."

Eugene Ch'en and I then strolled into the garden. When we got back to the house, my attention was attracted by the gay laughter in the drawing room. It was Ai-Ling Kung's high voice saying: "She's only a middle-class housewife! How can she ever qualify to be the wife of a budding leader? Something must be done about it."

"That's true," agreed Mei-ling Soong. "She symbolizes a wide social gulf in the nation's life." Then with sarcasm she added: "But I must say she has her good points. She makes a very good housewife for a Ningpo peasant." I could feel the lashing scorn of those words.

"What do you expect?" exclaimed Mrs. Liao Chung-k'ai. "She's only a child and not out of her shell yet. Oh, give her a chance to find herself. She'll learn. And I must say she is a really good woman; too good for that bad-tempered husband of hers."

"Out of her shell?" The words rang a bell. I had heard that expression before. Yes, it was Yi-min who had said those very same words to me years ago.

As Eugene Ch'en and I came into the drawing room, the three women shut up like clams.

Since Kai-shek had not yet come, I smiled and sat down while Eugene Ch'en went over to speak to Mrs. Liao. Ai-ling Kung and Mei-ling Soong squirmed in their seats, wondering if I had heard their remarks. They eyed me from head to foot as if they were judging a schoolgirl. At last Mme Kung asked: "Have you bought much jewelry, Mme Chiang? You can afford it, you know."

"People keep asking me what kind of jewelry and clothes I will buy when the country is united," I answered. "But I can't possibly say. I will wait until it all happens. You've heard the saying, "Don't count your chickens before they are hatched!'"

"You are very wise, my dear," said Mrs. Liao to me.

"Only diamonds and platinum will be good enough for a great leader's wife," said Mme Kung with the airs of a grand duchess. "I'd take nothing less!"

Mei-ling Soong widened her eyes and exclaimed in mock ecstasy: "I love platinum and solitary diamonds! They are fascinating!" Then turning to me she asked: "Don't you like platinum, Mme Chiang? I think gold is so vulgar and so cheap looking."

"I don't care at all for jewelry," I answered dryly. "Gold, platinum, or diamonds hold no special appeal for me."

Then they pumped me for information about my husband. The two sisters, no doubt, regarded me as a simpleton, so I led them on in order to see how far they would go.

"How do you find married life, Mme Chiang? Do you ever quarrel with your husband?" asked Ai-Ling Kung.

"No," I answered demurely. "We haven't had anything so far to quarrel about. Kai-shek respects my wishes and I respect his. We get along through mutual respect."

"But Kai-shek is well known for his horrid temper. Doesn't he ever scold you?" asked Mme kung with a sly smile. "No? Then you must be patience personified, not to have quarreled with him yet."

"According to Dr. Sun, Kai-shek flairs up at the slightest provocation. Is that so?" asked Mei-ling Soong. She looked at me and continued: "Of course, I don't believe it. But a bad temper in a man is preferable to a man without a temper. Don't you think so?" I pretended to agree with her by nodding and she asked again: "Tell us about the first wife, Mme Mao. Does she object to you? Does she put obstacles in your way? Is she nasty to you?"

"Mme Mao is the sweetest lady I know," I answered truthfully. "She is a devout Buddhist and is not concerned with any worldly affairs. Of course, Kai-shek secured her consent to a separation before we were married."

"And what about the second wife, Mme Yao? Do you ever see her?" again asked Mei-ling Soong. "What is she like?"

"Mme Yao lives in Soochow, and I have not met her. She is rather conservative and loves to play mah-jongg. Before we were married, she agreed to accept a settlement of $5,000 to relinquish all claims on Kai-shek for future support. But for good measure, Kai-shek still gives her a small monthly allowance. We now regard her as a relative. Kai-shek refers to her as Auntie."

I looked at Mme Kung and saw that she and Mei-ling were exchanging significant glances. Pumping in such vein went on and on and on.

At five o'clock, Kai-shek came in, all flustered and uttering profuse apologies for being late. Mme Kung pretended to be angry and gave him a black look. But he went up to her and mumbled some endearment.

Then we all repaired to the dining room. As we sat around the table, the seating was in this manner: Kai-shek was placed between Mme Kung and Mei-ling Soong, while I sat between Eugene Ch'en and Mrs. Liao Chung-k'ai.

When dinner was served, it was in European style. First came a jellied consommé, pigeon breast on a piece of diamond-shaped toast, served on individual plates, one for each person, and garnished with a sprig of watercress and chip potatoes. The golden-brown pigeons looked luscious, with their breast meat popping out. They looked most appetizing.

Before we started to eat, Mei-ling Soong made an announcement, and we all looked at her: "Pigeon eating is like eating mangoes. Both should be eaten with the fingers only, in the bathroom, without anyone looking on," she told us. "Since the bathroom of this house is so small, you are requested to eat your pigeons here and in silence. But I warn you! No one is allowed to talk or look at one another until the whole pigeon is consumed! All agreed? Let us begin now and enjoy it. Be sure to keep your eyes on your plate and don't look around. Otherwise it will be embarrassing." With this warning, we obeyed and ate in silence. I did not look at anyone at all but found the pigeon tender and even the bones were soft.

After dinner we exchanged a lot of small talk. And Kai-shek's manner revealed one significant fact: He was thrilled beyond words to be a guest of Mme Kung, who praised her sister incessantly. No one was as clever as Mei-ling Soong.

When it was time to leave, I shook hands with our hostess, who said to me: "Oh, don't go home, Mme Chiang. Do stay the night here and keep us company! There is so much we can talk about."

"Yes, why don't you stay the night here? We seem always to be saying good-bye to you, just when we are beginning to enjoy ourselves," exclaimed Mei-ling Soong.

Well, that was true enough, I thought. Our meetings together seemed always too short. It was always time to separate just when we were having the nicest time in settling down to a hearty talk. Yet, I could instinctively feel that everything these sisters asked me was for a purpose, and that purpose was to get more and more information about Kai-shek. I naturally felt reluctant to be pumped, so I said: "It is so hot and I have brought with me neither a change of clothing nor a set of pajamas. Anyway, I thank you both very much just the same. I've enjoyed a very interesting evening."

"Are you so much in love that you cannot stay away from your husband even for one night, Mme Chiang?" chided Mme Kung.

"Oh, do stay," urged Mei-ling Soong. "I do want to have a nice long chat with you. We planned on your staying and now you are disappointing us!"

The more they urged, they more determined I became. I disliked people pumping me about my husband's affairs. It was not right for any woman to talk about her husband behind his back, so I shook my head and said with finality: "Please give me a rain check. I'll stay as long as you like next time, but not tonight."

I could see how crestfallen they became. They blinked their sullen eyes, but I was firm and said good-bye as gracefully as I could.

The little party seemed to be just an ordinary get-together. I had no idea, and could not believe it possible, that it was the beginning of a long-range intrigue to usurp my position as the wife of Chiang Kai-shek.

On the following afternoon, I had a luncheon engagement with Mrs. Liao Chung-k'ai, who usually went by her maiden name Miss Ho Hsiang-ning. Her father was the rich Ho Tin, who had helped Dr. Sun with funds in his early revolutionary days. So she and her late husband were considered veteran revolutionaries who belonged to the Kuomintang inner circle. She and I had become very good friends since I arrived in Canton, and I grieved deeply over the assassination of her husband. But she was a very strong character and bore her sorrow most bravely.

As soon as she saw me, she spoke of the day before at Mme Kung's pigeon dinner. She was so indignant that her breath was jumbled with invectives; she was frowning and gesticulating. "I feel very distressed over your safety," she exclaimed angrily, and I was taken aback.

"Why be distressed when there is nothing to be distressed about?" I asked. "What's the trouble?"

"Oh, my dear, you are so innocent. You are oblivious of the danger that lurks about you! You must be wary. Life is a hideous nightmare with the enemy behind every hedge. You must be careful. Don't be too trusting!"

I knew she was saying this for my own good, for we were very close friends and she liked me as a sister. Her love was of the purely unselfish kind.

"Steer away from that woman," she warned me in a serious voice, "and don't let Kai-shek fall into her trap. I am telling you this because I love you, and I don't want you to be unhappy. So do be careful."

"But what harm can she do me?" I asked perplexedly. "We are not strangers. We have known her for at least four years, though I know she used to ignore Kai-shek as if he were a common soldier. She never did have any respect for him. In fact, I remember distinctly, when Dr. Sun introduced us, she rudely turned her head the other way. It embarrassed Dr. Sun terribly."

"I would not put anything past that woman," she exclaimed. "Today the situation is different. Kai-shek is the most important personage in Canton and is an attractive prize to be ensnared. You must remember that she still has an unmarried sister. Ah, there's the chief danger, and I can see it as plain as daylight."

"But Kai-shek and I are married. Surely she would not come between husband and wife. Besides, she is a Christian!"

"How very naïve you are, my dear," she retorted, shaking her head. "That woman is notorious for being unscrupulous, and when it suits her to grab, she simply grabs, right under your nose! She did that with her own husband, and I know what I'm talking about. Christianity has nothing to do with it."

She was so serious about it that I, too, was forced to become serious. But in my heart, I laughed at her suspicions and fears. Of course, I understood well enough what she meant, but I felt quite safe where Kai-shek was concerned. Had he not sworn to me eternal fidelity? Had he not wanted to cut off his finger to prove his love? Of course, I did not tell her about this. "I do appreciate your kind concern," I said gratefully, "and I shall take your advice. I'll accept no more invitations from that woman."

"That is wise," she told me. Then she hugged and kissed me and patted my hand. "After all, you are so young and so trusting that you can

Jennie.

be taken in very easily, and that is why I want to warn you in good time, before it is too late!"

In gratitude I flung my arms about her and held her very tight. Indeed, she seemed like a mother to me, and in our embrace there was more emotion than I could have expected.

"Of course, it is really wonderful," she said at last, looking at me with her tired, sad eyes. "Until the Waichow victory, Kai-shek as head of the Whampoa Military Academy was practically unknown outside of the Canton. But today, look at him! He is the most powerful man in South China. It's hard to overestimate his influence. And you, my dear, are our new leader's wife. There is so much you can do in social welfare work to help the underprivileged of Canton. Would you like to do that?"

"I certainly would like to help all I can," I told her. "Let me know exactly what I can do and I shall do my utmost to help in every way."

"That's the spirit," she said, patting my cheek.

Luncheon was then served and we sat down to a very nice repast.

Back at my flat in the academy, I was attending to Kai-shek's large pile of mail. Letter by letter, I opened each one. And then I came across an envelope that bore a Russian stamp. It was a letter from Ching-kuo. One paragraph read:

> *Last year, most of my clothing was lost when my suitcase was stolen. This winter I will urgently need some thick clothes to keep me warm. The slashing cold of a Moscow winter is more than I can bear. At present I have only the clothes I am wearing. Please send some money to buy clothes as soon as possible. I am in dire need. This is urgent.*
>
> *Ching-kuo*

That afternoon I showed the letter to Kai-shek. But after he had glanced at it perfunctorily, he merely handed it back without comment.

That night I asked him: "What about sending some money to Ching-kuo to buy winter clothing? He needs it badly since it will soon be very cold there."

He simply answered: "Young people must be taught to be more responsible with their things. How can he be so careless as to let his clothing be stolen? He must be responsible for his own losses. I cannot send him any money."

Three days passed, and Kai-shek did not refer to the matter again. So I asked: "Have you decided on how much you intend to send Ching-kuo to buy winter clothes? He is waiting for your reply."

"No," he answered indifferently. "I will not send him any."

Ch'en Kuo-fu, who was often called Kai-shek's "nephew," had recently arrived at the academy to take up a position. He temporarily acted as private secretary and came to the conference room to help me each morning with Kai-shek's large pile of mail. Feeling much worried over Ching-kuo's predicament in Moscow, I asked his advice as to what to do. He advised: "Since Kai-shek refuses to help, it is no use forcing the issue. It will only irritate him and cause ill feeling. You know his bad temper. What about raising a loan as an emergency measure? Later on, we can get Kai-shek to repay it."

"But where can we get such a loan?" I asked. "We used to get money from the Army Preparation Committee, but that department is now closed. Will you try to think of another source?"

"I'll try," he promised. For a week I worried over this matter. On the eighth day, as we sat together sorting the large pile of mail in the conference room, I asked Ch'en Kuo-fu anxiously: "Have you been able to arrange a loan?"

"No," he answered. "Money is tight everywhere, and each place I approached turned me down."

I went into my bedroom and took from my small jewel case a wad of Canton bank notes that was my only savings of the last two years. I had had to deny myself many things in order to save this sum. For dear Fu-mei's sake, I handed the money to Ch'en Kuo-fu and said: "This is all that I have in cash. It amounts to $2,000. Since the boy is so far away in a foreign land and without warm clothing this winter, you had better remit it to him at once so that he will get what is necessary. Write and tell him the money is from his father."

"What a kind and loving stepmother you are," he said, and I could see he was touched.

"Ching-kuo needs this money more than I do. So please send it at once. I promised Fu-mei I would look after her son, so I want to keep my promise to her."

"Yes," answered Ch'en Kuo-fu, "I will send it by telegraphic transfer without delay. Ching-kuo should get the money within three days."

20

The Blue Shirts

In their protest against Kai-shek's dictatorial behavior, many of the conservatives became his political opponents. But because he controlled the army, there was nothing for the conservatives to do but acquiesce in his wishes. When he wanted something from them, he usually got it. Below the surface, however, it caused much ill feeling and hatred.

For the sake of efficiency, Kai-shek insisted on further radical changes. To discuss this problem, a meeting of the legislators was scheduled for that afternoon. Kai-shek insisted that I accompany him to this meeting.

After lunch, the legislators assembled at the Kuomintang headquarters in the Treasury Building and were waiting for the details of Kai-shek's latest demands. Kai-shek and I, walking side by side, arrived on the second floor of the legislature hallway accompanied by a retinue of politicians, legislators, and bodyguards. Walking down the hallway, we met a young man dressed in uniform. He was holding a bunch of newspapers in his hands, which were folded in front of him. He strolled toward Kai-shek and said, "You stole my cousin's army and shot his two best generals in cold blood, so take this!" Then his right hand, holding a revolver, came out from beneath the newspapers.

Kai-shek's bodyguard saw the gun and jumped for it. But before they could snatch the pistol, it fired, though its aim had been deflected. Kai-shek and I, greatly alarmed, ran down the corridor while the bodyguards wrestled with the assassin. One bodyguard brought the man under control by disarming him, while another bodyguard emptied his revolver into the would-be assassin's body. Kai-shek and I were shaking like a leaf when we were told that the assassin was none other than Hsu Chi, cousin of General Hsu Ch'ung-chih.

When the newspapers reported the news, conditions in Canton became confused and unstable, for the death of any leader would mean a change in government. Fortunately, however, Kai-shek was safe and sound, although much shaken by the experience.

Ever since the *Chung shan* gunboat incident, and now this latest attempt on his life, I noticed that Kai-shek had become highly nervous and no longer found enjoyment in anything he did. He was obsessed with dark plots against him and his growing power. The fact that his life could have been forfeited so easily on two occasions served as a reminder of the dangers surrounding him. It became his firm belief that the enemy outside, however strong, could be easily defeated, but a traitor within was far deadlier. One did not know who the traitor was and hence could not defend against him. He did not mention anything about the assassin's attempt on his life because he felt that there was some justification for the hatred. But time and again he said to me: "How provident that you became suspicious of Becky Wang's telephone calls and warned me in time; otherwise I would now be a prisoner in Vladivostock or even stone dead. You really saved my life, my darling wife!"

He was always so appreciative, so I answered: "You are now a strong and powerful man and naturally have many enemies, so you will have to be very careful wherever you go."

Henceforth he became suspicious not only of strangers but of practically everybody, even friends who visited us. This proved a disadvantage, for he could trust no one, and I had to stay away from all my friends.

How to protect himself effectively became the critical question. After much deliberation, he finally said to me, "I will organize my Blue Shirts!"*

---

*Jennie seems to have been confused here and may have been referring to one of Chiang's secret-service organizations of a different name. The so-called Blue Shirts organization was not actually established until 1932. On the Blue Shirts in the 1930s, see Lloyd E. Eastman, *The Abortive Revolution: China Under Nationalist Rule, 1927–1937* (Cambridge: Harvard University Press, 1974, rev. ed., 1990), pp. 31–84 and Appendix. —L.E.E.

"Why Blue Shirts?" I asked.

"The Blue Shirts will be a completely secret system of private investigators. I know the Green and Black Dragon Societies of Japan and the Triad Societies of Shanghai. But I prefer the Black Shirts system of Benito Mussolini of Italy. It would be a splendid idea to organize my own group and call them Blue Shirts."

"Do you mean they will wear blue shirts?"

"Oh, no. They will be detectives in plain clothes. But for want of a better name, I will call them Blue Shirts. Do you like the name?"

"It is typical, because China is often called the land of the blue gown," I answered. "As you said, anything can happen under our noses, and the Blue Shirts will be our safeguard. They will keep us informed of plots that are being hatched and of crimes that are being planned. Yes, I think it is an important move, but their training must be highly specialized."

"Yes, it will be," answered Kai-shek. "Their work will be to gather vital information from our enemies, prevent plots from being carried out, make secret arrests, and quash all resistance to our government." He then mapped out his plans on a large sheet of paper. "Look at these," he said. "The organization will consist of two departments, namely, Department of Investigation and Department of Statistics. With this organization, I will extinguish all opposition, strengthen our government, and conquer all plotters."

With this scheme for his protection, he accomplished it at a minimum of cost, largely through the help of two trusted "nephews," sons of his former boss and mentor, the late Ch'en Ch'i-mei. These men were Ch'en Kuo-fu, who helped me with the mail, and his younger brother, Ch'en Li-fu. These men were assigned to organize the two departments, but I found the elder was the cleverer. He was a man of subtle intellect.

Kai-shek was impatient to get things done in a hurry, and he spent a good deal of time helping the two brothers to get organized. Of course, this matter was kept strictly secret. The Ch'en brothers were considered to be the leaders of the C. C. Clique. I kept the records and did a lot of the paperwork. The plan was to have a network of secret agents and informers who spied not only on the public, but on government workers as well. This apparatus was to outrank the police in importance, since it was a private branch of Kai-shek's own headquarters.

The Ch'en brothers were responsible for recruiting for the new organization, and they proved to be staunch workers. As things progressed, they were given sole charge of the organization. With the help of their assistants, they worked wonders.

A Blue Shirt was a detective who followed the same principles as a spy to gain vital information in secret. A network of listening posts and detection stations was duly established. This made it difficult for plotters to plan and scheme without it becoming known. With the Blue Shirts now at work, Kai-shek was given a daily report of what his adversaries were thinking and doing. It was reassuring information and gave him a strong sense of security.

To get the maximum loyalty from these men, they were given lectures on loyalty, on Dr. Sun's Three Principles of the People, and on Nationalism. They were to recognize only the orders of the leader, a principle that was to be their highest law. They were told to forget all other duties except fealty to their boss and to be ever ready to arrest, kill, torture, or mutilate any suspect or culprit that fell into their hands.

Since everything was highly secret, outsiders had but a hazy idea about them. Because of their name, it was commonly believed that they wore blue uniforms for identification. But in truth, they did not wear any uniform at all, and in this way the people were hoodwinked. Thus, it was not easy to ascertain who belonged to the Blue Shirts and who did not.

The Ch'en brothers fully realized that their work would become a powerful force in Kai-shek's government. It would become stronger as Kai-shek's power increased. They worked at their jobs indefatigably. Most of their recruits were from the middle and lower classes of Cantonese. Getting Ningpo men was important for Kai-shek psychologically because he felt that a clansman would not easily turn traitor. They were, therefore, for sentimental reasons more dependable. Regardless of whether they came from Canton or from Ningpo, however, they all had to swear the same oath—that they would protect their leader with their lives. As encouragement, they were promised a bonus each year and a pension after ten years of service.

There is no doubt that through the years, the Blue Shirts did their job well to protect their master. Just for the record, however, I cannot omit mentioning one crime placed at their door.*

---

*One wonders why Jennie Ch'en chose to recount this story in her memoir. The incident occurred more than a decade after the period of her marriage to Chiang. And the so-called Blue Shirts had been accused of numerous other assassinations during the 1930s. —L.E.E.

The whole of Shanghai was shocked [in 1938] by the gruesome axe slaying of veteran statesman T'ang Shao-yi. He was found bludgeoned to death at his home on Range Road, North Szechwan Road, Shanghai. The seventy-five-year-old politician was living in retirement after a colorful career under Yuan Shih-k'ai. Suspected motive for the killing was said to be his public utterances against the Nationalist government.

The murder was carefully planned. Because Mr. T'ang was an ardent connoisseur of Chinese art and a collector of porcelains, the murderer posed as a curio dealer. He telephoned his intended victim for an appointment to show him a genuine large Sung celadon vase, which he offered for sale at a very low price. Mr. T'ang made an appointment for ten o'clock the following morning. The assassin appeared at the appointed hour with the vase and was shown into Mr. T'ang's drawing room. As the man proffered the vase to Mr. T'ang, he stealthily pulled out from inside the vase an axe wrapped in paper. Raising the axe high in the air, the assassin made one swift movement and struck Mr. T'ang on the head, bludgeoning him to instant death. The murderer then took flight, leaving the axe and vase behind. It was two hours later before the gruesome deed was discovered by a servant. She gave the alarm. Police investigators found the vase and the blood-stained axe with strands of hair clinging to blood clots.

One man was subsequently arrested by the Shanghai municipal police. After days of intensive grilling, he signed a confession that he was a member of the Blue Shirts of the Nationalist government.

21

Northern Expedition

With the entire territory of Canton under his control, Kai-shek began to see the prospect before him of all of China being united. This was the most grandiose of his dreams. Once united, China would become one of the most powerful nations in the world. At the same time, he would become China's sole leader. This was his ardent wish. The people of China were sick and tired of the oppression of the warlords. They yearned for a united China, and they therefore rallied behind Kai-shek. I, for one, knew he would succeed and prayed hard and earnestly to the Great Buddha to bless and watch over him.

Kai-shek's power now increased rapidly. He was first elected a member of the State Council, followed by becoming chairman of the Central Executive Committee, and chairman of the Military Council. He was also the head of the Organization Department and of the Military People's Department [militia, or *min-t'uan* (?)] of the headquarters of the Kuomintang. The time to start the Northern Expedition seemed ripe, so he could assume the leadership, making him the undisputed leader of all the political and party organizations of South China.

Through Michael Borodin, the Soviets were now sending aid in the form of finances, arms, and ammunition. This solved the major problems that had held up the expedition against the warlords. All plans for the expedition were now thoroughly discussed and mapped out in consultation with Borodin and General Galen.

To assure the future stability and control of Canton, Kai-shek had appointed his most reliable men to take charge. General Li Chi-shen was appointed governor of Canton and commander in chief of the Cantonese Army. Old Mr. Chang Ching-chiang was appointed supervisor of the Kuomintang. The Political Department was headed by the Hunanese General T'an Yen-k'ai. These three important positions settled, Kai-shek breathed a sigh of relief.

On July 9, 1926, the ceremony for the oath-taking took place at the Eastern Parade Grounds. It was called the "Oath to Assume the Office of Commander in Chief of the Northern Punitive Expedition Ceremony." Kai-shek, resplendent in his best uniform, and I in my pale-blue silk gown, sat on the dais with six officials. The ceremony was simple but impressive; General T'an Yen-k'ai, the newly appointed political chief, officiated. After a number of speeches, Kai-shek spoke: "This Northern Expedition is being carried out according to our late leader's wish. The purpose is to restore independence to China and its people. I will lead my armies to advance and never retreat. In a revolutionary spirit I am ready to sacrifice myself for my country. I also call upon all our soldiers to obey orders and observe discipline. We must be united in spirit to destroy the enemy; otherwise the enemy will destroy us."

There followed thunderous applause. Then the Party Committee member Wu Chih-hui presented Kai-shek with a blue flag upon which was written, in bold calligraphy, this phrase: "Down with militarism, the tool of foreign imperialism." Immediately after Kai-shek received this flag, he gave the following oath: "I shall faithfully carry out the Three Principles of the People, obey the orders of party officials unconditionally, protect the nation, and discharge my duty as a soldier."

The ceremony was attended by all the dignitaries of the government and the party. There was a crowd of 50,000 spectators and guests. It was Kai-shek's great day, and I was thrilled to be at his side. Such a large crowd of people, I thought, was quite insignificant compared with the soldiers now under his command. He had under him eight armies, which consisted of more than twenty divisions. And the number of officers and men who took orders from him was more than 100,000. I marveled at his good fortune in having acquired so much power within such a short span of time.

But this formidable force had an even more formidable task waiting to be accomplished. That task was to unite China by defeating the warlords all over the country. The total number of soldiers under these warlords was estimated to be over a million. They outnumbered Kai-shek's Nationalist Army by about ten to one. I prayed silently that victory would be his, and I murmured, "Oh Great Buddha, protect and guard him!"

After the ceremony, Kai-shek spent most of his time inspecting his armies and giving his staff officers pep talks. Mrs. Liao Chung-kai and I then helped him draft a number of messages, declarations, and telegrams to various departments. In the message, he repeatedly reminded his officers and men that this Northern Expedition was to unite China so that a strong nation could be established, strong enough to defend itself against all outside aggressors and imperialism. The soldiers were the people's Nationalist Army, and so they must uphold the army's good name at all costs. In his manifesto to the people of the whole nation, he said that he was fighting to relieve them of misgovernment and would never cease until he had driven away the imperialists and their tools, the warlords. And he hoped the people would cooperate with the soldiers in their common task of fighting against the enemy. These words, widely publicized in all the newspapers, seemed like the explosion of bombs on the heads of the warlords. They realized their days were numbered.

The chief enemies were three: Wu P'ei-fu, Sun Ch'uan-fang, and Chang Tso-lin. To fight them all meant fighting almost a million soldiers. It would be no easy matter. The only redeeming feature was that although Kai-shek's armies were small in comparison, he was an outstanding strategist and would follow the classical strategy: Befriend those afar and attack those near. In other words, attack Wu P'ei-fu, humor Sun Ch'uan-fang, and forget Chang Tso-lin. But while Kai-shek was marshalling his forces to enter Hunan to fight Wu P'ei-fu's men, Sun Ch'uan-fang started to raid the branch offices and arrest members of the Kuomintang in Shanghai. Kai-shek cleverly pretended that he did not know about these events but continued to exchange polite telegrams in classical style with Sun Ch'uan-fang, both of them assuring the other that if one did not attack the other first, the other would never do anything to mar their excellent friendship.

So on July 27, 1926, Kai-shek was ready to launch the Northern Expedition. The Central Executive Committee placed him in command of the entire enterprise in collaboration with the Russian general Vassily Galen.

We all met on the Wangsha Railway Station platform to see Kai-shek off. A photographer asked us to stand in a straight line before the train to have our pictures taken. After two were snapped, Kai-shek, seeing that I was on the verge of tears, held both my hands in farewell and said: "I'm going to war, but don't cry, for to do so will give me bad luck. Order twenty copies of the photos and bring them to Shiukwan when I wire you. Be sure to keep the negatives, for the pictures will be of great historical importance to our revolution." Seeing that I was still sad and gloomy, he said encouragingly: "You will have a chance to work in the reconstruction of our country as soon as the provinces are united. I'm on the threshold of my third wish. Remember? Now wish me luck and smile." My eyes were welling with tears, but I smiled. Then he said: "This is the first phase of our Northern Expedition. On its victorious conclusion, when all the provinces are conquered, we will be the happiest couple in China. Just wait and see."

"All your instructions shall be carried out," I managed to say chokingly. Then I blurted, "Oh, do let us go help you at the front!"

He looked at my sad, pleading eyes and laughed. He was so amused at the idea that he could not control his laughter. He said: "When women hear the roar of cannons, they are so scared that they urinate in their pants! Remember the *Yung Feng* cruiser?"

To get back at him for this ridicule, I exclaimed, "Laughter before talking shows a cunning nature!"

"You should say shrewd nature," corrected Mrs. Liao Chung-k'ai.

Kai-shek came closer to me and asked, "Am I cunning or shrewd?"

"Both," I said with a pout.

He turned to Mrs. Liao: "I really love her most dearly. Do take great care of her for me."

"You know I will do that, Kai-shek, for I, too, love her as my own sister. You concentrate on your battles, and we will come to bring you 'war comforts' at Shiukwan."

As the train moved noisily away, I felt a wrench in my heart. I waved and waved to Kai-shek, with tears in my eyes. He waved back until I couldn't see him any longer. Now that he had left, I had no time for brooding. My job was to supervise the removal of all our personal belongings from our flat in the military academy to my house in Tungshan. This kept me busy for two days. Kai-shek had taken our servant

Sui-Chang with him, but Ah Shun was left to help me with the various chores, and he was as efficient as ever.

Wonderful Mrs. Liao Chung-k'ai was a great comfort. She came over to my place daily to discuss what we should take to Shiukwan. We planned to leave as soon as we received Kai-shek's telegram, for we had agreed that we would go to Shuikwan to see him on the first leg of his expedition, on the border of Kwangtung. Indeed, Mrs. Liao was really a most remarkable person. She was so experienced, so sane, and so down-to-earth. She seemed to know everything. On her suggestion, we bought large quantities of cloth for making bandages, tins of ointment, cotton wool, and two large bottles of iodine and other medical stores. Then we cut the cloth, rolled the bandages, and packed the wool into smaller packages. We didn't have a Red Cross brigade, but our two-women convoy was designed to augment the supplies of Kai-shek's Military Medical Aid Department.

The following week we received Kai-shek's telegram saying that it was now safe to proceed to Shiukwan. Mrs. Liao and I immediately took the train to the fighting zone. It was something new for women to appear in no-man's-land, but it was an example of our purpose and re-solve. We wanted to do our utmost to help relieve the suffering of the wounded, if possible. The weather was rather warm when we arrived there after an uneventful trip. Kai-shek with his bodyguards and Blue Shirts was at the station to meet our train. He looked thin but was tan and full of vigor and high spirits.

Greetings and pleasant amenities over, I handed him the batch of twenty photos that were taken at the Wangsha Railway Station, and he was delighted to see them. He examined them closely and critically. "They came out very well, much better than I expected," he said hap-pily. "One day these pictures will be very important, for they show the start of our campaign and the people who took part. Don't lose the neg-atives." He carried the photos under his arm proudly.

He had brought with him our boy Sui-Chang, so we handed over to this capable fellow all the medical supplies with instructions to have them delivered to the Military Medical Aid as a small contribution from Mrs. Liao and me.

Kai-shek told us that the border was clear of the enemy, and the sol-diers enjoyed high morale and were ready to fulfil their destiny. Then he took us to the home of Shiukwan's leading citizen, the House of Wu, a tall, imposing house with many rooms, all well furnished with rich blackwood furniture in the traditional style. Our host and hostess were gentle people who welcomed us with open arms. Kai-shek showed Mrs. Liao to her room and then showed me his. As he closed the door, he grabbed me savagely to his breast and murmured endearments. I could see how much he had missed me by the way he caressed me so passionately.

That night after dinner we retired to our room early, and Kai-shek embraced me, saying: "A soldier's life is so uncertain. I may get killed any time, but I want you always to remember that you are the only one I love, no matter what happens. You are the only person who holds my heart. Before I met you, my life was miserable and I wasted several years in wine, women, and song. How I regret it. After we were married, you brought me good luck and I have realized my three wishes. Do you remember what they are?" He kissed me ardently and I nodded.

"I never realized that I would be granted my wishes so soon," he mused. "You brought me good luck!" Then, referring to the photographs again, he added: "You and I came out very well. Do take good care of the negatives for me. The photos and our expedition will go down in history."

As I lay there with his arms around me, I thought to myself: This is the first time he has ever spoken of death to me. I pray that the Great Buddha will protect and guard him throughout this campaign. Then I clung closer to him and we became one.

Early the next morning, while Kai-shek was in conference with his officers, Mrs. Liao and I went out to visit the camps. Along the way, we saw a stream of straggling soldiers making their way to the advanced field hospital, which was nearby. We followed them there on an inspection tour and found that the makeshift surgeries were woefully ill equipped to handle the volume of desperate cases. We saw that the wounded lay unattended for many hours. We found that there was much we could do to help, so we pitched in. All that day Mrs. Liao and I helped the doctors and nurses in their work. Despite the care of the doctors and nurses, and our voluntary help, many of the wounded died.

On the third day, the whole expedition was on the move northward. Mrs. Liao and I, after bidding a sad farewell to Kai-shek, therefore, returned to Canton, where I was to settle our household affairs. I would then return to Shanghai to await Kai-shek's next telegram, which was to be sent from Kiukiang in Kiangsi province. The distance from Canton to Kiukiang was about 1,500 miles, and it was estimated that it would take approximately two months to conquer this territory.

′   ′   ′

The progress of Kai-shek's expedition after Shiukwan was extremely rapid. The newly reorganized Eighth Army, with fresh reinforcements from Kwangtung and Kwangsi, and part of the Fourth and Seventh armies, started a counteroffensive. Within a fortnight, Changsha, the capital of Hunan, fell. Before the end of August, the entire province of Hunan was almost clear of the enemy.

Hupei was Kai-shek's next target, and the fighting for control of that province was brisk. A decisive battle was fought between Wu P'ei-fu's crack divisions and the pick of the Nationalist Army. By late August the enemy forces were severely beaten. By this time, Kai-shek had moved his headquarters to Yo-Chow, a town on the northern border of Hunan. It was only some sixty miles from the field where this big battle was raging, and a little over a hundred miles from the triple city of Wuhan, which is composed of Hankow, Hanyang, and Wuchang.

Wu P'ei-fu was personally supervising this important battle. He and his generals were directing operations from Hsien-ning, only a few miles north of the battlefield. After four days and nights of intensive fighting, in which both sides suffered heavy losses, the enemy withdrew hurriedly into Wuchang, the capital of Hupei province. Kai-shek's Nationalist Army followed in hot pursuit and took the city of Hanyang on September 7, 1926. After occupying the city, they crossed the river to take Hankow. Meanwhile, a part of the army besieged more than 20,000 of the enemy in Wuchang. The next day, Kai-shek approached the city of Wuchang and demanded that the besieged generals surrender unconditionally within twenty-four hours. The enemy held out for more than ten days, however, before the city was finally taken. Then the Kuomintang flag proudly fluttered over the Wuhan cities, welcoming the arrival of Michael Borodin, the Kuomintang leaders, and their followers to Hankow. They came from Canton to assume the administration of Wuhan.

Kai-shek wrote to me on September 17, 1926, as follows:

My Dear Wife,

No doubt you have read of our victories at Wuhan. I am now in Hankow and am kept busy consolidating our positions. As soon as our armies are reorganized, I will set out for Hanchang and Kiukiang, and then I will send for you. The best way to come would be by the Taikoo River steamer. I wish you were here now to console and comfort me. There has been a great deal of dissension in our party, about which I shall tell you when we meet. It is nothing but prejudice, jealousy, and power politics—as usual.

Since Wuhan is our most important victory to date, I have insisted on several innovations. Each morning we hold a memorial service honoring our great leader Dr. Sun. These are similar to the services held at the Whampoa Military Academy, except they are more elaborate and with a brass band. The soldiers, officers, and officials stand and bow three times to Dr. Sun's portrait while I stand on the platform, read aloud his will, a sentence at a time, while the audience repeats it after me. After that we have silent meditation for three minutes before we discuss our military situation and other problems.

Borodin, his advisers, and others have shown a reluctance to attend these morning ceremonies. I have insisted, however, explaining that Dr. Sun is the great leader of our Chinese Republic and this honor must be upheld. I was happily surprised to get a telegram from Soong Mei-ling congratulating me on my victories and calling me a hero. I have telegraphed her my thanks.

I will write again before I leave for Nanchang. In the meantime think more and more of me. I am well but tired. Ask after your mother, brother, and friends for me. I do love you very dearly.

*Chung**

Now that Wuhan was well under control, Kai-shek ripped off his mask of friendship with Sun Ch'uan-fang, the commander in chief of the five southeastern provinces. Formerly they had addressed one another by their first names and called each other My Dear Elder Brother. Their language now was quite different. The old policy of humoring Sun Ch'uan-fang was no longer necessary, for Sun Ch'uan-fang had issued an ultimatum to Kai-shek to withdraw his troops from Sun's borders within twenty-four hours. He said in a telegram addressed to the whole country:

*Chiang Kai-shek's formal given name was Chung-cheng. Here, writing to Jennie, he uses an informal short form. —L.E.E.

Chiang Kai-shek, a nobody from some remote waterside, has no right to threaten me and impose himself on my borders. Falsely flying the flag of Sun Yat-sen, he is actually acting according to the policy of Lenin. He has spread Bolshevism in South China and has caused much suffering among the people. Such actions indicate that he is now an aggressor and a destroyer of the peace. His sins and crimes are without limit and incur the anger of both God and man.

Kai-shek replied by saying:

Sun Ch'uan-fang's plans to inflict harm on Hunan and Kwangtung are absolutely transparent. He is deceiving himself as well as cheating others. He has occupied Kiangsu and Chekiang during the past year and still will not rein in his ambition. Under the pretext of protecting his regions and maintaining peace for his people, he is actually an aggressor, causing suffering to the people.

To strike while the iron was hot, Kai-shek led his army in a southeasterly direction into the province of Kiangsi to capture the ancient city of Nanchang. His overwhelming success was like splitting bamboo, and he took over the city after strong resistance. He then turned his army northward to capture the city of Kiukiang.

In the meantime I had settled my household affairs in Canton and returned to Shanghai on the SS *Empress of Canada*. The first thing Kai-shek did after taking over Kiukiang was to send me an urgent telegram asking me to come to him at once. He had booked passage for me on the Taikoo River steamer *Szechwan*, which left Shanghai on September 28, 1926.

The distance from Shanghai to Kiukiang along the Yangtze River is around 400 miles. The journey took two pleasant days. The September weather was balmy, and along the winding river one could see many scenes of interest. I made it a habit to sit on deck watching the scenery. The second day on board I was standing on deck near the rail. There were pine-clad hills on one side of the river. On the opposite bank were stretches of bamboo groves, whose glistening stems and verdant plumes presented a remarkably beautiful picture. I thought to myself, no wonder Chinese artists love to paint bamboo. I now understand the reason for their admiration. As I was thus musing, two men who were standing nearby watching the passing scene, oblivious of my presence, talked about the political situation and the success of the Northern Expedition. One said to the other: "Warlord Sun Ch'uan-fang will surely be defeated by Chiang Kai-shek."

"What makes you say that?"

"He's got Russian advisers, Russian guns, and ammunition, but he is a bastard. He has no father!"

"How do you know?" asked the other.

"Well, he built a tomb for his deceased mother, but through all these years, he has never even mentioned his father."

"That is true," agreed his friend. "I wonder who his father was."

I walked slowly away and made up my mind to tell Kai-shek about this incident.

On my arrival at Kiukiang, Kai-shek with his bodyguards and Blue Shirts came to meet me. Kai-shek looked very ruddy and lively, but very thin. He was so very affectionate and tender that it made me think that husbands and wives should stay apart from one another once in a while, so that they would appreciate each other the more.

Kai-shek and I stayed at the home of Mr. and Mrs. Fong Tung, Kiukiang's society leader, whose beautiful house was surrounded by a typical Chinese garden with weeping-willow trees and a red-lacquered bridge and pagoda. Our host and hostess treated us most cordially, making us feel like honored guests. The string of servants waited on us hand and foot.

I was thrilled to be in this City of Nine Rivers, which is the literal meaning of the name Kiukiang. The city was noted for its beautiful monasteries and pagodas. It was also noted for its porcelains, silver wares, and silks. The porcelains were brought to Kiukiang from the famous area of Ching-teh-chen, where all the imperial pottery, so much appreciated by collectors, had been made for centuries.

The silversmiths' work, too, was interesting because of the primitive methods employed, mostly hammering, and the results attained were exquisite. Much silk was made in and about the city. And on the shelves of the local shops I saw rolls and rolls of luxurious brocades and satins of every shade and pattern. I seized the chance to replenish my wardrobe by having a number of new dresses made from these fine silks.

One day I said to Kai-shek: "Isn't it strange? While on board the *Szechwan* I heard two men talking. One said you were a bastard, that you had no father!"

"You should have had the men arrested."

"How could I on board? Any protest by me would have attracted a lot of attention."

This question troubled me. There was really some justification for the rumor because it was true that Kai-shek had always eulogized his mother and never mentioned his father even once. I wrote to my mother in Shanghai and asked her to engage an investigator to make extensive inquiries about Kai-shek's father.

ィ   ィ   ィ

By now Kai-shek's Nationalist Army had increased greatly in size. As its quantity increased, however, the quality decreased, and success thereafter came less easily. Beginning in September, the battle for Kiangsi was fought for two-and-one-half months before the province was cleared of Sun Ch'uan-fang's troops.

The attack on Fukien began in early October. By the end of November, that province, too, was occupied by Kai-shek's troops. As for Chekiang, Kai-shek's native province, prolonged fighting took place, and Sun Ch'uan-fang had several minor successes. But in the middle of February 1927, the Nationalists won out and took over the province.

Anhwei province fell to Kai-shek's forces in March 1927. The victory came when the military governor, formerly under Sun Ch'uan-fang, decided to throw in his lot with Kai-shek. He was named commander of the Thirty-seventh Nationalist Army.

Kai-shek's powers now grew to an unprecedented extent. As soon as he ousted a warlord, he would take over his area as a conqueror, assuming the new power through audacity, resourcefulness, and energy.

But with easy victories also came a bewildering string of problems and confusions. He had climbed the ladder of success, but all his victories had been gained with the aid of Moscow's guns and ammunition. He was, therefore, obliged to listen to Moscow's directives. Dr. Sun's slogan, after all, was Russia is our teacher. But if Kai-shek heeded Moscow's instructions, he did so reluctantly. And this displeased Borodin, who now regarded him as insolent.

22

Private Life

*I*n our private life, however, away from the turmoil of public affairs, Kai-shek's ardent love for me never changed. He was as considerate as ever, consulted me on all his decisions, and valued my opinions and suggestions. Since I was devoted to him, I shared all his interests and worries as if they were my own.

As victory after victory was won by the Nationalist Army, Kai-shek was kept busy accepting the surrenders of enemy commanders, as well as receiving offers of cooperation from neutral generals. When he started the expedition, he had only about 100,000 men in 8 armies. Now, within five months, he had 264,000 men under him, organized into 200 regiments. Many of the newly surrendered military leaders were rewarded with the rank of general or the title of commander of an army. This was done to encourage them, for often they had only a few regiments under them. Thus the number of so-called Nationalist armies had grown to thirty armies. When representatives from the minor warlords of Szechwan came to ask for "peace talks," Kai-shek exclaimed to me: "Everywhere they want to surrender to me. Their only fear is that I might not permit them to surrender. They are willing to ally with me or anyone else, just so they save their skins. They are all stinking opportunists!"

"Don't be so harsh," I advised. "Do you remember what you said about retiring gracefully? You are now a great man, and you must be generous. If they give in to you, it means they concede defeat."

At this time, Kai-shek truly believed that his Nationalist Army was invincible. Some of the armies, however, were formed primarily from troops that had recently capitulated. Few of the troops were experienced fighters, and most of them were leaving the warmer climes of South China for the colder zones of the North. Why was it, then, that they fought so well, won so many victories, and advanced so rapidly?

There were several reasons: The chief reason was that Kai-shek's forces believed they were fighting for the salvation of China, whereas the warlords were fighting solely for their selfish interests. Ever since the Chinese Republic had been established in 1911—for the past fifteen years—the country had suffered from civil wars. Most of the Chinese people, including many of the soldiers, were, therefore, war weary and wanted peace. They were willing to throw in their lot with the Nationalists so that China could become a strong, prosperous, and, above all, united nation.

Under the warlords, soldiers were commonly called yellow-uniformed robbers. They were undisciplined. Wherever they went, they looted, pressed people into forced labor, and demanded large sums of money and food. Naturally they were hated. It is understandable, therefore, why the Nationalists achieved their speedy successes.

Meanwhile, Kai-shek was busy mapping out his next campaign. The objectives of this campaign were Nanking and Shanghai, which were much stronger than any of the cities previously conquered. More planning was, therefore, required, and our stay in Kiukiang was necessarily extended. I nonetheless remained busy. Besides my studies of the English and Chinese languages, I resumed my job as personal secretary to look after Kai-shek's mail and open all his letters.

In answer to Kai-shek's secret invitation, the three big "bosses" of the Shanghai underworld came to Kiukiang to give a report of conditions there. How could Shanghai be captured?

These men were the notorious Tu, Wang, and Chang, commonly known as the "tripod" of Shanghai. They had their fingers on the pulse of Shanghai's organized gangland. If one appealed to them, one could within a few hours recover anything that had been lost or stolen. Their visit to Kai-shek was short and sweet, for they had but one idea in mind, namely, how to take over control of Shanghai. For this, silver bullets must be used. This was entirely satisfactory to Kai-shek, for he knew he could set the Nanking City mint in motion as soon as that city was captured.

As a result of overwork and constant worry, Kai-shek now felt seedy and had a fever of 103. I insisted, therefore, that he take a rest in bed. Besides, he was losing weight and not eating well. He was not at home to visitors.

Then, out of the blue, came a letter from Canton for Kai-shek. I opened it and showed it to him. After perusal, he handed it to me. It read:

Dear Big Brother,

For a few months I have not been near you to receive your profitable instruction. In your busy military life you have wired inviting me to accompany my sister and family to visit Wuhan (Hankow) to see our Nationalist Party's new achievements. For this I am very grateful. But the day before yesterday I left Canton for Shanghai to see my mother. Big sister is still in Canton and may shortly return to Shanghai. When I have time I shall certainly accompany her to visit the Yangtze cities. I am now taking advantage of Yung-chih's (H. H. Kung's) departure for Hankow to write you these few lines to ask after your well-being.

Mei-ling

After reading it, Kai-shek said: "That's a reply to my telegram thanking her for her congratulations. I invited her to come to Hankow. I haven't seen her since that pigeon dinner." He mused as he read the card again. "It shows how important it is to hold high position," he continued. "Once you are up, people flock to you." He lay there and was silent.

I took hold of his cold hand and warmed it by holding it tight. I felt him shivering. I held it for what seemed an hour, and gradually I could feel him relaxing.

"Would you mind if I invited her and her sister to visit us in Kiukiang?" he asked hesitatingly.

I immediately thought of Mrs. Liao Chung-k'ai's warning and therefore hesitated. I also thought of what he had previously said: I want to get closer to the Suns and the Soongs. As I sat there in silence, he asked again: "Will you say yes?"

"If it pleases you to invite them, naturally I have no objection. Go ahead and ask them to come if it makes you happy."

"Not now, but later," he said cheerily. "Perhaps next week, when I am not so busy."

As Kai-shek was mentally fatigued, I thought a trip to Kuling would cheer him up, for he loved outdoor life. He had spoken of Kuling so very often that I seemed to know the place. He told me that in the old days, Kuling was the most fruitful field for the propagation of Buddhism after the religion had been introduced from India, back in A.D. 67. The mountains, 4,500 feet high, were dotted with famous temples, which were visited by thousands of pilgrims annually. Kai-shek was delighted with this suggestion, and I made arrangements for our trip.

On the journey to Kuling, we stayed at a pleasant bungalow near the Chih-Sen Monastery, belonging to our host, Mr. Fong Tung. To reach our destination, we were carried up the steep mountain in sedan chairs. It was ironical to see Kai-shek's twelve bodyguards and six Blue-Shirt detectives accompanying us on foot for protection, for it seemed so unnecessary. But it was their job, so there they were as excess baggage. The two servant boys, Ah Shun and Sui-chang, with Mr. Fong Tung's man acting as guide, looked after all our comforts—as they always did—and carried out Kai-shek's orders most competently.

For two days we inhaled deeply the sweet exhilarating air and enjoyed the glorious sunshine. We climbed the hills and slopes and looked at the Yangtze Valley in the distance. We also visited the various monasteries. At each shrine we bowed respectfully to Buddha and gave a small donation, paid out by Ah Shun, as our contribution for "incense and oil," which was the custom. Most of the monasteries had little income and depended on gifts from the devout for subsistance. If some monks tilled their vegetable plots or grew wheat on their terraced fields, their income was still negligible.

As long as I live I will never forget the first afternoon of our arrival. Kai-shek and I walked for miles. We visited the White Deer Grotto and saw the spot where the illustrious poet Li Po, of the T'ang Dynasty, made his studio. Li Po had built a large artificial grotto there. It is said that he had a tame white deer as a pet, from which the name of the grotto is derived. Owing to the fame of Li Po, the grotto had become a favorite resort for scholars during the turbulent years when the T'ang Dynasty was tottering to its fall. Scholars came here and opened a school, which had the rank of a university. Thus the place acquired the name "Oldest University" of China.

Because Kai-shek loved the mountains, we climbed the high slopes until our feet ached. As the afternoon wore on, we sat on a large rock to watch the sunset. The whole western sky was aflame with a deep crim-

Chiang Kai-shek and Jennie, probably about the time of their visit to Kuling.

son color. It was certainly a magnificent sight! It was the manifestation
of the Supreme Being in all his glory. Kai-shek and I marveled at the in-
definable splendor of the sinking orb below the far-off horizon. Silently
we looked with wondrous awe at the sublime spectacle, and I thought
to myself, how insignificant is man! How futile are our struggles! And
how great is the universe! We were only a speck in the midst of this
grandeur! The radiance of the western sky blazed with a thousand hues
of gold and rich vermillion that blended through every shade of red, orange, blue, green, and purple. I myself had never watched a sunset before. I was so thrilled that I closed my eyes and made a silent wish: May
Kai-shek succeed in his Northern Expedition and may he live long and
enjoy good health. Kai-shek, too, was silent and I knew he was in deep
thought. At last I said: "No wonder the Buddhists regard this mountain
as sacred. We are standing on consecrated ground."

"Yes," he agreed readily. "This is a wonderful spot. We must come
here again when we can spare the time."

Kai-shek looked at me for several minutes so intently, I thought
there was something stuck on my face. I raised my hand to wipe away

whatever it was, but each time he seized my palm in his and said: "It is extraordinary how much I love you. I just asked Buddha to protect and guard you. You won't believe it, but it is true. At the front, in all my spare moments I thought of you, day and night! Did you think of me too?"

"No," I replied jokingly. "I am not a sentimentalist or an emotionalist."

Then he caressed my cheek and remarked, "I don't believe you, for I know you love me just as much as I love you."

As the first sign of darkness began to spread over the mountain, we walked silently back to our bungalow with a strange, happy feeling that we had seen the great Buddha and that he had blessed our love.

23

The Ordeal

*I*t is often said, Happiness penetrates the soul, but what afterwards gushes forth is springs of tears. This saying proved to be very true where Kai-shek was concerned, for on our return from Kuling the first thing that was handed him was an urgent telegram from Hankow. We had hardly entered our drawing room when Kai-shek tore open the envelope and read it. In disgust he threw it away. Then he banged his head with both his fists, took up a vase from the table and smashed it to smittereens, slumped into an easy chair, bent down his head, and wept bitterly. For an instant I became terrified and pleaded: "Oh, please be calm. What has happened?"

"They have snatched the leadership from me! All my plans are finished! All my hopes are shattered!"

I picked up the telegram from the floor and read it; the gist of it stated:

> Eighty Kuomintang party members, a Committee of the State Council, and the new Central Executive Committee have voted themselves to be the highest authorities in the Hankow government. Please await orders.

This was a crushing blow. Kai-shek was head of the government, a member of the State Council, chairman of the Central Executive Committee, and chairman of the Military Council. Why had he been ignored so completely, without even being invited to the meeting? Was it to make him lose face? Or was it a trick to discredit him? No wonder this news came as a shock. Besides, it was Kai-shek's intention to establish a government in Nanking after that city was captured. Now, however, the Communists had seized the initiative and jumped a step ahead. In other words, they had snatched from him the fruits of his labor. I perfectly understood Kai-shek's fury. All his fond hopes of leadership were ended. He had been betrayed, stabbed in the back!

For an hour Kai-shek behaved like a madman. He banged the table, shouted to high heaven, and cursed Borodin in no uncertain terms. I allowed him an hour to blow off steam and then advised: "Why distress yourself in this manner? Why not wire Hankow and ask them to send a representative of the National Assembly to come at once to thrash out the matter with you face-to-face? Hankow is only 145 miles away. That would be more sensible. At least you will know where you stand. Shall I draft a wire for you?"

His eyes gleamed with hate and he nodded. I scribbled out a draft and handed it to him. He read it over, made a couple of changes in the wording to make it more effective. Then I had Ah Shun dispatch it immediately.

From the time I sent off the message until the representative arrived, it was almost twenty-seven hours. And during that period I lived in agony. Kai-shek was upset, fidgety, and restive. Nothing I did calmed his ruffled nerves.

Late the following afternoon, our old friend Mrs. Liao Chung-k'ai arrived, and I was relieved to learn that she was representing the Hankow government. She was the best person they could have sent because she was our close friend and an upright, honest woman. Indeed, it was a clever and tactful move to use her as mediator between Kai-shek and the new government.

We welcomed her cordially and ushered her into our drawing room, where she got down to business straightaway. Mrs. Liao tried to make her position clear by saying: "First, I want you both to understand that Borodin and Wang Ching-wei thought I was the logical person to represent the Hankow government in bringing you the news of their decision. They, and both of you, are my friends; and whatever I have to say now is not necessarily what I would personally endorse. The reason I promised to act as liaison is that I feel for you an intimacy akin to that of a family relationship. And this matter concerns the Kuomintang, of which my late husband and I have been pioneer members. As soon as I have made my report to you, I will return to Hankow by the same steamer this evening."

Then she opened her dispatch case and took out a sheet of paper. Looking at it, she said: "There have been great changes since Shiukwan. The Kuomintang headquarters has moved from Canton to Hankow, and now it has formed a government with Wang Ching-wei as chairman. He recently returned from France. Eugene Chen is the minister of foreign affairs, and T. V. Soong is the minister of finance. In fact," she added, "Madame Sun gives the government her blessing. She and her mother, her two sisters, and the Kung family children are all in Hankow to celebrate the occasion. Now I am here to answer any questions you may have."

Kai-shek was furious and shouted: "Everything was carried out so sneakily! I was not consulted at all! Was it done deliberately to make me lose face or to threaten me?"

"It was neither," she replied firmly. "The Hankow government was formed legally to carry out the wishes of our late leader Dr. Sun. It symbolizes the hope for an early completion of our revolution. So far, great things are being achieved both by you and Mr. Borodin. Mme Sun has announced that the Hankow government is the legitimate interpreter of Dr. Sun's ideology. No one will deny that. You are not consulted because you were out of contact, moving from one front to another. You know that is the reason."

At this Kai-shek was silent for a moment. He had nothing to say against Mme Sun and her blessing of the new government. Seeing his silence, I said: "We were in Kuling for two glorious days and imagine our surprise when we heard the news. It was such a shock. In fact, Kai-shek was stunned."

Mrs. Liao then handed a sheet of paper to Kai-shek. "Read this," she advised. "Probably you have not seen it because you have been on the move." Kai-shek held it with both hands and I could see his hands tremble. It was a letter from General Hsu Ch'ung-chih, his former boss. Having been silent for two years and seeing that the Hankow government had become a reality, Hsu wrote:

Dear Brother Kai-shek,

You may recall that, ten years ago, you and I followed our master to work for the revolution. Because of our indomitable spirit, we devoted our lives hoping for success. Unfortunately our master died, and you asked me to let you temporarily take over my army in order to reorganize

it. This I agreed to. Subsequently you established the Nationalist
government in Canton and called my army the Nationalist Army.

   Ever since I handed the army over to you, our party affairs have been
confused and split; administration has become corrupt and inefficient.
You have thus made yourself the target of arrows from all sides. Those
who used to call themselves your subordinates, supporters, or friends
have now risen as one man to oppose you. According to the theory of
censure you cannot really be excused from this responsibility.

   Now that the Hankow government is a reality, I hope you will reflect
and do what is right: Obey orders and confess your mistakes. Censure
yourself for bad faith and keep your promise so that the country will be
at peace. For you, this will be an honorable way out; for our people it
will be a great blessing. Consider and reconsider my words calmly and
dispassionately.

Hsu Ch'ung-chih

Kai-shek looked at our guest, then at me, and merely blinked without saying a word. Then Mrs. Liao took out another sheet of paper and
handed it to Kai-shek.

"This is a handbill," she explained. It read, "The Revolution Will
Never Succeed Without First Striking Down Chiang Kai-shek!"

"There is an anti-Chiang movement going on," she continued. "It is
largely carried out by members of the Kuomintang who consider themselves more revolutionary than you. I understand that the most outspoken participants in the movement are none other than your own men:
two officers, Hsu Ch'ien and Teng Yen-ta, whom you call your protégés.
These two men are now with the Hankow government and they shout
aloud, 'Down with Chiang Kai-shek, the dictator!' They not only shout
one by one, but they shout like cheerleaders, leading large crowds at
mass meetings! Two days ago they actually led the masses to shout until they were hoarse, just as the revolutionaries did in Russia. Both Teng
Yen-ta and Hsu Ch'ien have denounced you as a new warlord!"

I looked at Kai-shek and saw that his face had turned an ugly white.
He fumed with rage. He clenched and unclenched his hands convul-
sively. I was truly frightened. The behavior of his two protégés in con-
ducting an anti-Chiang campaign—it was as though his two protégés
were biting the hand that had fed them, and he was nauseated by their
actions. It was a severe blow to his pride. Fearing that in such a state of
mind, he might do something desperate, I rose quietly from my chair

and went into our bedroom. I then took Kai-shek's revolver from its holster, which was dangling from the clothes stand, and hid it in one of his high leather riding boots at the end of the bedstead. I also warned the boys, Ah Shun and Sui-Chang, to stand by and be wary of their master's actions. When I came into the room again, Mrs. Liao handed Kai-shek yet another paper and said: This is an Open Letter from Wang Ching-wei:

> When our leader Sun Yat-sen saw the rapid decline of our country, he promoted the Three Principles as the basis of our revolutionary policies. These policies and principles were designed to sweep away all difficulties that beset the nation. In the declaration of the Northern Expedition, Dr. Sun's aim had been not only to destroy the warlords but also to guarantee that no successors to these warlords would arise. But now a crafty fellow has snatched power for his own aggrandizement.
>
> Chiang Kai-shek thinks he can pursue his private interests because he now holds supreme authority. His despotic ambition runs unchecked. He violates party regulations and browbeats congress. To rally support, he promises important official posts to all his friends. All he thinks of is his personal interests. He regards the nation as his private property. People's lives depend on his whims. Under him, life is cheap, and there is no security. Our comrades, some of whom are revolutionary pioneers, having followed our late leader for years, and who are firm believers in democracy, have now vowed to sacrifice their lives for the party and the country. They all regard Chiang Kai-shek as their common enemy and are determined to eliminate him. As soon as this declaration reaches you, rise up in arms and wipe away this rebel before it is too late! Only in this way can we save our country from annihilation and save the people from servitude to the imperialists.
>
> *Wang Ching-wei*

Mrs. Liao explained patiently, in a modulated voice: "Borodin considered Hankow a more desirable seat of government than either Canton or Nanking, and so the Kuomintang approved it as the capital. Now there are a number of reforms going on. A committee combining the State Council and the Central Executive Committee has been organized. In fact, this new committee held its first meeting on December 13, 1926, and voted itself, temporarily, to be the highest authority of the party and the Hankow government. Borodin and many comrades were present, and Wang Ching-wei was elected chairman. Since there are so many anti-Chiang movements going on in Wuchang, Hankow, and Hanyang, intensifying by the day, all Kuomintang members regard you as a new warlord. Your portrait, which used to decorate walls and banners as the savior of the people, now has two companions: the Kaiser on one side and Mussolini on the other. In view of your unpopularity, the Hankow government orders your dismissal from all offices and expels you from the party! Needless to say, it was passed legally and unanimously. The combined forces of our comrades secured a majority in all their decisions."

Kai-shek retorted: "I am a member of both councils and have not been informed of these decisions. How can they push me out altogether? You mean I am deprived of all my positions except that of commander in chief?"

"Yes, but even as commander in chief, your powers will henceforth be greatly reduced. One of the few resolutions passed by the Hankow government was that the commander in chief is just a member of the Military Council. Orders for mobilization must first be passed by a majority vote of the Military Council and approved by the Central Executive Committee before being issued to the commander in chief. He, then, may issue the orders."

She thereupon handed an official document to Kai-shek that read:

An Order to All Kuomintang Members:

Since the Northern Expedition began, all military, political, and party affairs have been concentrated in the hands of one individual, Chiang Kai-shek. This has meant that the political administration could not be directed by the party, but only by the military. Such a system has many defects. Not only does it protect all the useless and decadent elements of the party, but it also draws into the party all the bureaucrats and crafty opportunists. So it has produced an individual who is a dictator and a military autocrat. We cannot tolerate this for another day.

Wang Ching-wei
Michael Borodin

After reading the document, Kai-shek rose as though in a trance: So the Hankow government could do without him! Ridiculous! But he could see the disaster. He saw his position, his future, his reputation slipping from him. Hitherto he had thought the country could not possibly do without him. He was Dr. Sun's heir. The country and the party needed his leadership to carry out Dr. Sun's principles. But now he was to be discarded like an old shoe! All was lost! He walked to our bedroom. I could feel how utterly desperate he was. As I expected, he went to look for his revolver. But it was not in its usual place. Like one in a dream he pulled open one drawer after another and then searched the wardrobe. But he could not find his gun.

Thus frustrated, an intense hate and fury poured out of him, shattering all sense of proportion. He foamed and fumed, pulled the two suitcases off the chair, and dumped their contents on the floor. But the revolver was not there. Mrs. Liao and I stood at the door trembling while he raved, "Where is my revolver?"

I could see a strange gleam in his eyes. By this time I was weeping, and Mrs. Liao tried to calm him.

"Where is my revolver?" he repeated desperately. I could see his face was livid and his hands were shaking. "It should be in its usual place. Where did you put it, my dearest?"

Then he ran amok. He swept things off the table and broke the furniture by smashing chairs and overturning tables.

Mrs. Liao pulled at his arm to restrain him. She shouted sternly: "Don't act like a spoilt child! Only patience and tolerance will win out for you. This is not your home! How can you destroy other people's property? Don't lose your head!"

Then, like a baby, he broke down and wept bitterly. All that afternoon and evening, he refused to eat or talk. All military matters came to a standstill. He was not at home to anyone. Even the servants were kept outside our room.

That evening I insisted that he lie down in bed. "You get upset too easily. Matters can be thrashed out to your entire satisfaction," I said sympathetically. But he refused to listen or talk to me. He merely stared into vacant space. As the hours passed, I asked old Mr. Chang Ching-chiang and Mr. Ch'en Kuo-fu, the Blue Shirt chief, to come in and comfort Kai-shek. Meanwhile, Mrs. Liao, having completed her mission, returned to Hankow by night steamer.

By the next day, Kai-shek had adjusted somewhat to the initial shock. He was now much calmer, but he still looked pale and gaunt.

"What happened to you, my dearest?" I asked softly. "You lost all sense of proportion. Won't you tell me about it?"

"I don't know. Anger blinded my eyes. I wanted to kill myself to relieve the tension."

"Oh, my darling, you were desperately unhappy. How monstrous those people are! Don't ever try to kill yourself again! You must never lose your temper again! Your temper is your worst enemy!"

"I didn't actually want to die. I was blinded by rage, and it was the only way to relieve my anger," he confessed contritely, holding my hand.

I could sense the tremor in his voice and knew he was still very much agitated. I embraced him tenderly and kissed his cheek.

"Thank you for saving my life!" he murmured at last. "In my fury, I really would have shot myself. My temper gets the better of me so often. It was providential that you thought of hiding my revolver and thus saved my life! How good you are to me! I'll never forget it as long as I live! I am a man reborn!"

"I was so frightened at the color of your face. It changed to a pale green and then to a terrible white. Oh, how you must have suffered! Don't ever try to kill yourself again. Will you promise me that? Do say you will not do it again!"

"I hope there will never be another occasion to drive me to it," he said weakly. "But whether in life or in death, I will love you just the same. In death even more so ..."

He lay there and closed his eyes. I brushed away the tear that trickled down his cheek. He looked so worn and weak. But I knew his mind was alert and that he was in deep meditation. He evaded my plea not to attempt suicide again. His Hankow adversaries had played him false, and I knew he would plan retaliation. Knowing him so well, I could feel that he would conceive a plan to outwit them. Of that I was certain. He was vindictive by nature and was an outstanding strategist. He could afford to wait to take his revenge.

Kai-shek scorned the Hankow government's orders when they arrived. He saw no reason why he, the undisputed leader of the day, should be forced to obey what he called a pseudogovernment, for he believed that no legal government could be formed without his participation. Moreover, he called himself the true heir to Dr. Sun and had his own plans to establish a government in Hanking as soon as that city was captured. Still, for the sake of expediency, he would pretend to obey the orders from Nanking until his own preparations could be further advanced. Taking stock of his strength, he knew that Canton was safely under his control. Thanks to his foresight, he had placed men who took orders only from him in all key positions in the province. And he now set out to consolidate his control over the territories that had recently been conquered, namely Kiukiang and Nanchang. So, to build up his strength, he worked with renewed efforts to make these two cities as invulnerable as possible.

He began at Kiukiang. He called an emergency military meeting in our drawing room. He was tense and highly excited. The meeting began at 8 A.M. and continued all day and far into the night. With the exception of three hours off for three meals, and half an hour for his siesta, the discussion actually lasted almost sixteen hours.

Those who took part were Kai-shek's most trusted officers, the top brass, who bore the rank of general. These included General Ching Chin, General Pai Ch'ung-hsi, General Ho Ying-ch'in, and a dozen others who headed the various armies.

The chief topic of discussion was the strengthening of the defenses of Kiukiang and Nanchang. What methods should be adopted in case of a sudden attack by the Hankow government? Every angle of this question was debated. In fact, Kai-shek had his own plans regarding the strategy, but he thought two heads were better than one, so he convened this meeting to get a second opinion.

The whole morning was devoted to reports on the present situation, the duplicity of Borodin and his clique, the treacherous behavior of Hsu Ch'ien and Teng Yen-ta, and, finally, how the outer borders of Kiangsi province and the two cities of Kiukiang and Nanchang should be protected.

After lunch, Kai-shek said: "This morning I made a detailed report to you of the true situation and requested each of you to make suggestions. Can you now give me your opinions? What are your recommendations?"

Strange to say, all the generals gave recommendations that coincided with Kai-shek's own secret plans, and he was pleased to see that they all were of the same school of thought. Then he issued orders and placed his most loyal officers accordingly.

Kai-shek next concentrated on Nanchang. He ordered the strengthening of the fortresses there to make them more effective in case of a sudden government siege.

Primarily because of his fear of raids, Kai-shek secretly sent his Blue Shirts to Hankow to seek inside information. Meanwhile, he and I packed up and left Kiukiang by railway for a more or less extended stay in Nanchang.

I enjoyed Nanchang because it was a unique city with a fine wall around it, twenty-two miles in circumference. Kai-shek told me that this wall had not been scaled by an enemy during the last 900 years of its existence. It was the only large city in Central China that the Tai-pings had been unable to take, and during subsequent revolutions and civil wars it had suffered little damage. Credit for this remarkable record belonged to the town's great deity, Protector Hsu Chin-yang, who in the year A.D. 200 had saved the province from a disastrous flood. As a result he was deified by the people as the "Universal Lord of Happiness."

I found Nanchang, as a city, most charming and interesting. It was second only to Kiukiang; yet it was an important distribution point for the famous Chinese porcelain made in the nearby district of Ching-teh-chen. Grass cloth, too, was a famous local product. What attracted me most were the large stocks of curios and works of art. They were perhaps more numerous than in most other cities because this place had never been looted or tapped by foreigners. Of historic interest, the city was located on the old Ambassador's Route, so called because it led directly from Canton northward through Kwangtung and Kiangsi provinces to Kiukiang. It was over this route that the MacCartney Mission passed in 1793 on its way to Peking.

Nanchang was very conservative, proud, and wealthy. The people still looked with suspicion upon any innovations brought in by foreigners. Western influence had not yet penetrated the city to any noticeable extent. Foreign goods were exceedingly scarce, and Western methods of doing things had not been adopted by the local merchants.

Kai-shek and I stayed at the House of Yuan, and our host and hostess showed us every courtesy. They were a charming middle-aged couple of the old school, who were most solicitous of our comfort. They made us feel like members of their family.

Since Hankow exercised the "supreme power of the party," although done secretly upon Moscow's instructions, I told Kai-shek: "Don't fall into their trap. If you disobey orders, the government will find fault with you and accuse you of trying to split the party. You must be wise and try to humor them. Don't throw down the gauntlet. Pretend to accept all the government's directives, even if you have to exercise the utmost restraint."

While Kai-shek took my advice, he busily reorganized his armies and his Whampoa cadets and dug in at Nanchang and Kiukiang, tightening his control over the whole of Kiangsi province. At the same time, he planned his next move against the Hankow government. Fortunately he had the support of the conservative members of the party in Canton, as well as of those who had from the beginning been actively opposed to communism.

Another source of strength was derived from the Blue Shirts. They worked among the Kuomintang members and promised them high positions in the Nanking government. This bait worked because there was soon an exodus of veterans leaving Hankow. They went to Shanghai, where they stayed in the International Settlements, to await their chance to join Kai-shek and his new government.

Now, for a whole week, the strengthening of the Nanchang defenses continued without cease, though it seemed improbable that Hankow would launch an attack on either Kiukiang or our city. Like busy bees, Kai-shek and I plied between the two cities on inspection tours to make certain that his orders had been carried out to the letter.

24

Chiang's Father

One day the Nanchang postman delivered a letter to me from my mother. It was a reply to my inquiry regarding Kai-shek's father. She enclosed the report that the investigator had given her. It read:

First Report Regarding Chiang Kai-shek

Chiang Kai-shek outwardly appears to be the son of the late Mr. and Mrs. Chiang Shu-an of Hsi-k'ou, in Feng-hua County, Chekiang. A thorough investigation reveals, however, that old Mr. Chiang Shu-an was merely Chiang Kai-shek's stepfather. This is the story:* Chiang Kai-shek was originally surnamed Cheng, with the given name San-fa-tzu. He lived with his parents in Hsu-chou in Honan province. Born on October 31, 1887, he was the third son of his parents. His eldest brother, seven years his senior, was named Cheng Shiu-fa. His second elder brother, four years his senior, was called Erh-fa-tzu. His father, who owned twelve *mu* of land, was a farmer. His mother, née Huang, a capable woman and a fine seamstress, was tall and thin and nicknamed Lanky Mama Cheng. The

---

*Jennie Ch'en's account here that Chiang Kai-shek was originally surnamed Cheng is probably erroneous—although the story has had much currency over the years in China. But all of this warrants further investigation. During the war against Japan in the 1940s, a man from Honan, surnamed Cheng, suddenly appeared in Chungking, claiming to be Chiang's brother. Chiang had his secret police remove the fellow from public view. But he was reportedly well treated, and after the war he was given a minor government post. Some Chinese say that such kindly treatment of a possible political inconvenience suggests that there was truth in the fellow's claims; otherwise he would simply have been disposed of. —L.E.E.

231

little family of five was able to eke out a fairly comfortable living. San-fa-tzu, being the youngest and constitutionally weakest, was pampered by his mother.

In 1894, the larger part of Honan province suffered a severe famine. Thousands of miles of land did not have even an inch of grass. This was due to the disastrous floods of the Yellow and Huai rivers. The former is known as China's Sorrow. Indeed, the inundation took a toll of thousands of lives, and those who survived suffered starvation. The rich farmers of Hsu-chou quickly moved to the larger cities; the poorer farmers tried to stick it out. But after a time, San-fa-tzu's father decided that he, too, must move his little family to the city of Loyang. He told his wife: "If we stay here we will surely perish. Hopes of getting relief grain from the imperial government are remote. Our little stock of roots, husk, and bark will soon be exhausted. Look at the streets and roads! They are scattered with the dead. We cannot survive if we remain here. Let us leave while we have the strength in our bodies to carry us away."

"San-fa-tzu and I cannot make such a long, strenuous journey on foot," said Lanky Mama Cheng. "So what shall we do?"

"I can carry you piggyback," said Father Cheng. "At least if we leave, we may hope to survive together. But to remain means certain death for us all."

"How can we leave without our belongings?" protested Mama Cheng. "We will need warm clothing and blankets. If you carry San-fa-tzu piggy-back, who will carry our luggage?"

"We'll have to sacrifice all that," said Father Cheng impatiently. "Life is more precious than clothing and blankets."

"If we are to die, I would rather die in our own home and on our own land," said Lanky Mama Cheng with finality. "With my small bound feet, I will not be able to make that long journey. It will be better for you to take the boys and leave. I will stay here and await government aid."

Father Cheng came over to his wife and pleaded: "How can I leave you behind? It's not human. Let us go together. Don't depend on government aid. Here, I kneel to you and beg you to listen to reason and come with us."

But Mama Cheng was adamant and refused to budge.

Papa Cheng sighed deeply, for he knew it was futile to persuade a stubborn wife. So he sheepishly rose to his feet and spoke to his three sons, thus: "My sons. The three of you are sensible lads. Since your mother refuses to leave with me, I will not force her, but I, myself, have decided to leave. So you three may decide for yourselves. Those who wish to remain will stay with your mother. Those who wish to go with me should make up your minds now."

The two elder boys, Shiu-fa and Erh-fa-tzu, said they would go with their father. After a tearful farewell, the trio left.

As the days passed, Lanky Mama Cheng and San-fa-tzu consumed the remaining food, the tree bark, roots, and grain husks that were in the house. Soon they found that the few remaining neighbors were leaving. Not wishing to stay behind, Mama Cheng said to them: "Let me and my young son accompany you." So saying, she hurriedly wrapped some clothing in a bundle, threw it over her shoulder like a knapsack, and followed the slow-moving caravan, whose destination was Kaifeng, the ancient capital of Honan.

Outside their village the little band could see more and more groups of people converging on the highway to join the exodus. Many people weakened by starvation simply fell down on the roadside to die. When this happened, their family members howled with grief and refused to go on until the dead were buried in an improvised grave.

After three days of painful trudging, Mama Cheng and her son left the crowd to seek refuge in a small, broken-down temple. An old man was worshiping there. Mama Cheng watched him burn joss sticks and joss paper and kneel in prayer. She and her son followed suit. When the praying was over, the man said to her: "I know you are a refugee, but you will not get any handouts here. You will have to go to the Hsiang Kuo Monastery in the city, fifty *li* from here, where they serve congee to refugees twice a day. The monastery does a lot of charity work to help the destitute. That is where you should go."

So to the monastery Mama Cheng and her son went. They were given congee and some bean cakes, and at night, they slept upon a straw mat in the monastery's spacious courtyard among hundreds of other refugees. Thus they lived for a week.

One day Mama Cheng was mending San-fa-tzu's torn coat when an elderly monk passed by. Mama Cheng rose from her straw mat and after bowing, asked: "Reverend Master, I wish to earn my living. Where can I find work in this strange city?"

The monk looked at her and answered: "You seem to sew well. I understand there is a merchant named Chiang. He is looking for a nurse to care for his motherless baby. Whether he has found one or not, I do not know, but you may go there and inquire." So saying, he gave her instructions how to get there.

Mama Cheng thanked the monk most profusely, rolled up her mat, tied up her baggage, and carrying these over her shoulder, dragged along her son, heading for the address given. After searching for some time, mother and son came to a doorway of a rich man's home. The tall, stately doors were of the richest black lacquer, of such a fine quality that she had never before seen. Looking up she saw hanging on the eaves a pair of large white and blue lanterns, and at once she knew that the house was in mourning, for ordinary lanterns were always painted red.

Summoning up courage, Mama Cheng adjusted her dress and hair and knocked at the door. In answer, a dog barked fiercely, which frightened the intruders. When a manservant appeared, Mama Cheng told him the purpose of her call.

Old Mr. Chiang, the owner of the house, was a salt merchant by trade. He had been very much worried after he had lost his second wife, née Hsu, who had died at childbirth. He had had difficulty in finding someone suitable to care for the motherless babe. Although he had three children, one boy and two girls, all of them were too young and playful to take on the responsibility of nursing. Besides, being a salt merchant, he had many other activities. A part of his time was spent in writing indictments for those unfortunates who were involved in litigation. Indeed, Old Mr. Chiang was a busy man, and it was his intention to send word back to his native village to engage an elderly clanswoman to nurse his newborn babe and to act as governess over his household. But he did not get around to it.

When Mama Cheng was brought in to his presence, he did not notice her shabby appearance but saw that she was a tall, handsome woman with a strong, healthy body and walked with a pleasant gait. He liked her looks and demeanor and asked her name.

"My maiden name is Huang, but my married name is Cheng," she answered respectfully. Then she told him her story and added, "I do not know if my husband is dead or alive."

"Since you have no home, you may work here and be a nurse to my motherless baby and also act as governess to my other children. We will call you Mama Huang. I have seen many prospects, but you are the best of them all, and since you have a son of your own, you will have to keep strict control over him so that the children will not fight or quarrel."

"Since you are so kind to take me and my son in, I will make it my business to do that," she promised gratefully and added, "Although my son is sensitive and sometimes morbid, he will obey me implicitly."

It did not take long for Mama Huang to learn that Old Mr. Chiang was a native of Hsi-k'ou village, Feng-hua County, Chekiang province. Fifty years before, he had accompanied his father, Chiang Yu-Piu, to Honan to became a salt merchant. Therefore, Old Mr. Chiang, on his father's death, acquired through inheritance his father's business and palatial home.

Being a capable woman, Mama Huang worked hard in the house and looked after the children as if they were her very own. As the years passed fleetingly by, Old Mr. Chiang, feeling homesick and senile, sold his business and moved his family back to his native Hsi-k'ou home in Chekiang. He told Mama Huang, "Fallen leaves return to their roots and my yearning for my native home is similar." He looked at her admiringly and said: "Ever since you came to work here, you have been very hardworking, faithful, and kind. I am grateful to you for all what you have done. Will you marry me and come to Chekiang to be a mother to my children?"

"But what about my own son?" she asked. "He is a Cheng."

"Let him change his surname to Chiang."

"That solves the problem," said Mama Huang wisely, and that night Old Mr. Chiang made Mama Huang his wife.

So that in a nutshell is how Chiang Kai-shek acquired the surname of Chiang.

Whether true or not, this was the report my mother sent me.

25

The Great Intrigue

*I*n an attempt to keep Kai-shek in harness, the Hankow government refused to send him any more supplies, ammunition, or money to pay his soldiers. Each day also brought new condemnations of his insubordination. Borodin was a good psychologist and understood the way Kai-shek's mind worked. Thus, Kai-shek became frustrated and disspirited. He asked: "Why does Hankow slander me? I know that Borodin wants to see me overthrown! I suppose it is his jealousy and hatred of my candid criticisms. He started the government behind my back, and now he expects me to kowtow to him. But I will not do it. He is in the wrong."

"You are tired and overwrought," I said tenderly. "Do what is right and don't worry about Hankow. How do you feel now?"

"Not too good," he answered. "In fact I feel like a horse with a spear stuck in its body, a tiger coming in front of me, and a wolf behind. The situation is desperate!" Then to my utter surprise he shouted: "Oh, my master and the martyrs of our party in Heaven! Will you have pity on me and protect me? I'm doing what is right. Do prevent me from falling into a hopeless situation."

I became alarmed and asked worriedly, "How do you feel?"

"My misery is indescribable," he answered painfully. "I can only say that I am suffering as much as the Buddha when he faced his adversaries in his great trial of strength."

"Then you must have strength," I said. "Have patience as did the Buddha! It took him seven years to achieve enlightenment."

"I know I am right. What I do is right. If I don't carry out my resolutions, how can I save our party and save China?"

"Other men have said the same thing when it comes to fighting for power," I ventured to say. I did not mention that Generals Ch'en Chiung-ming and Wu P'ei-fu had also announced publicly that their desire was to save China. As these men were his bitter enemies, the mere mention of their names by me would have infuriated him. So, for the sake of peace, I remained silent.

"The difference between me and other men," he retorted, "is that I am saving China for our leader, Dr. Sun, while other men do it for personal gain."

To guarantee his success, Kai-shek conceived of yet another strategy. To undermine his enemy, he would follow the classical strategy of depriving him of his source of power. An important source of power, of course, is money. At present Kai-shek was without money. But he thought to shift the balance of power with the Hankow government by winning over the finance minister of Hankow, T. V. Soong. The subtle way to accomplish this would be through the minister's sister, Mme Kung. Thus decided, he wrote to her, inviting her to come to Kiukiang for an important meeting.

On receipt of the letter, Mme Kung came posthaste, sailing on the Central Bank of China's cruiser. On arrival, she did not disembark but stayed on board and sent for Kai-shek. She did not come ashore because I had accompanied Kai-shek on this Kiukiang trip—and she had reasons for avoiding me. On the cruiser, she and Kai-shek spent twenty-four hours discussing the political situation.

As Kai-shek expected, Mme Kung was a formidable negotiator. She was the most able of the Soong sisters, a hardheaded female possessed of great energy and a strong will to power. She was shrewd, cunning, and ambitious. Kai-shek knew that her passionate interest was money, for she speculated on the exchange market and took a fierce joy in business manipulations and enterprises. She had been educated at Wesleyan College in Macon, Georgia, U.S.A., and when she returned to China, she became Dr. Sun's secretary. It was she, and not Mme Sun, whom Dr. Sun had first dated and had hired as his secretary. But she married H. H. Kung, who was secretary of the Tokyo Y.M.C.A. She then recommended her sister Ch'ing-ling to replace her as Dr. Sun's secretary.

After the twenty-four-hour meeting between Mme Kung and Kai-shek on the cruiser, she returned directly to Hankow. Kai-shek came home to tell me in great detail what had transpired. He said: "I have not kept any secrets from you, and I don't want to begin now, especially now when I need your help. Mme Kung said this to me: 'You are a rising star. Will you allow your star to set as quickly as it has risen? Will you allow the Communists, using their treacherous intrigues, to throw you out? Today, Borodin plans to take over your powers and hand them to General Galen. It is only a matter of time until they eliminate you. Will you accept defeat without a fight? I will be honest with you. In fighting alone for the Nationalist cause, you do not have enough personality, although I must say you have the spirit. But spirit is not everything. This gigantic task of liberating and reconstructing China, and framing the Chinese constitution, needs great influence, money, personality, and prestige. As it is, you have none of these. You are surrounded by weak men and women whose interests are altogether selfish. They just want to further their own goals, not yours. You know what I say is true.

"'But the situation is not hopeless. I will make a bargain with you. It is this: I will not only convince my brother T. V. to leave the Hankow government as you wish, but will go one better. He and I will rally the leading bankers of Shanghai to back you with the necessary funds so that you can buy the ammunition you need to carry on the expedition. In return, you will agree to marry my sister Mei-ling. And you will also agree that as soon as the Nanking government is established, you will name my husband, H. H. Kung, prime minister and my brother T. V. your minister of finance.'"

Kai-shek looked at me and said: "I am desperate. She has struck a very hard bargain, but what she says is true. I cannot expect any more money or ammunition or supplies from Hankow. So her offer is the only way for me to achieve my plans to unite China. I now ask you to help me. I beg you not to say no. After all, true love is measured by the size of the sacrifice one is willing to make!"

"What do you want me to do?" I asked.

"To step aside for five years so that I can marry Mei-ling Soong and get the necessary help to carry on the expedition without the support of Hankow! It's only a political marriage!"

My heart almost skipped a beat. Ever since our marriage I had tied my life to his. And now he was asking me to step aside, as though our marriage was merely a plaything.

My first impulse was to tell him to go to hell—as any respectable wife would do. But because I had been immersed in the politics of the nation for so long, the unification of China now, to me, came first, above everything else. So I could understand clearly Kai-shek's desperation. It was his only chance to defy Hankow and carry on independently. Without my agreement, a marriage with Mei-ling Soong was impossible. And without the marriage, Kai-shek would not get even a single cent from the Shanghai bankers. I knew the attitude of Mme Kung. With her, everything was business.

I stood there in shocked silence, unable to answer. I tried to view the problem as Kai-shek viewed it. He looked at me, waiting for my answer. But I had nothing to say. In fact, I turned away without a word. He caught me by the arm, however, and said softly: "I haven't promised Ai-ling Kung anything yet. I wanted to talk to you first."

With the flash of a woman's intuition, I knew this was untrue. I knew the matter had already been decided. He forced himself to smile at me—a false smile.

I pulled my arm from his grip and thought to myself: So, Mrs. Liao Chung-k'ai's words have at last become a reality. Mme Kung had successfully alienated his affection from me.

He pleaded: "Will you listen to what I have to say? When we have established our government in Nanking, we will need qualified administrators. To achieve this, we will need a supervisory training department to provide courses on supervisory training of young men and women so that they will be ready to take up their prospective duties when the government is formed." I listened woodenly, without comment.

Then he continued: "I understand American universities provide the most wonderful courses on these topics. There are so many technical courses, such as political science, that cover city management, government administration, and international relations. All these will be most useful. But someone has to go abroad to study these subjects." I still listened without comment.

"Of course," he continued, "our culture and civilization are fundamentally sound. But we do not have the means to compete with the modern nations of today. As you know, we need modern technical and economic knowledge. As a result of our contacts with the West, we know that our own culture has shortcomings. Even in Dr. Sun's Three Principles of the People, it is clear that we need foreign ideas to raise up our distressed nation. We need new ideas and new spiritual forces. And the only way to acquire these ideas is from abroad."

He looked at me and forced a smile: "Would you like to go abroad to study in America for five years? You will not be lonely, for I shall get Therese and Helen Chang to accompany you. It will only be for five short years. By the time you return, the Nanking government will have become a reality and we can resume our life together. Our love will be the same. I swear to that. You know I love no other woman but you. We will work shoulder-to-shoulder as we have always planned! Will you agree to this?"

"Five years is a long time," I said chokingly. "Don't make any promises or swear any oaths! I have heard enough of them from you. I still remember the oath of eternal love you swore to me at French Park in Shanghai—when you even wanted to cut off a finger to prove your sincerity—and the promises you made at Hsi-k'ou on the Dragon's Pulse! So far, all your promises have been worthless. So don't make any more that you will not be able to keep."

Kai-shek blinked his jet-black eyes and changed tactics. Instead of smiling, he became very grave and said brokenly: "My position is precarious. You know that. I must take decisive action with your help. The Northern Expedition has a great mission, the salvation of China. If I can carry on, then China will be saved, and I myself can live. Otherwise, I will die—die as a result of failure or disappointment. You don't want that, do you?"

I stood there with reddened eyes, and his sentences burned into my brain. "Here is my chance to make good," he explained. "I must grasp the opportunity—I have ambitions—I want to reach the top and stay there. I want to carry on our leader's teachings, and this means to me more than anything else in life! Without it I would prefer death."

I looked at him and memorized his words. I felt a sudden hatred for Ai-ling Kung, that husband snatcher. I shook my head dumbly, and he continued: "During his lifetime, Dr. Sun personally told me," he continued, "that he expected me to be as brave and as faithful to the national cause as was Minister Lu Siu-fu, the most loyal Sung Dynasty minister. I hope you will help me so that I can achieve the goals of the Northern Expedition. You will then be like a female Lu Siu-fu who paved the way for the success of the Northern Expedition. Please, help me, and go abroad for only five years. I will give you anything you ask. Only promise to help me in my hour of need."

"If I do agree to step aside," I said angrily, "it will only be for the sake of the unification of China. It will not be for you or for Ai-ling Kung."

There followed days of terrible misery. I felt as if my soul was on a rack. But Kai-shek was exceedingly amiable and patronizing, praising me on this and that. But I kept quiet and only spoke coldly when occasion demanded. I had to think the matter over thoroughly before I could take the final step of leaving him for good. Many a time he stretched out his arms as if he wanted to embrace me, as he had often done previously. But I turned my head away, and he thought better of it and desisted. It was an intolerable situation.

On March 19, 1927, he said to me: "I am leaving for Anking tomorrow to inspect the front lines. We are making great progress there. Here are two letters I have written. You may give them to Ah Shun to dispatch after you have read them. It is only a matter of business and no love is involved. I want to keep you informed of what is going on and of all new developments. So please, please, don't be angry with me."

The letters read:

March 19, 1927
(To Mme H. H. Kung)
Dear Elder Sister,

Please accompany your mother, your second sister, Mme Sun [Soong Ch'ing-ling], your third sister (Mei-ling), your son David, your daughter, and others, to come to Kuling to stay. Under no circumstances remain in Hankow. I will leave Kiukiang tonight and will arrive at Anking tomorrow. I am aware of why Mei-ling did not previously come to Kuling (because of my wife).

After you return to Hankow, find out third sister's (Mei-ling's) attitude. If you have letters I hope you will send them by special courier to deliver to Anking. Each week we can have a special messenger deliver letters so that they are not lost. Do you agree?

Chung-cheng [Chiang's formal name]

March 19, 1927
(To Miss Mei-ling Soong)
Dear Mei-ling,

I presume your sister has given (you) my special message. Tonight I will leave Kiukiang and will stay over at Anking for a few days to await

*your reply. After I receive your letter, I will proceed to the front. What do
you think? Write me in detail. Can you send me a copy of your latest
photograph so that I can look at you constantly? I believe it would be
much better if your mother, Mme Sun, Mme Kung, and the children
quickly leave Hankow and come to stay in Kuling. Thinking I was still in
Kiangsi, you thought it inconvenient (because of my wife) to come to see
me. But I have now left Kiangsi, so you need not entertain any such
doubts that will cause you embarrassment.*

These two letters spurred me to make up my mind to leave Nanchang. The matter had now reached a point of no return as far as I was
concerned. For days I had weighed in my mind what steps I should take,
and now the situation was untenable. I therefore packed my four suitcases and took the train to Kiukiang, where I took a steamer for Shanghai. Before leaving, however, I handed Ah Shun the bunch of keys to
Kai-shek's trunks and a short letter addressed to his master. Saying
good-bye to this servant, who had served me so loyally and capably, I
was swept by many emotions.

Back in Shanghai I was irretrievably on my own, and it was not easy
going back to my dear mother's home. All mothers love their daughters, wish them happiness, and worry when anything goes amiss. Returning home to stay indefinitely was an admission that all was not
well.

When I had told Mother that I had left Kai-shek, she was shocked beyond words. She pleaded in despair: "Oh, my dear daughter, go back, go
back to the husband you love. Your duty is at his side."

"I do not love him any more," I retorted.

"You do, I know that, and you know he loves you. Everyone knows
you are his only love."

Poor Mother did not understand the true situation, and I didn't have
the heart to tell her the details. I did not want to talk either about the
vile woman who had come between husband and wife or about the sister who staged the "great intrigue" to steal my husband. The joke was
on Christianity because these "fine" people hid behind the cloak of religion to suit their purposes and to draw benefits from their religion.

"Oh, go back to your husband. He belongs to you and you to him,"
repeated Mother. "Despite your ages, you are ideally matched. You may
never meet with such a love again. He is fast becoming a great leader.
Don't throw away such an opportunity!"

With pain and sorrow in my heart I went over to where she sat and tried to comfort her: "Very well, Mother dear, I'll tell you the true situation. But promise me you will not repeat it to a living soul. Kai-shek doesn't want any publicity, for it may hurt our cause."

When I had finished telling her the intrigue of Ai-ling Kung and my promise to Kai-shek to step aside so that he could realize his dream, she embraced me, broke down and wept: "Oh, my dear daughter, you are such a good wife. Chinese history will one day record your sacrifice for our country!"

Now that I was back home, many friends and relatives called. The house was full of people, all wishing to see me and ask me questions about my "wonderful" married life. Ironically, they congratulated me on my husband's many victories. Although the house was crowded, more and more friends came. They laughed and joked and stayed for tea or dinner. Without exception, they spoke of Kai-shek's bravery and his strategy, his great future, and how lucky I was. They predicted he would rule the whole of China as soon as the northern provinces were conquered.

Such talk only cut deeper into my wounded heart, but I had to hide my feelings, look pleasant, and thank them for their good wishes. It was not easy to adjust to this changed atmosphere, and every time I answered questions about my happy married life, I felt like a hypocrite.

26

Nanking

*L*iving at my mother's home in Shanghai, I continued to watch Kaishek's military activities. He had consolidated his positions in Kiukiang and Nanchang, and his armies were placed on the alert. He realized his best chance of survival would be to capture Nanking and to quickly establish a rival government there. Thus, with renewed energies, he hurriedly worked toward that end.

On March 24, 1927, he directed his soldiers to advance on Nanking, which surprisingly fell like a house of cards. But before he could arrive there to assume control, the Communists there incited thousands of screaming hooligans who set fire to British and American homes, stoned foreigners, burned cars, and rampaged through the city.* The foreign homes on Second Hill were the chief targets. The raids were so well organized that homes, hospitals, missions, and schools were systematically looted and inmates ill treated. This was a reply to Kaishek's defiance of the Hankow government's authority. It was designed to discredit him in the eyes of the world. The raiders called themselves Bolsheviks and acted like Bolsheviks.

Fortunately, a landing party from the U.S. naval ships in the river fired a salvo of shots on the city, which so completely frightened the

---

*C. Martin Wilbur writes that it is still uncertain who was responsible for this Nanking Incident, although the Nationalist version is to blame the Communists, as Jennie does here. See Wilbur, *The Nationalist Revolution in China, 1923–1928* (New York: Cambridge University Press, 1983), p. 92. —L.E.E.

raiders that not a single armed soldier was encountered when the landing party arrived. British bluejackets also joined in. Although nine lives were lost, the rest of the foreigners escaped uninjured. Had it not been for the shell fire, there would have been a massacre.

On arrival the following day, Kai-shek speedily issued a declaration in which he asked the foreigners to be calm and announced that he would assume full responsibility for all damages and losses to their properties. This announcement had a calming effect on all foreigners in Nanking. The proclamation read: "In all matters pertaining to foreign relations, the new Nanking government will be willing to deal fairly and sincerely, if the powers do not in any way impede the Nationalist Revolution." In addition, he made the following statements: "All discussions must be entered into on the initiative of the Nationalist government and without coercion from outside influences or unconditional demands. All questions pertaining to the settlement of the case must be discussed in a spirit of equality."

Kai-shek quickly organized his Nanking government, and the outrages soon redounded to Hankow's disadvantage. The plot to discredit him had, instead, worked in his favor. The people at large voiced admiration for his leadership and condemned Hankow for its treachery.

Although thwarted, the Hankow government did not give up so easily. In fact, its propagandists hurled all kinds of accusations at Kai-shek, denouncing him as a new warlord. They made the most of their opportunities to spread the gospel of communism as widely as possible among the peasants, students, and laborers all over the southern provinces. The propagandists told the masses that Kai-shek, in his madness for power, had put aside Dr. Sun's teachings and betrayed his cause. A new warlord had been born!

But without losing precious time, Kai-shek led his forces to capture Shanghai. The Blue Shirts instigated a general strike to signify their support for the Nationalist cause. The Communists again tried to capitalize on the situation by organizing Shanghai labor pickets and generously supplying them with arms. Their scheme was to start an uprising so that they could set up a labor government in the city or, at least, to cause conflicts between the Western powers and the newly arrived Nationalist forces.

By March 26, 1927, Kai-shek had taken personal command of Chinese Shanghai territory in order to protect the international metropolis and to forestall a repetition of what had happened in Nanking. To prevent Communist intrigue, the Nationalist Army, in cooperation with local labor unions and the Chambers of Commerce, disarmed the Red labor pickets and kept Communist saboteurs under surveillance. Only then was the Shanghai situation brought under control. In a fiery speech, Kai-shek shouted: "Down with communism! Get rid of the Reds! Borodin go home!"

Tension was high. Ironically, the former slogans, Down with imperialists, Drive away all foreign capitalists, and Soviet Russia is our teacher, had been shouted too often and too loudly and too long to be checked easily. It was embarrassing to see the about-face. The Communists were challenged, yet their organized labor groups were anxious to injure the imperialists and capitalists in the International Settlements as a last mad fling to get even. But fortunately, foreign forces of the British, Americans, and French were guarding the concessions jealously with machine-guns behind sandbags and barbed-wire barricades. Street fighting and bombing were expected at any time, but little happened. All was quiet within the Shanghai concessions.

Now that the agreement with Mme Kung had been settled, Kai-shek's Blue Shirts were ordered to give the Communists a dose of their own medicine. They instigated a raid on the finance minister's headquarters in Hankow so that T. V. Soong could have an excuse to escape being "killed." This done, Kai-shek announced from Nanchang a declaration of his position. It read:

It is claimed that I have no more confidence in the Communist Party, and that I have even prohibited the introduction of Communist elements into the Kuomintang. As a matter of fact, I never supported the Communist Party, even at the beginning. As I said last year in the Whampoa academy, I had invited other minor revolutionary organizations to join hands with us in the revolutionary movement only on the condition that I reserved the right to suppress any group that might go beyond the limits by endangering the Nationalist cause. In the interests of, and for the welfare of, the Kuomintang, I now suppress the Communist movement because it has gone beyond the limits.

Chiang Kai-shek

As head of the Nanking government, Kai-shek demanded that all the Communists under Borodin in Hankow leave China. The demand was scorned. Negotiations ensued but failed. "If you do not leave, I will lead my armies on a punitive expedition to smash Hankow," threatened Kai-shek.

Seeing the futility of further resistance, Borodin and his wife had no alternative but to sheepishly leave Hankow on July 15, 1927. Thus did this Red leader and his entourage fade out of the Chinese political limelight. Then followed a persecution. Communism was outlawed. Even Sino-Russian diplomatic relations ended.

Communism now outlawed, Kai-shek took over and wielded greater power than ever before. With his government at Nanking, he became the undisputed military leader and heir to Dr. Sun's Kuomintang. His greatest power came from the military academy, which produced an unending supply of crack cadets. He held a total of half a million men in the hollow of his hand.

It may be said that his ascendency came like a tidal wave that was born from the disturbance on the China ocean bed. It billowed across the surface of Central China as mountainous breakers on the far-distant northern plain. The warlords of the North now, for the first time, felt uneasy and knew that unless they threw in their lot with Nanking, their days were numbered.

Now head of his own government, Kai-shek's first thoughts were of money—silver bullets. The old mint was hastily reorganized and the printing machines set in motion to turn out a new currency, under the supervision of the minister of finance, T. V. Soong. This money was called *fapi*, which meant legal tender. The press was kept printing the bank notes from dawn to dawn without a stop.

The men who had helped Kai-shek in some way or other in the past were given important positions in order to fulfil obligations. For instance the two men who had supplied Kai-shek with personal loans over a number of years during his "lean" days were old Mr. Chang Ching-chiang and Yeh Cho-t'ang. The former was appointed governor of Chekiang, while the latter became manager of the Szu-ming (Ningpo) Bank of China. The joke of the matter was that Mr. Yeh knew next to nothing about banking.

Other parvenus who were also richly rewarded paraded in their gleaming new cars, flashed huge rolls of newly printed money, and

made themselves conspicuous wherever they went. They belonged to
the new ruling class of Nanking.

One of the important measures taken by the government was to
clean out the Communist poison. The remaining Communist elements
had to be uprooted. The persecution was carried on ruthlessly and thoroughly, not because Kai-shek necessarily disagreed with their theoreti-
cal assumptions, but because communism's basic loyalty was to Soviet
Russia, whose interests now clashed with the Nationalists. Soon the
streets of the old section of Shanghai City literally ran with the blood of
beheaded victims. More than 5,000 workers were executed, and another 5,000 or more jailed. To save themselves, the rest of the Communists went underground. But Mme Sun, having lost her Hankow government, came back to Shanghai to live at her home at 29 Rue Moliere
in the French Concession.

⸗   ⸗   ⸗

Nanking was chosen as the Nationalist capital because Dr. Sun had
wished it. Formerly, Nanking had been the capital of the illustrious
Ming (1368–1644), a pure Chinese dynasty that Dr. Sun wished to emulate. At an emergency meeting Kai-shek told the Kuomintang members: "In our new government we will uphold the principle of party
rule. The constitutional form of government was tried in China after
the Revolution of 1911, but it failed because our people lacked political
consciousness. There is no use trying it again. I have decided that China
will be ruled under a tutelage government. I will therefore rule China
through the Kuomintang, which is now China's only political party,
and, for the time being, through you party members. We also need urgently to enhance our intelligence service in order to mop up the rem-
nants of communism. We must also centralize all taxes under our central government's Ministry of Finance, which will be headed by T. V.
Soong.

"Uppermost in my mind," he continued, "is the elevation of our
great leader Dr. Sun Yat-sen to the rank of "Father of our Chinese Republic." Dr. Sun worked for forty years to lead our people in the Nationalist cause, and we cannot allow any other personality to usurp this
honored position."

He looked at Chen Kuo-fu and asked: "What about that photograph
you were supposed to have purchased? Did you get it yet?" Kai-shek
was referring to a photograph that had been taken in Japan in about

1895 or 1898. The photograph showed members of the Revolutionary Party; Yang Ch'ü-yün was seated as the chairman of the party, and Dr. Sun was standing in the background as leader Yang's secretary. Kai-shek had ordered Ch'en Kuo-fu, "Buy this picture and the negative as soon as possible."

"But it is not for sale," exclaimed Ch'en.

"Offer a million dollars!" exclaimed Kai-shek impatiently. "The party must have this picture and the negative at any price. They must be destroyed as soon as possible. It would be most embarrassing to have our Father of the Chinese Republic shown in a subordinate position."

ϝ ϝ ϝ

Although regarded as China's newest supreme leader, Kai-shek astutely recognized that the many recent protests were not merely against communism but also against himself and his blunt, aggressive, dictatorial tactics. The loudest of all the protests came from a group of veteran Kuomintang members whom Dr. Sun had esteemed and honored, but whom Kai-shek now ignored and bypassed when making appointments.

One of the principal complaints against Kai-shek was his high-handed dismissal of Borodin. Dr. Sun had invited Borodin to come to China as an adviser. And now, out of personal enmity, Kai-shek had dismissed him without even convening a meeting of the Kuomintang to obtain the party's approval. Thus, although Hankow was rid of Borodin, the Kuomintang officials were highly incensed, saying that Kai-shek's behavior differed little from the northern warlords, whom they were trying to oust.

Leaders of the Hankow government had duly confessed their mistake in putting the government into the hands of the Communists and serving as their tool for several months. They were, nonetheless, unwilling to make peace with the new government in Nanking. Supporters of the Hankow government, under the leadership of Wang Ching-wei, continued to shout, "Down with the Dictator Chiang Kai-shek!" Wang Ching-wei claimed that Hankow was struggling against two enemies: the Communists and Chiang Kai-shek! "These two enemies," he declared, "were worse than the warlords themselves!"

Kai-shek realized there was some truth in this accusation. He thought, therefore, that if he went into retirement there would be no further reason for the people to shout, "Down with Chiang Kai-shek."

The fact is that as long as he remained as commander in chief, there was no hope that the Northern Expedition could succeed. This was because the Hankow forces would not defend Kai-shek against the northerners' eastward march against him. And Kai-shek's forces couldn't fight the northerners alone because they had to defend against a possible attack from Hankow.

In addition to all this, certain dissident factions in territories nominally under Kai-shek's control were threatening civil war. First there was the Hunanese Army that challenged Nanking, followed by a threatened uprising in Canton. Nanchang, too, had protested and talked of civil war.

These threats resulted from dissatisfaction with Kai-shek's ruthless and dictatorial ways. Many of his subordinates were dissatisfied with conditions, which they considered worse than those in warlord days. And so they had no respect for Kai-shek and defied his authority. Actually, the situation was not as unfavorable to Kai-shek as it appeared because generals who were loyal to Kai-shek controlled all key positions in these territories. It nevertheless caused him much worry.

As matters worsened, Kai-shek on August 13, 1927, announced his "resignation." The newspapers called this a face-saving maneuver because Kai-shek's resignation was analogous to the boss's going on furlough for a month or two. He actually retained control of the army and could resume his military powers whenever he was ready to come out of "retirement." To outsiders, however, news of Kai-shek's retirement came as a shock because they interpreted the word *retirement* in the literal sense of the word.

27

My Exile

*I*t was on the morning of August 1, 1927, a very hot, sunny day, when Kai-shek came to Mother's home in Shanghai. He came into the house alone, leaving his bodyguards and Blue Shirt detectives standing in the courtyard. Normally it would have been a very exciting occasion to have a celebrity visit our home. Under the circumstances, however, I did not even bother to ask this uninvited guest to sit down. I looked at him and said sarcastically: "To what do I owe this visit? It is commonly said, Without a purpose, one does not go to the Great Buddha's shrine. So, your coming here today must mean that you have a favor to ask!"

"You have guessed right, my dear Chieh-ju," he said patronizingly. "I've come to talk to you about your trip to the United States! I have arranged for Therese and Helen Chang to be your companions and to look after you while you are gone. You will only be away for a period of five years! Here are your steamship tickets!"

I ignored his extended hand and answered: "I've stepped aside to allow you to realize your ambition. What more do you want from me? You've always said that people can impose their will upon me! Do you now want to force me into exile?"

"Don't talk like that!" he pleaded, coming nearer to me. "The trip abroad is for your own benefit. I want you to study and increase your knowledge. And later when you come back, you can work for the government. You did promise to work shoulder-to-shoulder with me! Remember?"

"The past is past," I replied. "I am perfectly content to stay here with Mother." I looked at him and smiled within my heart. So the great Chiang Kai-shek was begging me to go abroad! I knew the reason why. Soong Mei-ling could not feel comfortable as long as I was in Shanghai, for I was well known in political circles as Mme Chiang Kai-shek. She wanted to get rid of me before her wedding. But my pride prevented me from agreeing too easily. I said nonchalantly: "I don't want to listen to your line of talk that you are doing everything for my benefit. I've stepped aside very quietly for your convenience, since you have said the yardstick of love is measured by the size of the sacrifice one is willing to make. I am doing this for the unification of China and nothing else. Another woman would scratch Ai-ling Kung's eyes out."

"But you don't understand," he pleaded nervously. "Your departure for the United States is one of the demands of Ai-ling Kung. I know it is a great deal to ask of you, Chieh-ju, but it is entirely for the unification of China that I dare call upon your patriotism to help the country. As long as you remain in Shanghai, the deal is off. Don't you understand my problem?"

I looked at him contemptuously but felt a deep pity in my heart. He looked so very pale, tense, and gaunt. His color was bad and his expression was filled with desperation. For a while I ignored him and went over to the shrine to add more oil to the lamp suspended before the Buddha. I lit some fresh incense sticks and placed them in the pewter urn. At this moment, Mother and brother Bun came home from shopping, and they were surprised to see our guest.

Mother invited him to sit down, and brother Bun offered him a cup of tea. Brother Bun also took a pot of tea and some cups into the courtyard to serve the bodyguards and the Blue Shirts.

Kai-shek spoke politely to Mother for a few minutes and touched upon the complexities of the national situation. Then he worked up courage to explain to Mother that he wanted me to go abroad for five years in order to study political science and public administration. And when I returned, I could serve the government.

"Here are three steamship tickets—one for Chieh-ju and two for the Chang sisters," he said as he looked them over and with tremulous hands gave them to mother. The steamer is the *President Jackson*. It is a large and luxurious ship, 40,000 tons!"

Mother looked at me and asked, "Do you want to go abroad, my daughter?"

"I don't want to go," I said petulantly. "Why should I go so far away? It's like going into exile!"

"It's only for five years!" he exclaimed flippantly.

"All your promises are worthless!" I said in a loud voice. "After breaking so many promises, how can you expect me to believe another word from you!"

Mother was a wonderful woman. She sat there and listened. She knew my situation and thought I had acted wisely. She also realized Kai-shek's predicament. She turned to him and asked bluntly, "When you say five years, are you telling the truth or are you merely saying it to deceive my daughter?"

"Of course, I am telling the truth!" he said earnestly.

"Don't say things you don't mean," I said in a grave voice. "We are not used to your political double-talk."

"I swear to it!" he exclaimed heatedly. "When I say five years, I mean five years!"

"Do you know that swearing is invoking a spirit to witness an assertion you wish to make? So beware of the curse you will bring upon yourself if you tell a lie!" said Mother, quoting a proverb.

"Of course, I mean what I say! I will swear to it! Don't you believe me?" he asked protestingly.

"Very well then, let us hear you swear it before the Buddha!" said Mother, going toward the shrine. She picked up three joss sticks and a pair of candles and lit them. Then she placed them in the incense burner. The candles burned brightly. Without hesitation, Kai-shek stepped over to the shrine, stood at attention before the image, and swore: "I promise to resume my marital relationship with Chieh-ju as husband and wife within five years from today. Should I break my promise and fail to take her back, may the Great Buddha smite me and my Nanking government. And if within ten or twenty years I do not do my duty toward her, then may Buddha topple my government and banish me from China forever." He looked at mother and asked, "Now, do you believe me?"

"Yes," sighed mother sadly, "I believe you."

Then Kai-shek picked up the three steamship tickets from the table, handed them to Mother, and said: "Chieh-ju will not be lonely. All her expenses will be paid by the government. She has two companions who will look after her. You must remember she is going abroad to broaden her education, to better herself. She is not going into exile, as she says. So don't look so unhappy about it."

After Kai-shek left the house, the spell of my unhappiness lingered on and I felt a flash of pain shoot through my heart. I cried: "Oh, Mother. I don't believe him anymore. I know this is the end of my marriage!"

I sat close to her and she put her arms around me and said comfortingly: "He has sworn a solemn oath. If he does not keep his promise let him be burdened with the curse for the rest of his life!"

I clung helplessly to her like a child lost to the world, and there we sat for a long while, watching the dove-gray ashes of the burning incense and the flickering candles playing shadows on the Great Buddha's face.

On August 19, 1927, accompanied by Therese and Helen Chang, I sailed from Shanghai on the SS *President Jackson*, bound for the United States. Facetiously friends called my companions my "ladies-in-waiting." Leaving home for the first time for a strange country for a relatively prolonged absence was a sad experience. My home now broken up, all that was left to me were my sweet mother, my brother, and a few friends, whose love and affection were the very light of my existence. Parting from them after my tragic failure as a wife seemed to be a sorrow almost too great to bear. But because it was Kai-shek's wish that I leave, and since I had committed myself to sacrifice for the unification of the nation, I could not turn back. Yet it is impossible to describe the misery that I felt when the hour of parting, especially from my aging mother, at last arrived. Mother and brother Bun had come on board to see me off, and our hearts were wrenched, for we felt that at least five years must elapse before we would meet again.

However, I tore myself from my loved ones when compelled by the ship's warning gong for visitors to leave for shore. My mother placed her hands affectionately around my body and reverently invoked Buddha's blessing. The ship was docked at midstream on the Huang-p'u. In a few minutes the passenger launch began to move slowly away from our ship, and crowds of people waved their hands or handkerchiefs in farewell. As soon as the launch left, our ship weighed anchor and began to move, churning the yellow water of the Huang-p'u River. I continued to lean over the ship's side to wave my handkerchief long after the faces of the people on the launch ceased to be recognizable.

Now heading for the open sea, I continued to look at the Shanghai shoreline and could see the famous tall buildings of the Bund. They appeared as if enveloped in mist—a mist caused by the tears that blinded my eyes. Then we passed the Woosung Forts, and I looked over the rails to watch the churning of the muddy water against the ship. Gradually the water began to change to a yellowish-green, which meant the yellow, muddy waters from the Yangtze had entered the ocean. Shanghai had completely vanished from view, so with an aching heart, I retired quietly to my cabin, leaving Therese and Helen on deck.

After a beautifully smooth passage of two-and-a-half days, we reached Kobe, where Therese showed me a Japanese newspaper she had just bought. It contained a report saying:

Mme Chiang Kai-shek Sets Sail for America

London, Aug. 19, 1927 (AP) Mme Chiang Kai-shek, wife of the former commander in chief of the Nanking Nationalists, sailed for the United States today aboard the SS *President Jackson,* according to a report from Shanghai to the *Daily Mail.* Friends said that she expected to make a tour of the United States before reaching New York.

It was reported today, the dispatch adds, that Chiang Kai-shek would leave on Monday for Germany.

A Reuters dispatch from Shanghai says that Chiang has issued a statement declaring that his resignation as commander in chief should be accepted and that he should be prosecuted for gross neglect of duty.

A deputation of thirty military leaders recently visited Chiang and begged him to withdraw his resignation. Both moves, the dispatch said, were regarded as "face-savers."

In view of the increasing demoralization at Nanking caused by the onslaught of the northerners, Rear Admiral Tyrwhitt, in command of the British naval forces in China, left for Nanking aboard his flagship *Hawkins* today with a force of 150 marines, says a Shanghai dispatch to the *Daily Mail.*

I was shocked at this unwelcome publicity, and it killed my desire to see Kobe. But Therese and Helen Chang went ahead and took the train to Tokyo, where they spent the day and then met our ship at Yokohama, our next port of call. As we were only to remain at these ports a few hours, I stayed on the steamer, pacing the deck and looking at the surrounding scenery. I did not go ashore because I could not get over my self-consciousness and the humiliation that gripped my mind.

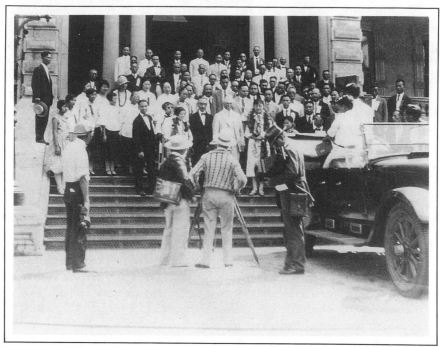

Photo session welcoming Jennie (first row, center), probably in San Francisco.

Leaving Yokohama, it took thirteen miserable days to reach Honolulu, where the steamer stopped for six hours. Then we proceeded on our passage to the mainland, reaching San Francisco in another five interminable days.

If I had a shock at Kobe, there was a greater shock in store for me at the Bay City, for the newspapers proclaimed:

Chiang Silent on Wedding
Denies Having Wife Here, But Says Nothing of Marrying Again

Shanghai, Sept. 19, 1927 (AP)—General Chiang Kai-shek, former Nationalist commander in chief, is quoted as declaring in a recent interview in Feng-hua that the woman who arrived at San Francisco aboard the liner *President Jackson* from China early this month is not his wife. He asserted that the report that she is his wife is "the work of political enemies" seeking to so embarrass him. He added that he does not know the "Mme Chiang Kai-shek" mentioned in the dispatches.

To avoid any further publicity, Therese, Helen, and I agreed among ourselves that we would henceforth avoid all reporters. We decided to say "no comment," no matter how persistent the newsmen would be.

In San Francisco we took the express train to New York. On our arrival there, the three of us were mobbed by a large crowd of reporters, all trying to get us to say something to them. Cameras flashed on all sides of us! It was all confusion, and our paths were blocked. There were about thirty men and women all milling around and trying to get us to say something. But as planned, we were firm and answered their question with "no comment."

"Give us just one statement please!" "Oh, ladies be kind!" "Please don't brush off the press!" "Be a good sport!"

But we hurried on to our taxi and left the reporters staring after us. The next day the *New York Times* reported:

> Chiang Blames Foes for Talk of Wife
> Indignant over Story Revived
> as He Plans Marriage with Miss Soong.
> Wedding Is Not Certain
> She Won't Marry Unless Mother Gives Consent—
> Chiang Going to Japan to Seek It.
> By Henry F. Misselwitz.
> Copyright, 1927, by the New York Times Company
> By Wireless to the New York Times.

Shanghai, Sept. 24—Political enemies are blamed by Chiang Kai-shek for what he denounces as false reports concerning the young woman now in the United States who is said to be his wife.

The retired Nationalist leader returned to Shanghai from Ningpo yesterday with Cupid, not Mars, as his patron deity. As previously announced, he hopes to wed Miss Mei Ling Soong and is on his way to Kobe, Japan, to see her mother and request parental sanction of the proposed marriage. If married, the couple plan a honeymoon in America, spending at least a year in Washington.

Chiang was more indignant over the position in which the aforementioned reports place his fiancee than over possible political injury to himself, as he sat at tea this afternoon in the French Concession. He was dressed in flowing Chinese robes and told me a story that throws into striking relief two phases of present-day China—political intrigues and their ramifications and a struggle between new and old Chinese customs.

"The reports concerning my first wife and this young woman who recently went to America," he said, "were circulated widely in order to discredit not only me but my proposed marriage to Miss Soong. I want to clear up the matter. The reports were instigated by political enemies desiring to embarrass me as much as possible and prevent my return to the revolution, as well as to obtain personal advancement. In 1921, I divorced my first wife. Since then I have set free two concubines. I was surprised to learn that one of them went to America as my wife.

"Only cowards would strike at me in this manner, seeking to harm me through Miss Soong. They are hiding behind a woman's skirts, the most cowardly thing a man can do.

"Our marriage is not yet definite. I have known Miss Soong for five years. Before we can be united in marriage, we must gain her mother's consent. Hence I am proceeding to Japan shortly in order to see Mrs. Soong, who is convalescing, and request permission to marry her daughter. If she is willing, we will be married as soon as possible, probably in Shanghai. Later we desire to go to America.

"I do not propose to return to politics for several years. I hope the new Nanking government will succeed, but feel I must stand aside. I want to spend a year in America and two years in Europe. I intend to study political and financial affairs in the United States and to learn something by inspecting the naval and military academies. My primary interests are related to the future of a unified China, and I want to study American government and military science and tactics."

I asked Chiang where he intended to live. He replied: "Wherever Miss Soong wants to live we live."

Miss Soong, seen later, said she thought if her mother granted permission for the marriage, they would live in Washington during most of their stay in the United States. "The General wants to study government affairs; hence I think we shall live in Washington," she said. "Of course, this all depends on Mother's consent. If the idea of this union distresses her too much I shall bow to her will. But I hope she can be persuaded to give her consent."

Miss Soong is a Methodist, and she said the ceremony would be according to the Methodist ritual.

At the Foreign Office this evening I saw a copy of a passport application by the girl the general denies is his wife. She signed the form Chiang Chieh-ju, not stating whether she was Miss or Mrs. She gave her occupation as a student, her age as 20, and said that the purpose of her visit abroad was to travel.

The official who issued the passport denied that he did so on the understanding that she was Chiang Kai-shek's wife.

So, I was Mme Chiang Kai-shek no more! The name to me was a mockery. I knew I was now ruined—my soul was on a rack. There was

Jennie sight-seeing in the United States.

no joy, no peace for me. I walked as if I had a dangling chain on my leg and a placard around my neck proclaiming who I was—a discarded wife—an unwanted woman!—an imposter! I had to avoid people and look the other way, as if I were a leper. Whenever I came across anyone, the fear of being recognized gripped me. This terrible feeling of self-consciousness framed itself on my mind, and I could not get rid of it. My future was bleak and I fully realized there were all those hard things to be faced. Nothing could ease my anguish. Nothing could heal my wounded pride.

Thus my first few days in New York proved to be much more miserable than I could ever have imagined. Therese and Helen had their own friends to contact. And although they urged me to accompany them on their outings, I felt too unhappy and self-conscious to go anywhere with them.

The two girls were, indeed, very sweet. Ever since the day we left Shanghai, both sisters tried all kinds of antics to cheer me up. They would joke and tell funny stories to amuse me. Unfortunately, all their efforts were in vain, for I was too despondent to respond cordially. I must confess I was a "double-sized wet blanket" and must have gotten on their nerves. But they were too gracious to say so to my face.

Therese seriously advised me: "Oh, my dear, return injustice for injustice, deceit for deceit, but don't cry. I know you have been wronged unjustly. Their deceit is monstrous. But snap out of it and pay them back in their own coin!"

She had waited for me to go out, but I stayed in our apartment. I was too angry, confused, and uncertain after reading the newspaper article. "Oh, Therese, please let me think," I pleaded.

She looked at me, frowning as if it was not necessary to think. "Don't wait, darling," she said. "You are not divorced yet! Assert your rights; telegraph Kai-shek and give him a piece of your mind! You can make it hot for him here!"

I had not told either Therese or Helen of my pact with Kai-shek, nor what my departure from Shanghai meant, nor how important it was that I step aside so that Kai-shek could acquire the Soongs' help by marrying the third sister and get finances from the Shanghai bankers through T. V. Soong and Madame Kung.

Thus Therese and Helen could not understand my deep pain, sorrow, and the injustice I suffered. They simply regarded my gloom as incomprehensible and baffling. After a week, they both went their own way; Helen to take up dressmaking and Therese to study in a teacher's course. They had their own plans, and I was left all alone to work out my own destiny.

After ten days in New York, I was anxious for news from Mother. So I went to the Chinese consulate hoping to get some mail. I was coldly received by the vice consul, Mr. Kiang, who invited me to go into his office. He explained: "Please do not have your private mail sent in the care of this office. We handle only official business here and I hope you will understand our position."

I was shocked and asked angrily: "What kind of people are you? I am a Chinese woman alone in the United States and you talk to me like that! I had no New York address when I left Shanghai, so how could my mother know where to send letters to me except in care of this consulate! I thought a consulate was at the service of its nationals!"

"You need not worry," he answered politely enough. "Your mother has been given instructions. She will send your allowance and mail directly to your private address, 310 Riverside Drive, I believe. Is that address correct? I am sorry we have no time to handle any of your private business or problems. We cannot do anything for you here. We are acting on instructions."

"On whose instructions!" I demanded to know.

"Instructions from Nanking."

"So that's the attitude!" I said heatedly. "Tell me by whose instructions from Nanking? Are they from General Chiang Kai-shek!"

"I'm not permitted to say."

"By that female's orders, then!"

"I didn't say that," he answered in trepidation. "Please, please, don't misquote me! I beg of you!"

Our voices were raised in animated talk, and when I left the office I could see the curious glances of the various members of the consulate, as if I was a tainted person. Seeing this, I stood there a minute and looked at them with infinite contempt. Most surprisingly, they scattered like frightened birds. I told myself, it was usual for sycophants to know which side their bread was buttered on, and in a way I felt more pity than anger for them.

I walked home, blinded with tears. What had I done to deserve this insult? What atonement could be made for the wrong done to me? There was no atonement possible, I told myself. I was disgraced, not he. It was the usual story of a man and a woman. I gave him my life—he took it, used it, spoiled it, and now I am degraded. So even in faraway New York, I could feel the hand of persecution reaching out to strike me down. I was an outcast! They did not want to have any more contacts with me—not even with my mail! All that night I sat in my room and brooded, for I could not sleep. The thoughts of my life's tragedy kaleidoscoped before my eyes.

Stealing a husband was not news in the world. I had read about it in both Chinese and American magazines many times, where prominent people took their troubles to court, but I never dreamt that it would happen to me. When a man or woman acquired wealth or power, their former spouses were often discarded like old shoes. The question I asked myself was, To what extent must I bow gracefully in giving up my husband? As a Chinese national, I wasn't even welcome at my own consulate!

Only someone who has experienced such degradation can realize the humiliation, the mental torture, the excruciating pain. I sat in my room and brooded all night. When dawn came I simply went berserk. I stood at the table laden with all the untouched food and with both hands shook at it madly. I shouted at the top of my voice: "I didn't want to marry him in the first place! But he swore an oath of eternal love and even wanted to cut off a finger to convince me. I was too young and too inexperienced to know his fickle character. But my father saw through him and that is why he was not allowed to come to our house to bother me. Oh, how blind I was! How stupid! I should have known!" I ran up and down the room, with both my hands tearing at my hair, raving and shouting.

My outbursts frightened the tenants, who called the janitor. He came to my door to inquire what had happened to the Chinese lady. When I opened it, I could see his frightened eyes and gaping mouth. He asked fearfully, "Is something wrong?"

"No," I lied. "I just had a frightful nightmare. Sorry if I caused a disturbance. Please pardon me!"

In a melancholy mood, I sat in my room all day, and when dawn broke I walked out of my apartment into the street, not caring where I was going. Finally I found myself walking up and down 79th Street, and then on and on I wandered, making a loop until I doubled back on Riverside Drive. I became very tired. Then, crossing the street, I came to the water's edge and looked groggily into the Hudson River. The water flowed gently. How calm and peaceful it all seemed. It fascinated me, despite the early morning traffic. "Please, Great Buddha…" I wailed, but I could not finish my sentence. My hysteria had abated, replaced by a deep, indescribable melancholy that gave me a feeling of the futility of life. Nothing mattered anymore. Sick and weak, I leaned on the iron railing overlooking the flowing waters. A cool breeze blew in from the North, and my hair streamed out over my forehead. The wind seemed to emphasze the words: "Discarded woman—abandoned wife—she's an imposter!"

Dazed, I looked at the river's current and murmured, "Extricate yourself from your heavy grief!" Then an irresistible impulse to jump in and end it all assailed me. Life was not worth living. Everywhere, people pointed their fingers to jeer at me! I suddenly cried: "Oh, darling Mother and brother Bun! Please forgive me. My suffering is more than I can bear! We shall meet again the next world!"

I placed one foot on the lower railing, raised my body, and tried to climb over it. But before I could raise my body, a strong hand suddenly seized my shoulder from behind. I started and looked around. It was an elderly gentleman with gray hair. He warned: "Don't do anything rash! Suicide is a cowardly way out! You should know better than to throw your young life away! Go home and learn to lead a useful life. Stop pitying yourself."

I was trembling from head to foot. After a few minutes I became a little steadier. The kind old gentleman walked me home to the entrance to my flat. "Don't do it again," he advised. "In this life we all have our problems, and our problems keep growing day by day. But if we have hope and faith, we will win out in the end. You are young, so very young indeed. You are alive and healthy. The world has in store for you unending opportunities and all the good things of life. Don't ever do it again. Will you promise?"

I nodded my head and stood there dazed, while he turned and walked briskly down the street.

Back in my flat, I sat in a chair and thought over what the old gentleman had said. He had saved my life, and I had not even said thank you to him. He was right. In destroying myself, my body would float in the water and perhaps be carried out to the ocean to feed the fishes, and what then? My own grief and misery would come to an end, but what about my mother and brother Bun? They would grieve over my death so terribly. Mother gave me life and it would be unfilial of me to destroy it.

I knelt down on the floor and muttered: "I'll spend the rest of my life to make you happy, dear Mother. I'll not die to cause you grief." I bowed my head in sorrow and asked, "Oh, Great Buddha, in your infinite grace and mercy, please help and guide me to do the right thing. ..." I bent my head in prayer and could hear the thumping of my wounded heart. Then I thought of Joseph Auslander's words:

Because You knew black nights of unbelief,
The sleepless agony, the stark despair,
Sustain us when we struggle with our grief;
Help us to find the strength You found in prayer.

Thirty-six years have now passed since that memorable day, and although the whole of China was unified in 1929 by Kai-shek, he never made any attempt to keep our pact or to support me. To him I am a woman he does not know. He has conveniently forgotten that he married me according to lawful Chinese ceremony and that I stepped aside quietly to enable him to realize his ambition to complete the Northern Expedition to unify China. But I did not know that in helping him, I had to pay and pay and pay again for the stigma he inflicted on me. All these bitter years I have never remarried. I live a life of embarrassment, concealment, and repression. To eke out a living, I give tuition in both the English and Chinese languages to private pupils. If I should be recognized on the street by those who know about my past, I am invariably stared at curiously and pointed out as the woman that Chiang Kai-shek discarded in order to marry Mei-ling Soong.

ABOUT THE BOOK

This engrossing memoir tells the fascinating story of one of China's great leaders during the Nationalist revolution of the 1920s and of the woman who paid a staggering price so that he could attain his ambition. The tale begins in 1919 when the thirty-two-year-old Chiang Kai-shek met the naïve thirteen-year-old whom he would call Ch'en Chieh-ju. He pursued her relentlessly for two years until she finally agreed to marry her brash and forceful suitor. Chieh-ju was at her husband's side constantly for the seven years of their marriage, which enabled her to chronicle with immediacy and vivid detail his single-minded pursuit of power in the Kuomintang (KMT).

So explosive were her revelations that the KMT used threats and bribes to block U.S. publication plans in the 1960s. Now, her long-suppressed memoir finally reveals Chiang Kai-shek's human side, which has been shrouded in myth. Chiang Kai-shek emerges as a lustful, ill-tempered, quarrelsome, stubborn, and boundlessly ambitious man. In pursuit of his goals, he abandoned the young wife he seemingly loved to make a politically expedient alliance with Soong Mei-ling, now famed as Madame Chiang. Despite his betrayal, Chieh-ju's love for her husband is clearly evident. She paints here a stirring portrait of their personal life as well as of the infighting and intrigue that marked her husband's early political career. Above all, her story conveys a keen sense of the texture of upper-class life in the China of that period, a quality academic studies rarely capture.

Ch'en Chieh-ju was the wife of Chiang Kai-shek from 1921 to 1927. **Lloyd E. Eastman** is professor of history and Asian studies at the University of Illinois.

INDEX